Political Philosophy

FUNDAMENTALS OF PHILOSOPHY SERIES

Series Editors
John Martin Fischer, University of California, Riverside
John Perry, Stanford University

Biomedical Ethics
Walter Glannon

Mind: A Brief Introduction
John R. Searle

A Contemporary Introduction to Free Will
Robert Kane

Political Philosophy
A. John Simmons

Political Philosophy

A. JOHN SIMMONS
University of Virginia

New York ◆ Oxford
OXFORD UNIVERSITY PRESS
2008

Oxford University Press, Inc., publishes works that further Oxford University's objective of excellence in research, scholarship, and education.

Oxford   New York
Auckland   Cape Town   Dar es Salaam   Hong Kong   Karachi
Kuala Lumpur   Madrid   Melbourne   Mexico City   Nairobi
New Delhi   Shanghai   Taipei   Toronto

With offices in
Argentina   Austria   Brazil   Chile   Czech Republic   France   Greece
Guatemala   Hungary   Italy   Japan   Poland   Portugal   Singapore
South Korea   Switzerland   Thailand   Turkey   Ukraine   Vietnam

Published by Oxford University Press, Inc.
198 Madison Avenue, New York, New York, 10016
http://www.oup.com

Library of Congress Cataloging-in-Publication Data

Simmons, A. John (Alan John), 1950–
   Political philosophy / A. John Simmons.
      p.cm.— (Fundamentals of philosophy series)
   Includes bibliographical references and index.
   Contents: Morals and politics—States?—Obligations—Justice—Democracy—
The world of states.
   ISBN-13: 978-0-19-513801-6 (cloth)
   ISBN-13: 978-0-19-513802-3 (pbk.)
      1. Political science—Philosophy. I. Title.

JA71.S476 2008
320.01—dc22
                                                                2006052479

9 8 7 6 5 4 3 2 1

Printed in the United States of America
on acid-free paper

Contents

Acknowledgments

Much of this book was written during a year of sabbatical leave from the University of Virginia, and my first thanks must go to the university for making this research time available to me. The first three chapters of the book were composed during a several-month stay in Puyricard, France (just north of Aix-en-Provence), where I nobly overcame many temptations in order to get words on paper. To our friends in Puyricard, Eguilles, and Aix goes my gratitude for making our life there pleasant and easy. My daughter Sarah also deserves special mention; she not only filled our lives with light in her unique ways, but she also braved the terrors of French preschool so her father could sit at home and write. My friend and wife, Nancy Schauber, as always read and improved all that I wrote, both in France and in the United States. I trust she knows how much her help and companionship, in this and in all else, means to me. Of the many others who have helped me, I thank especially the main participants in the Georgia State manuscript workshop on this book (Andrew Altman, Andrew I. Cohen, Andrew J. Cohen, David Copp, Christie Hartley, Peter Lindsay, Chris Morris, George Rainbolt, and Kit Wellman) and the reviewers for Oxford University Press (Craig Duncan, Chris Morris [again], James Skidmore, Ajume Wingo, and two anonymous readers). Finally, I would like to thank John Fischer for his support and encouragement of this project and the many students in courses and seminars, during three decades of teaching, who have so often forced me to think better and more clearly about political philosophy.

Preface

The books of this series are intended to be compact and generally accessible studies of the central areas of philosophy. *Political Philosophy*, accordingly, aims to identify and explore the central arguments of political philosophy in a way that makes plain their structure and logic while combining breadth with brevity. Such a combination is not easy to achieve, and any attempt to do so is forced to make hard and often questionable choices about what to include and what to pass over in silence. Indeed, the extraordinary diversity of themes in works identified by their authors as "political philosophy" virtually guarantees that a book forced to make these choices will be unsatisfying to many. Different academic disciplines, different cultures, and different philosophical traditions identify differently the proper orientation and essential subject matter of political philosophy. I here offer the reader one interpretation of what matters most (and how it matters) in political philosophy.

Books on our subject tend to be of three general types. One type is historically ordered, consisting of summaries (and sometimes critical discussions) of the works of the principal figures in the history of political philosophy, perhaps including a few prominent contemporary works for balance. A second type focuses on the major themes and positions in contemporary (primarily post-1950) political philosophy, with passing reference to historical contributions on these themes but oriented throughout by contemporary concerns. A third and less common type simply explores a unified set of problems that is taken to define the core of political philosophy, examining the ways in which these problems have been and could be addressed, and seeing how historical and contemporary work in political philosophy fits together and constitutes a continuous preoccupation with the same basic problems.

This book is of the third type. While the book contains regular and often extended treatment of the arguments of the great historical figures in political philosophy, it is not intended as a history (with appropriately careful historical scholarship), nor does it proceed by discussing problems in the "historical order" in which they arose. The book's ordering is logical, not historical. Neither is the book intended as a summary and discussion of contemporary themes in political philosophy, though again it certainly touches on, and often offers reasonably detailed discussions of, most of these themes as well. In fact, the book's orientation, as we will see, often displays my disagreements with the emphases and foundational concerns of much mainstream contemporary political philosophy. What the reader will find here is simply a consideration of what I take to be the key issues and arguments of political philosophy, issues and arguments with which philosophers have struggled for many hundreds of years. These philosophers, of course, were speaking to their own quite diverse communities and have been oriented by their own quite different assumptions and preoccupations. But there are common threads of concern running through their works down through the ages, and their arguments have been addressed not only to their contemporaries but to thoughtful persons of future times—like ourselves. This book tries to identify and helpfully discuss these common threads. Whether or not the voice in which it does so is the right voice for my audience, the reader must judge.

Political Philosophy

CHAPTER 1

Morals and Politics

1.1. Political Philosophy

While there is certainly real and substantial disagreement about the nature and proper scope of political philosophy, we must, to begin, attempt to define our subject matter at least at the most general level. *Political philosophy* is the evaluative study of political societies. Vague as this definition may be, it allows us to immediately identify some basic ways in which political *philosophy* both overlaps with and is distinct from the discipline of political *science*. Political science in its purest form is an essentially descriptive discipline; its primary task is to *describe* and analyze the nature of political societies—to describe their structure and organization, the principles that guide them, the (actual or likely) behavior of their subjects and leaders, and so on. The core subject matter of political science is *de facto* (existing) political societies (though political science also describes past and possible societies). When political scientists begin to evaluate real or possible societies—as good or bad, just or unjust, legitimate or illegitimate—their work shades into the domain of political philosophy (or what political scientists like to call "normative political theory").

Political philosophy must, of course, share with political science its concern for accurately describing the realities of political life, for one can hardly defend a form of political life as good or ideal without first taking account of the facts of (e.g.) psychology and economics, without seeing clearly how various kinds of people can be expected to act and interact and how various kinds of institutional structures can be expected to function. Similarly, political philosophy shares with political science a purely analytic, conceptual side, where its job is to sort out and clarify the essential concepts of politics.

What is distinctive about political philosophy, however, is its *prescriptive* or evaluative concern with justifications, values, virtues, ideals, rights, obligations—in short, its concern with how political societies *should* be, how political policies and institutions can be justified, how we and our political officeholders ought to behave in our public lives. The principal subject matter of political philosophy can accordingly be said to be *de jure* (legitimate, justified, just) political societies. Political philosophy can thus be aptly characterized as a branch or an application of *moral* philosophy. Not all evaluations are moral, of course (as my judgment that I'm writing these lines with "a good pen" plainly shows); but the evaluations made in political philosophy are in fact distinctly moral. Where moral philosophy examines the more general questions of how we should act and be, political philosophy examines the more specific questions of how we should act and be in our political lives and (consequently) of what kinds of political societies we should (and should not) create or oppose. A familiar way in which political philosophers of all ages (from Plato in *Republic* to John Rawls in *A Theory of Justice*) have pursued these questions is by describing an ideal or model political society, against which past, present, and possible political societies can be compared, analyzed, and criticized. The ideals in question are moral ideals for our political lives, and in defending such ideals, political philosophy secures for itself a special and immediate practical relevance that much other philosophical theory at least appears to lack.

Exactly *how* political philosophy is related to moral philosophy (i.e., exactly what the former's being a "branch" or an "application" of the latter amounts to) is a subject of some controversy among political philosophers. In the simplest and most traditional model, the principles of political philosophy are thought to just follow directly from perfectly general moral principles, conjoined with the facts of political life, in a roughly syllogistic way.[1] Thus, certain general moral principles, taken to apply to all people in all contexts (and serving as major premises)—principles such as "All persons should be treated as equals" or "All persons' rights should be respected"—might be taken to imply (when the facts of political life, serving as minor premises, are taken into account) principles (conclusions) more specifically political—such as "All basic goods and liberties should be distributed equally by governments," "All political authority should be created and employed democratically," or "No person should be subjected by government or law to unmerited harm." Much of traditional natural law theory, from Aquinas to Locke, viewed the relationship of moral to political philosophy in this way, with the (universally applicable, always binding) rules of natural law (i.e., the moral rules laid down for humankind by

God/reason) directly determining the moral rules for the structure of and limits on political societies and their inhabitants. The same general view of the relation of moral to political philosophy was in fact shared by many of natural law theory's most ardent opponents (e.g., utilitarian moralists), and this view continues to be well represented among today's moral and political philosophers.

According to a second, more contemporary model, the principles of political philosophy are viewed instead as an autonomous region of moral philosophy, neither derived from more general moral principles nor applicable to the nonpolitical aspects of our lives.[2] Political philosophy, in this view, is a body of separately justified moral principles that are special for political contexts, governing how political institutions should be arranged and how persons in their public lives should act and be, but irrelevant to our private lives or to our conduct in non-political settings (e.g., where the rule of law has completely dissolved). Thus, it might be a principle of political philosophy that governments must treat all their subjects (and citizens must treat their fellows in public life) impartially and as equals; but it might still be perfectly permissible (or even obligatory) for people in their private lives (or in "the state of nature") to show special favoritism to their friends and family, there being no generally applicable moral principle requiring impartiality in our dealings with others.

There is still a third model of the relationship of moral to political philosophy that seems in many ways more satisfactory than either of the first two we've considered. In this model, the principles of political philosophy are a mix of those advocated by the first two models, with some directly derived from more general moral principles and others separately justified for specifically political contexts.[3] It seems plausible, for instance, to argue that, on the one hand, governments and citizens must scrupulously respect the moral rights that all persons possess simply as persons—just as these rights must be respected in nonpublic, nonpolitical contexts—while, on the other hand, the principles specifying the best form for political institutions to take (within the constraints imposed by this respect for rights) are not simply derivable from more general moral principles but are justified in a special way for political contexts.

1.2. Moral Philosophy

I have been referring to "moral philosophy" and "moral principles." But aside from offering a very general characterization of the former and a few examples of the latter, I have not said anything about the substance of morality (but have only mentioned a couple of substantive moral theories without explaining them). Nor will I try to do a great deal more on that topic now. Moral philosophy is, of course, a very large subject, a subject for another book (or for two or three other books). But a few very general observations here may help to make a bit clearer the idea of political philosophy as a "branch" or an "application" of moral philosophy. I will mention here just two basic divisions in moral philosophy,[4] both of which are features of the most general kind of map of moral philosophy's terrain and both of which are important to understanding prominent disagreements in political philosophy.

Moral philosophy, I have said, is the study of how we should act and be—or, more generally, how we should live. Perhaps the most basic division among moral philosophers concerns whether moral philosophy should focus first or primarily on the kinds of acts we should perform or on the kinds of persons we should be. Those who opt for the former orientation defend what we can call *conduct-based* (or *deontic*) moral theories, whose central moral concepts are right action, rights, or obligations/duties. After telling us how we should act, such theories typically conclude, secondarily and derivatively, that we should be the kind of person who reliably performs right actions, respects rights, and discharges obligations. Those who opt for the latter orientation defend *virtue* (or *aretaic*) theories, whose central moral concepts are virtue, excellence, and moral character. After telling us what kinds of persons we should be, virtue theories typically conclude, secondarily and derivatively, that we should act in the ways that a good or virtuous person would act (in the circumstances). While moral philosophers have, of course, attempted to defend comprehensive (or genuinely mixed) moral theories, which give priority to neither conduct-based nor virtue-based concerns, these attempts have almost invariably allowed one category or the other to dominate in the end.

Modern and contemporary political philosophers have mostly regarded political philosophy as a branch or an application of some conduct-based moral philosophy. Influenced by conduct-based natural law, utilitarian, or Kantian moral theories, they have derived principles of political philosophy that primarily concern how states/governments and subjects should act, what their respective rights and obligations in political society amount to. Worries about natural and human rights, political obligation and authority, property and the just division of social goods, freedom of expression, freedom of religion, freedom of political participation, and so on all naturally take center stage in a political philosophy oriented by conduct-based moral theory. Government's proper role is to try to control how its subjects act (within reasonable limits) and to secure their freedom to choose for themselves, not to try to determine who those subjects shall be (or how they shall become that way). By contrast, representatives of ancient and republican traditions in political philosophy, more directly influenced by virtue theories (such as those of Plato and Aristotle), have often taken government's primary function to be precisely that of promoting the process of virtuous character formation in its subjects in order to insure that those subjects will be suitable participants in civic life. With virtuous citizens, it may seem, the details of political life can largely be safely left to sort themselves out.

A second basic division in moral philosophy—primarily, but not exclusively, at issue in debates within conduct-based moral theory—is the division between *consequentialist* and *deontological* moral theories. Here, the division concerns more directly the ways in which we can defend or justify claims that a particular kind of action is right (or that a particular character trait is good or virtuous). And it is a division in moral philosophy that has been, as we shall see, at the very center of prominent debates in contemporary political philosophy. According to consequentialist moral theories, the rightness (or wrongness) of actions (or the excellence of character traits) depends solely on the goodness (or badness) of their consequences.[5] Deontological moral theories, by contrast, maintain that at least some actions are right or wrong (or character traits are virtuous or vicious) "intrinsically," or at least for reasons other than (or in addition to) the goodness or badness of their consequences.

The most widely discussed and defended consequentialist theories have been varieties of ethical egoism and utilitarianism, both of which view rightness in action (or virtue in character) as a function of the promotion of "utility." According to egoistic theories (e.g., that defended by Hobbes), actions are right by virtue of promoting the good of the agent's "personal utility"—that is, the actor's own pleasure, happiness, or desire satisfaction. According to utilitarian theories (e.g., those defended by Bentham, Mill, and Sidgwick), actions are right by virtue of promoting "overall utility" (i.e., pleasure, happiness, or desire satisfaction summed over all persons or all sentient creatures). There are also non-utility-oriented consequentialist theories, such as perfectionism—which (as in Nietzsche) makes rightness a function of the promotion of the good of human excellence—and mixed consequentialist theories (e.g., Aristotle's).[6] The great strength of all of the many varieties of consequentialist moral theory is their identification of plausible candidates (e.g., happiness) for the good and their adoption of the seemingly quite natural view that rightness or virtue is simply a matter of producing goodness in the world. The great weakness of these theories is a simple function of this "natural" view: if rightness or virtue is simply about producing goodness, then in some sense "the ends justify the means" and right or virtue could in principle turn out to involve (seemingly) quite awful acts or traits.

Deontological moral theories, by denying that rightness turns exclusively on the production of goodness, can avoid this apparent weakness and can square more easily with the central intuitive, pretheoretical moral commitments of many (to, e.g., the sanctity of individuals, the absolute wrongness of certain kinds of acts, etc.). But in thus divorcing rightness or virtue from the simple production of goodness, deontological theories have been forced to identify alternative ways to justify judgments of rightness or virtue. And these ways have seemed to many to involve weaknesses as great as those ascribed to consequentialism—in particular, the weaknesses of dubious metaphysics or undue reliance on moral intuition (which, after all, these critics point out, is a mere cultural artifact, not the proper basis for a rational moral theory). Of the best-known deontological moral theories, the first charge (dubious metaphysics) has often been leveled against both "divine command theories" (which identify right actions with those commanded or willed by God) and Kantian theories (which, following Kant, identify rightness in action with a certain kind of nonconsequentialist practical consistency or rationality). Other deontological theories have been attacked using the second charge (undue reliance on moral intuition)—theories such as intuitionism (which identifies right actions with those so identified by mature moral agents), ideal observer theories (which identify right actions with those so identified by a hypothetical ideal observer), or some contemporary theories inspired by Kant that jettison Kant's metaphysics (e.g., those defended by Rawls and Nozick, which we discuss in Chapter 4).

Given our account of political philosophy as a branch or an application of moral philosophy, it should be unsurprising that many of the deepest disagreements in political philosophy simply reflect deep underlying disagreements in moral philosophy. In what follows, we will repeatedly see evidence of this fact. And we will see that keeping in mind the simple distinctions in moral philosophy noted above, even without pursuing any fuller account of the nature of moral philosophy, will enable us to understand much about the structure of many basic debates in political philosophy.

1.3. Political Society

Suppose we understand moral and political philosophy as they have been characterized above. This will help us to understand what I meant by emphasizing political philosophy's evaluative character. But even so, at least two obvious and immediate questions will remain concerning our initial definition of political philosophy as "the evaluative study of political societies." First, what *is* a "political society"? Second, precisely what is it about political societies that gets evaluated by political philosophy, and how are the various evaluations related to one another? Let us deal with these questions in turn.

We all, of course, have some more or less sophisticated intuitive response to the question "What is a political society?" Even if we cannot provide a precise definition of *political society,* we mostly have the sense that we would "know one if we saw one." After all, anyone at all likely to be reading this *lives* in a political society. But any reasonably precise answer to our question is bound to be controversial, for neither *political* nor *society* has a sufficiently precise meaning on its own to permit real precision in a definition of their conjunction. Indeed, once we give the matter some thought, there are a variety of ways in which the answer to this first question is not as plain as it may initially seem. There are many social groupings that clearly do not qualify as "societies," and there are many societies that clearly do not qualify as "political." While we are all familiar with many of the chief characteristics of the kinds of political societies in which we currently live, there are some societies about which most of us would be uncertain if asked to classify them as "political" or "nonpolitical": consider the variety of migratory, tribal, and religious societies, for example. Must a "political society" be a *state* (of the sort with which we moderns are all familiar)? Must it have a government, a fixed territory, law with coercive law enforcement (etc.)? Notice that this vagueness in the term *political* leaves equally vague the boundaries between "political philosophy" and the disciplines commonly called "social philosophy" and "legal philosophy" (a vagueness that most practitioners of these disciplines cheerfully acknowledge).

We can attempt now, though, at least a rough-and-ready answer to our question so that we can begin productively discussing the problems of political philosophy. Let us say, as adequate for our purposes here, that a "society" is a stable (e.g., multigenerational)[7] group of persons characterized by generally peaceful, cooperative (even if economically competitive), rule-governed conduct within a reasonably wide range of important interpersonal activities. Further, members of a society, properly so called, typically accept a certain view of themselves and their relations[8]: most of them (at least implicitly) accept that the social rules that mandate peaceful, cooperative conduct are binding on all of them.[9]

In this account (and in any other plausible account), many social groupings fail to count as societies principally because of the limited range or limited importance of the activities over which the grouping operates. So, for example, most clubs, teams, neighborhoods, churches, unions, and even groups that refer to themselves in their names as "societies" (e.g., "The Southern Society for Philosophy and Psychology" or "The National Debating Society") do not constitute societies in the relevant sense. Indeed, it is often (though by no means necessarily) the case that the political organization of a social grouping is what gives it its character as a society, for political organization generally involves the coercive imposition (on some group of persons) of requirements of peaceful, cooperative conduct within a wide range of important activities.

A political society, we can say, is a society that is governed, a society that has a functioning government. And a government (again in our rough-and-ready, intuitive sense) is a set of institutions that empowers people to make (or to authoritatively interpret) and coercively enforce (with significant sanctions) laws for all of that government's subjects, laws that require at least peaceful, cooperative conduct within a wide range of important activities.[10] Further, a real government's control must be at least broadly effective so that it can largely deter (if necessary) domestic lawbreaking, rival domestic lawmaking or law enforcement, and external control or aggression.[11] Finally, a government must claim to (or be generally understood to) exercise this control legitimately or rightfully.

We can, by extension, call something a "government" that does not effectively perform but that only has or claims the right to perform these functions (as in the case of a legitimate "government in exile"); but a society that has only a government in this extended sense is not governed, nor is it a "political society" in our sense. We could also, I suppose, call something a government "by analogy" that imposed only insignificant sanctions for lawbreaking (say, a maximum penalty of $1) or that required peaceful conduct only in small or unimportant areas of life (say, when inside a large building or when buying or selling vegetables) or that deliberately enforced the law only against some of those it took to be its subjects (say, redheads or lispers); but, again, a society with such a "government" would be governed little more than one with a government in exile. Most important for our purposes here, if we count such deviant and bizarre possibilities as instances of "political society," it will be very difficult to see how to argue for or against political life, by virtue of the difficulty in distinguishing political from nonpolitical life.[12] Let us, then, accept our definition of *political society* as at least reasonably intuitive and as sufficiently clear to allow us to focus on what has been chiefly at issue when political philosophers have performed their evaluative study of political societies.

1.4. The Problems of Political Philosophy

As for our second question ("What is it about political societies that gets evaluated by political philosophy?"), we can make a start toward an answer by observing that political philosophy has during its history focused principally on two main "evaluative" problems (or, better, two main families of problems): that of the proper distribution by political societies of basic social goods (e.g., wealth, privileges, and liberties) and that of the conditions for the rightful possession of political power or authority. Political philosophy, in short, evaluates both political distributions of goods and the distribution of the authority to control those distributions of goods. Which of these two problems is given priority largely determines the approach to (or style of) political philosophy that is practiced. Contemporary political philosophy has tended to give priority to the first problem (distributive justice), with the second problem (political authority) falling mostly into the background. The authority to govern is often taken, in this contemporary view, to follow simply from a government's justly distributing basic goods. After all, if a particular distribution of goods is morally ideal (say, being such that any reasonable person would favor it over all others), then it seems clear that we should all pursue and support such a distribution and that those who "impose" on us such a just distribution do so rightfully.

Early modern (i.e., sixteenth- to eighteenth-century) political philosophy, by contrast, focused more centrally on the problem of political authority, with the problem of distributive justice being either largely ignored or solved in a derivative fashion. For instance, those who were taken to rightfully wield political authority (or "the right to rule") were often taken to have as well (as a part of their authority) either the right to choose how to distribute social goods within their political societies or the right to control such distributions within the moral and contractual terms under which their political authority was held. The principal concern was with which specific governments were—and with which kinds of governments could be—legitimately instituted and maintained.

It is possible, then, to approach the two central problem areas of political philosophy in ways that make the solutions to one or the other primary, with solutions to the other being secondary or derivative. It is also possible, however, to regard the two problems as distinct and equally important aspects of political philosophy, the solution to each being largely independent of the solution to the other. Thus, it might be that a government that justly distributes basic social goods nonetheless acts without rightful political authority or that a government possessing such authority nonetheless acts unjustly in its distributive capacity.

It is this last approach to political philosophy, according to which neither of its two basic problem areas is primary, that I will defend and exemplify in this book, with the early chapters devoted mostly to the problem of political authority and the later chapters concentrating on the problem of distributive justice. More accurately, I should say that the later chapters deal with what some will take to be a more general problem than that of distributive justice: namely, what is the best form or structure for a political society to have (which includes, of course, the traditional problem of "the best regime")? Here, we mean, of course, "the best form" of political society for beings like ourselves in a world like ours. (The best societies for beings with no needs or impenetrable exoskeletons, say, or for beings living in a world of fantastic abundance are the province of the science-fiction department of political philosophy.) There are legitimate questions about just how utopian serious political philosophy can be, but there is also general agreement that political ideals feasible only on the assumption of dramatic changes either in human nature or motivation or in the material condition of the world are not the ones over which political philosophy should exert itself.[13] (Marxist political philosophy, e.g., has been widely condemned on precisely these grounds.)

This conception of the fundamental problems of political philosophy leaves some obvious possible topics untouched. Perhaps most important, this book will not try to address the various forms of what we can call "meta-political philosophy"—that part of political philosophy which offers a further interpretation, a social-scientific account, or a deep analysis of the long-standing orientation of political philosophy, typically suggesting that its arguments and positions are disingenuous, self-deceptive, or otherwise not to be taken at face value. Many take this project of "unmasking" politics (and unmasking philosophical arguments about politics) to be the only political philosophy worth doing.

The classical source of this approach to political philosophy is the stance of the character Thrasymachus in Plato's *Republic*. According to Thrasymachus (in Book I of that dialogue), the much revered "justice" being discussed by Socrates is really nothing but "the advantage of the stronger"; the strong make rules to enhance and preserve their own power, call obedience to these rules "justice," and (ideally) "con" the less strong into thinking that these rules are mandated by objective morality, required by the gods, or for the good of all. This style of argument is more familiar to modern readers from the writings of Karl Marx, who regarded the state (including the liberal-democratic state) as a mere tool of class domination and political philosophy (like all philosophy) as a form of ideological manipulation designed to support this domination. The kinds of arguments and positions we will consider centrally in this book are characterized by Marx as no more than devices by which the bourgeoisie (who control, and want to keep controlling, the principal means of production in society) maintain their power over the proletariat. Even if this project of control and manipulation is not fully deliberate or conscious (i.e., even if those in power sincerely believe in the force of the arguments they advance), this is in fact all that politics and political philosophy amount to. Both will disappear when economic class distinctions (and the private property relations that define them) disappear.

This Marxist project in political philosophy is still very much alive, both in its classical form and through its various contemporary offspring in political and legal theory. But it is also interesting that powerful, but non-Marxist, analogues of this approach have been developed by contemporary political philosophers. Much recent feminist political philosophy, for instance (though by no means all of it, as we will see in Chapter 4), has a similar meta-philosophical form: politics, along with the political philosophy that accepts its terms, is alleged to be really about gender domination, about the maintenance (and camouflaging) of the power that men exercise over women in society, in order to allow men to preserve their traditional social privileges (including especially that of free sexual access). Politics is really just sexual politics. The analogy to Marxist theory is perhaps clearest in the influential work of Catherine Mackinnon, where *gender* essentially replaces *class* in otherwise familiar Marxist arguments.[14]

None of these "meta-arguments," or any of the other possible skeptical meta-approaches to political philosophy,[15] is centrally discussed here. They are obviously important, for we can hardly claim to fully understand our subject (political philosophy) unless we appreciate the reasons for accepting, modifying, or rejecting the force of such arguments. Why, then, not consider these arguments here? Unhappily but inevitably, not everything can be considered in a book of this limited size; and we cannot, in my view, fairly analyze or interpret (in, e.g., the Marxist or feminist "meta-" fashions) the positions of political philosophers until we first know and fully understand those positions. It is toward that first step—the step of understanding the structure and force of the long-standing projects in political philosophy—that this book is intended as a contribution. The second "meta" step I must leave to others.

1.5. Ideal and Non-ideal

As we have seen, much political philosophy proceeds by trying to describe a political ideal—a form of political life that is best (morally and/or prudentially) for beings like ourselves in a world like ours. The ideal typically includes both an account of the best political institutions (or government) and an account of how governors and subjects ought to behave within the ideal political society.[16] It seems clear, though, that none of us actually lives in a political society that could be reasonably described as "ideal" in all respects (unless our "ideals" are ridiculously modest). What, then, is the relevance of some abstract philosophical ideal of political life to our actual lives in quite non-ideal circumstances?

One popular answer to that question follows the lead of John Rawls, who distinguished between (what he called) "ideal theory" and "non-ideal theory" in political philosophy. Rawls wanted to carefully separate philosophical reasoning about the best form for political society to take from philosophical reasoning about the rules we should follow in the very imperfect political societies in which we find ourselves. Roughly, the principles of ideal theory should collectively define a political ideal—a model of the best possible political society that is consistent with realistic assumptions about persons and societies (what Rawls eventually came to call "a realistic utopia"[17])—that could serve as the "target" for non-ideal theory. The principles of non-ideal theory would then specify the best path from here to there, the rules for accomplishing a fair, efficient, politically possible transition from our current state to one closely approximating the ideal target.

Rawls' ideal theory assumes "strict compliance" with the institutions of the basic structure of society (i.e., that people act justly and help to uphold just institutions, so far as it is possible for them to do so) and then asks which principles could "well order" a political society under those conditions. What, in short, would be an ideal political arrangement that could realistically hope to motivate such compliance, to (in Rawls' phrase) "generate its own support"? What is the best political life that we could bring into existence by our own choices, given the limits set by our moral and psychological natures and by facts about social institutions and how humans can live under them? Our answer will set the goal for non-ideal theory, which will then proceed to specify the rules for advancing toward that goal by dealing with two kinds of obstacles to its attainment: deliberate noncompliance with ideal principles by institutions and persons (to be addressed according to non-ideal rules specifying how to deal with unjust governments and persons) and unfavorable historical, social, or economic conditions, which make achieving ideal arrangements very difficult or impossible.[18]

Rawls himself concentrated throughout his career on ideal theory, for obvious reasons. While philosophical judgments about the fairness of transitional rules will be a necessary component of non-ideal theory (as will judgments about the acceptability of the moral costs of transition[19]), much of the rest of the work in non-ideal theory will either be better suited to social scientists (making judgments about what policies will "work" best in our actual political lives) or be highly relativized to the particular societal circumstances under consideration (i.e., how we should get from here to there depends very much on where "here" is).

The current book, like Rawls' books, will discuss principally questions of ideal theory in political philosophy. To those who insist that the more urgent work in political philosophy is work in non-ideal theory—after all, we want our practical philosophy to help us understand what we should do here and now—the only possible reply is the one that Rawls would no doubt make. We can properly understand what we should do here and now only after we have understood where we are trying to go from here. To those who suggest that the ideal target set by ideal theory should be not only feasible but "accessible"[20]—thus bringing the ideal closer to our immediate practical aims—the response should be that weakening the ideal in this way leaves it unclear why even further weakenings are not equally defensible, resulting in a morally anemic "ideal" (say, of the best political society that is "easily achievable"). But to thus lower our sights is to effectively abandon the conception of an ideal as our ultimate target in political philosophy. It is, in my view, the first job of political philosophy to specify a robust political ideal toward which our efforts in our non-ideal world should be aimed.

1.6. The Book

The remainder of this book will proceed in the following fashion. In Chapter 2, we will examine the traditional project of justifying the state, though in a rather different way from what is usual. Where most political philosophers have asked (following the great social contract theorists) "How is the state justified; that is, how can the state be shown to be prudentially and morally superior to the state of nature (i.e., to a condition of anarchy)?" we will ask instead the more general and open question "What is the best form of social organization (for beings like ourselves in a world like ours)?" For there are, as we shall see, more choices to consider than merely anarchy or the modern territorial state, and there is no reason to begin by assuming that the state *must* be justifiable. There are both more cooperative nonpolitical options to weigh as well as quite different political options (including, e.g., less territorial and world-state possibilities). In Chapter 3, the discussion turns more directly to the nature of the moral relationship between states (of the sort in which we currently live) and political subjects (such as ourselves). How can a state achieve legitimacy with respect to us, and what are the nature of and limits on the moral obligations we owe to our states? Modern states typically claim rights to obedience from their subjects, rights to independence from the control of those external to the state, and rights to sovereignty over a particular geographical territory. Chapter 3 focuses principally on the first of these claims, while later chapters (especially Chapter 6) will address the others.

Chapters 2 and 3 of the book thus deal (broadly) with questions about the nature and basis of political authority. With Chapter 4, the book turns to the second basic problem area of political philosophy: the proper organization or structure of political life. Assuming that political society can be justified and legitimated, how should it be ordered? The first requirement and principal virtue of a state is justice, and Chapter 4 explores the meaning and substance of political justice. Contemporary political philosophy has been so thoroughly dominated by discussions of justice that it will seem to some futile and misguided to devote to the subject (as I do here) only a single chapter. And it would be irresponsible of me not to note accordingly that my perspective on the terrain of political philosophy is a minority view (or, at least, an unfashionable one). As we will see, my approach to political philosophy comes closer to exemplifying the "Lockean" approach to the subject than it does the "Kantian" approach. I concede that my approach here will be forced to treat quite briefly much that merits more extended discussion. But I do hope that the first three chapters of the book will persuade readers of the propriety of my emphases.

We continue in Chapter 5 by examining the purported justifications of democratic government, exploring both the possible varieties of democratic order and the various values in light of which democratic government is said to be superior to its rivals. Many have argued, of course, that both state legitimacy and distributive justice require the operation of democratic political institutions, so the discussion in Chapter 5 will constitute a natural extension of those in Chapters 3 and 4. Finally, Chapter 6 considers the importance to political philosophy of relationships other than the simple citizen–state relationship: for instance, the moral relationships between states, between a state and those outside the state's boundaries, and between a state and distinct (e.g., tribal, national) groups within its boundaries. We conclude, then, by addressing both international and intranational dimensions of political philosophy, returning at the same time to themes touched on only quickly in prior chapters; our discussion here will center on questions about international distributive justice, state claims to territorial sovereignty, the rights of minority and national groups, and the justification of secession. Thus, this last chapter deals with issues central to a proper understanding of both political authority and distributive justice.

Suggested Reading

David Copp, *Morality, Normativity, and Society* (New York: Oxford University Press, 1995).
Margaret Gilbert, *On Social Facts* (Princeton: Princeton University Press, 1989).
Jean Hampton, *Political Philosophy* (Boulder: Westview, 1997).
Gerald MacCallum, *Political Philosophy* (Englewood Cliffs, NJ: Prentice Hall, 1987).
Thomas Nagel, *Equality and Partiality* (New York: Oxford University Press, 1991).

CHAPTER 2

States?

2.1. Why Have Political Societies?

If political philosophy is the evaluative study of political societies, its most fundamental question must be "Why have (create, support) political societies of any sort?"[1] Are political societies better (for us, here and now) than their alternatives and, if so, better in what way(s)? Why should we not live completely nonpolitical lives—not in the sense that many of us do now (i.e., by ignoring political matters, despising politicians, declining to vote, etc.) but in the sense of living with others without any political organization whatsoever to structure and control our interactions? None of us should have much trouble thinking of at least some respects in which we might be better off without political societies, but the positive case for political societies has always seemed to most so obviously strong that anarchist arguments to the contrary have earned their authors reputations ranging from wildly eccentric to dangerously subversive. Political life seems to most of us to plainly be at least permissible and prudent (if not morally obligatory) for us, with anything that threatens its continuation constituting an attack on our most basic interests.

As these quick remarks may have already suggested to the careful reader, however, it is easy on this topic to run together a variety of related but importantly distinct questions. To start, we can distinguish three such questions. First, what is the best form of social life (for us here and now)? Second, what forms of social life are acceptable? It could, of course, turn out that there is a range of permissible, advantageous forms of social life, all of which are acceptable, with all but one being less than ideal. Provided that it is morally permissible for us to create and sustain a form of life and that that form of life offers us clear advantages over at least some kinds of obvious alternatives, we might want to claim for that form of life a kind of justification—even if not the same kind of justification we would be giving if we showed it to be the best or the ideal form of social life.

This way of thinking about justification—in the dual terms of permissibility (i.e., acceptability) and optimality (i.e., what is best)—should not strike us as odd or unnatural. After all, when we attempt to justify our everyday actions, we reason in similar ways. We frequently try to show only that it was morally permissible and prudentially rational[2] for us to act in the way we did, all the while acknowledging that what we did was not the very best that could have been done[3] and that an even better action would have been equally, or even more strongly, justified. (Thus, I can justify going hiking this afternoon by showing only that it will wrong nobody else and please me, even though I know that I can do better morally [e.g., by spending that time helping the needy] or even better prudentially [e.g., by spending that time enhancing some more useful skill].) We can say, analogously, that a form of social life is justified if it is (at least) morally permissible and prudentially rational (in these senses) for us to create and/or sustain it.[4]

So the question "Why have political societies?" can be understood as asking either "Are political societies (or political societies of some specific kind) *best* for us?" or "Are political societies *acceptable* for us?" Both are ways of asking "Are political societies *justified*?" But there is still a third, distinct question with which these two might be confused: "Must we *create* political societies where none exist or *support* political societies (such as those in which we live) that do exist?" This can be seen to be a distinct question from the other two by noting that (1) a form of political society could be ideal without it being incumbent on us to create or support it, given that we do not ordinarily take ourselves to be bound always to do what is ideal or best, so long as what we do is at least permissible, and (2) a form of political society being merely acceptable seems to leave open to us the option of creating or supporting an alternative arrangement that is equally as acceptable as or better than the society in question. The question of whether or when we must create and/or support political societies, then, I will (for the most part) treat separately, leaving it largely for Chapter 3. Here, let us concentrate on our first two questions about justification (i.e., whether political society is best or acceptable).

There is one final potential ambiguity in the question "Why have political societies?" that must be quickly mentioned. In the contemporary mind, a question like "Why have political societies?" is almost bound to be understood as the question "Why have *states*?" The modern state is the only form of political society with which we have had much real experience, and a world consisting of a large plurality of sovereign, territorial states seems to most of us perfectly natural and virtually inevitable. But we should keep in mind that there have been in human history good examples of rather different kinds of political orders and that it is easy to imagine as well alternative political arrangements of which we have as yet seen no clear historical instances. For example, to name only a few obvious cases, the ancient Greek polis, the Roman Empire, and feudal relations in the middle ages all constituted (or included) plainly political orders but ones that differed in a variety of significant ways from our current political organizations.[5] Similarly, various migratory tribal and clan societies resembled modern political societies in certain salient fashions but were (among other differences) far less territorial in nature—either claiming as their own no fixed territories at all or claiming only rights of use (rather than rights to complete and permanent control) with respect to land and water. And organizations like the United Nations, the World Court, and the European Union suggest to an even moderately active imagination the possibility (even if not in the near future) of political orders like a world-federation or world-state, again quite different from our current political order.[6]

In short, in asking "Why have political societies?" we are not asking only "Why have states (of the modern sort)?" but instead whether *any* form of political life—past, present, or possible—is best (or acceptable) for us and (indirectly) whether the political world of modern states is to be preferred both to nonpolitical life and to alternative kinds of political life. We must remember as we proceed the ways in which our account of political society (in Chapter 1, section 1.3) was not simply a definition of the modern state. The modern state is characterized most saliently by (1) its claim to (and exercise of) sovereignty and (2) its claim to (and thorough control over) a relatively fixed geographical territory. *Sovereignty* (as we will see later in more detail) is usually understood to be the property (of the state) of being the final authority and sole source of binding law within its territory and of being independent of any external authorities (such as other states). Our definition of *political society,* by contrast, presupposed neither that such a society controls or claims a fixed territory (a political society's government could, say, make and enforce law for a people, identified nongeographically, rather than for all within a territory) nor that it is (or even claims to be) sovereign in the familiar senses (a political society could, e.g., accept other sources of law [e.g., church or custom] beyond its own government's creation or authoritative interpretation and even other kinds of law enforcement).

2.2. Justifying the State

The traditional project in political philosophy of "justifying the (modern) state," then, involves justifying only one possible kind of political society. Even were such a justification successful, some other kind of political society might still turn out to be better than the state. But let us at least begin with this traditional project, for two reasons. First, that project can certainly be plausibly described as the most central and familiar project in the history of political philosophy. And second, there is good reason to suppose in advance that the moral and prudential advantages of the modern state (i.e., those appealed to in its justification) will be shared in at least some measure by alternative forms of political society. Political life, we might say, seems likely to offer a mostly fixed range of benefits, regardless of its precise form. So in examining the justification of the state, we are likely to have placed before us as well most of what can be claimed (to a greater or lesser degree) on behalf of any other kind of political society.

The traditional justification of the state—best known to most students of political philosophy from the writings of Hobbes and Locke—involved an attempt to demonstrate that the state (or that a certain kind of state) is preferable to that nonpolitical condition called "the state of nature" (and, thus, that the state is both acceptable and best for us, relative to the state of nature). The state of nature is often equated with the condition of "anarchy," which seems perfectly fair if we are using the word *anarchy* in one only of its familiar senses, where it means "absence of government." The state of nature is then simply the absence of political society, which adequately captures the meaning intended by those who originally helped to popularize the phrase. If, however, we allow the term *anarchy* (and the associated idea of the state of nature) to convey as well its broader connotations of "chaos," "confusion," and "mayhem," we unfairly prejudge the anarchist's position. For the anarchist maintains that life in a state of nature is preferable (both morally and prudentially) to life in the state (or, for that matter, in any other kind of political society), precisely because such a nonpolitical existence can avoid the necessary evils of politics *without* paying the price of social chaos and confusion. We must in fairness also avoid thinking of the state of nature as simply that largely prehistorical period that preceded all political society (or that preceded it in some geographical area)—an interpretation of "state of nature" that is common in secondary works in political theory and that leads inevitably to unfairly charging (e.g.) Hobbes and Locke with doing "bad history." For while both Hobbes and Locke thought of the state of nature as having actual historical instantiations that included prehistorical times, both maintained as well that the state of nature characterized many recent and contemporary social conditions.[7] (Indeed, there is good reason to believe that both Hobbes and Locke viewed their own contemporary England as having existed in the state of nature for substantial periods of time during their lives.[8]) The best-known state of nature stories were not intended to describe (only) the lives of primitive savages but, rather, to reveal the problems common to life without government in *any* era.[9]

By "the state of nature," then, we can mean simply any condition (at any point in human history) in which people live together without political society (i.e., without real, effective government),[10] and our basic (traditional) justificatory question will thus be whether the state (or, at least, whether some kind of state) is better for us than would be a life in the state of nature, so understood. Now, on its face this question looks like one that cannot be answered without considerable qualification. Surely, we might say, despite the obvious advantages of states, it is too easy simply to respond that life in a state is necessarily better than nonpolitical life. For states can be quite unpleasant and dangerous, either because of their structures (e.g., in certain hereditary monarchies, where by law massive, unchecked power is placed in haphazardly selected hands) or because of their leaders (e.g., when a well-structured polity has the misfortune to empower a group of government officials who turn out to be corrupt, avaricious, and sadistic). And even when it is compared to quite decent states, it seems, the state of nature might be preferable for certain groups of people—for instance, for a group of rugged, independent, rough-and-tumble types (say, mountain men) or even just for a group of peaceful, cooperative, like-minded persons (say, Quakers)—or for groups living in certain geographical areas, such as those with small populations and substantial natural bounty (a particularly nice South Pacific island, say). More plainly needs to be said to sharpen our justificatory question.

And more, of course, has been said. In the first place, almost nobody but Hobbes has seriously argued that life in just any kind of state is preferable to life in any kind of state of nature. Political philosophers since (and famously including) Locke have generally allowed that without substantial institutional safeguards designed to secure justice in the state and to protect subjects from their rulers (among others), the state of nature might in fact be preferable to the state.[11] Similarly, though less often explicitly acknowledged, it would be foolish to deny that nonpolitical life might be preferable (at least prudentially) to even life in a decent state under certain realizable conditions or for certain groups (such as those mentioned above), particularly where those groups would be unlikely to come into regular contact with others.[12] Any plausible justification of the state must be a justification of decent states for normal populations in normal material conditions. Such a justification, of course, will "reach" virtually all of us (i.e., it will give us all compelling reasons to favor decent states) since we are in fact part of normal populations in normal conditions. It is thus enough of a justification to aspire to.

As we have seen, to justify a form of social life is to show it to be an acceptable (or the ideal) life for us, to show it to be morally permissible (or ideal) and prudentially rational (or ideal) for us to create and sustain that form of life. So to justify the state in the traditional way—that is, with the state of nature as the sole alternative considered—is to show that the (or some kind of) state is preferable to the state of nature on either moral or prudential grounds (or on both) and not condemnable (as inferior to the state of nature) on either. More specifically, the justification will need to identify moral or prudential advantages of the state over the state of nature, advantages that are not outweighed or equaled by disadvantages in other areas.[13]

The prudential advantages of the state are perhaps the most obvious, for states plainly provide (or make it possible for us to provide for ourselves) many important goods that virtually all of us want and depend upon, goods that it seems it would be very hard (or perhaps even impossible) for persons to create for themselves in a state of nature. For instance, the governments of most states create or support a single secured currency for exchange, a unified highway and transportation network, an ordered communications and postal system, a system of public schools and hospitals, various "legal opportunities" (e.g., making enforceable contracts, wills, marriages), assistance for the poor and disabled, cultural and recreational resources (e.g., museums, parks), and environmental protection.

But these kinds of prudential advantages, substantial as they may be, all pale before the chief good supplied by the state, the good stressed centrally in virtually all justifications of the state: namely, *security* (from violence, theft, and fraud). All of us are vulnerable to attack, particularly while sleeping, ill, or working to provide for our needs. States, through their armies, police, and legal systems, seek to deter and (where deterrence fails) to punish those who would prey upon their subjects, providing a substantial level of security for persons and their possessions, security against both domestic and foreign aggressors. While the level of security provided by the state plainly varies from state to state, as well as from place to place within individual states, some reasonable level of security is required if the "state" is even going to qualify as a political society (since political societies, remember, effectively enforce with significant sanctions broad requirements of peaceful, cooperative conduct). And all states that do not tyrannize their own subjects would seem to provide a level of security superior to that which could be hoped for in a state of nature. For without government, it appears, aggressors would be neither deterred before the fact (by the threat of legal punishment) nor disabled after the fact (by the use of legal punishment), forcing persons to rely for their security solely on their own quite limited strength and powers of anticipation. The prudential advantages of the state (over the state of nature), then, seem clear and considerable.

The moral advantages have seemed to most political philosophers quite obvious as well. One could, of course, still try to justify the state while admitting that the state and the state of nature are moral equals, neither being superior on moral grounds to the other, both being merely permissible conditions for people to create and sustain. The case for the state would then rest entirely on its prudential advantages. But even Locke, the classical political philosopher whose position comes closest to this view, clearly regarded the (limited) state as morally superior to even a quite civilized state of nature. While Locke stressed that persons were morally free to choose between the state and the state of nature, both choices being permissible,[14] he held as well that persons' natural rights are much more effectively and reliably secured in a (limited) state than in the state of nature.

All persons, Locke argued, are born to (and, at maturity, fully possess) moral rights not to be harmed in their lives, health, liberty, or possessions, provided only that they themselves respect the rights of others (through obedience to the law of nature that defines those rights). In a state of nature, persons are entitled to secure their own rights by threats and defensive actions, as well as by punishing and taking just compensation from those who violate their rights.[15] They are entitled as well to help defend others and to punish those who wrong others. But in a state of nature, this private (or group) securing of individual rights is likely to be sporadic and only unreliably effective, for people in anarchy will both often disagree about exactly what their rights are and often lack the power (or the courage) to enforce their rights against dangerous aggressors.[16] In a (limited) state, by contrast, there are both impartial judges to determine the nature of people's rights and sufficient force at hand to back up those judgments. People's natural rights, then, are more likely to be respected—and, when not respected, more likely to be vindicated by punishment and/or compensation—in a state than in a state of nature. Since it is better morally that rights be respected and enforced than that they be violated, the state is clearly morally superior to the state of nature for Locke (not to mention its superiority on prudential grounds), despite the fact that Locke sees us as under no moral obligation to choose the state over the state of nature[17] (or to remain the subject of a state, unless we have freely agreed to a permanent obligation of subjection).

Other political philosophers have identified different (or additional) moral advantages of the state over the state of nature, at least partly because they have embraced different moral theories than Locke's. Utilitarians, for instance—who have usually denied the existence of natural rights (and thus denied the moral advantage of the state identified by Locke)—have typically argued that the state is justified instead by virtue of its producing a greater expectable utility (i.e., total happiness, well-being, pleasure, desire satisfaction) than would be produced by nonpolitical social life.[18] Whether or not the state can be expected to make each person better off in this way—increasing the personal utility of each over a state of nature—it can at least be expected to improve the total (aggregate, summed) utility of its subjects over what they would enjoy in a state of nature, precisely by virtue of the state's provision or facilitation of the various goods appealed to in the prudential justification of the state. Since utilitarians maintain that we are obligated to maximize expected utility (or to obey rules, general adherence to which will maximize expected utility), it follows for them that we are obligated to create states where they do not exist and to support them where they do. The state is not just morally superior but optional, as in Locke; states are morally required.

Interestingly, that same conclusion is defended by that great antiutilitarian philosopher Kant and by his equally antiutilitarian contemporary followers. For Kant, there is only one basic (innate) right possessed by each of us: the right to be free. But real freedom is impossible in the lawless condition of the state of nature, where other rights can at best be only "provisional."[19] Accordingly, each of us has the right (derived from our innate right to be free) that others quit the state of nature to help to create and/or support a form of social life in which we can be genuinely free and can enjoy real rights. That form of social life is the state, which all are duty-bound to sustain. Contemporary Kantians have mounted similar arguments for the morally mandatory nature of the state, now stressing (in place of the rejected Kantian idea of the state as realizer of innate rights) the state's role as the provider of distributive justice and aid to the needy (the latter usually being viewed as one central aspect of justice, as we will see when we return to the subject of justice in Chapter 4). It is not enough, the argument goes, that people merely refrain from violence (theft, fraud) toward others and help the needy with their surplus property (which is all that Locke's morality requires of us)—requirements that could be satisfied even in a state of nature, making the state (and political society generally) look morally optional. Without the state, there can be no justice, which requires an institutional structure to insure fairness in large-scale distributions of liberty and material goods. Justice is morally imperative. So the state, as a necessary condition for a just life, is morally superior to the state of nature, and each of us is duty-bound to help to create and/or sustain the kind of political–institutional structure that can alone make justice possible.

Other arguments for the moral advantages of states are, of course, possible. But it is worth noticing here the ways in which the moral arguments for states that we have considered thus far are all in a way "parasitic" on the prudential arguments for the state enumerated earlier. It is because the state provides security (and other goods important to and wanted by virtually all people) that rights are more likely to be respected in the state than in the state of nature (giving the state its Lockean moral superiority); that the state is likely to produce more aggregate utility (giving the state its utilitarian moral superiority); that the state can make real freedom, real rights, and justice possible (giving the state its Kantian moral superiority). This suggests that if it were possible to enjoy the goods to which the prudential argument for the state centrally refers without the state—in a state of nature—then the state of nature might be able to enjoy as well the moral advantages ascribed to the state by its defenders. That, of course, has been the (or, at least, one) anarchist project: to show that the most important goods said by statists to be tied necessarily to the state can in fact be provided by nonpolitical persons in anarchy. These goods, anarchists contend, can (or will) be created by individuals without governments, as a result of (according to the individualist–anarchist line) self-interested co-operative conduct and market forces or (according to the communitarian–anarchist line) natural community harmony.

So why couldn't a state of nature produce the various goods we have listed, possibly reaping as well the moral advantages that the provision of those goods makes possible? After all, it is easy enough to imagine even unextraordinary people, with no government direction or assistance at all, still managing to settle on a system of exchange, or a common "currency," or linking their private roadways into a continuous route for shared use, isn't it? Even if imagining that does seem easy, it is probably less easy for most of us to imagine other kinds of goods being reliably produced in anarchy, chief among them the paramount good of security. For if the cold war taught us anything, it taught us how unsupervised individual quests for security (or, in the case of the cold war, unsupervised quests by individual states) can produce quite astonishing collective *insecurity*. Nobody who was taught in school how to "duck and cover" (in order to survive a nuclear blast) or who cowered through the Cuban Missile Crisis will ever need to be reminded of that lesson. On the other hand, the terrors of the cold war also make it unnecessary to remind us that the presence of states in the world hardly solves all security problems. It was Hobbes who first fully appreciated the problems associated with attempts to produce collective goods—and, in particular, the collective good of security—in anarchy, and it is to his famous arguments (and their contemporary descendants) that we need to turn now.

2.3. Hobbesian Games

Hobbes' *Leviathan*[20] paints a very different picture of life in the state of nature from what we see in anarchist writings, or even in Locke's *Two Treatises*. For Locke, life in the state of nature can be expected to be tolerable but "inconvenient," with people generally respecting each others' rights and living cooperatively and productively but with the threat of attack and the prospect of open warfare sufficient to render life reasonably (but not insufferably) insecure. For Hobbes, by contrast, life in the state of nature will inevitably be (in his famous phrase) "solitary, poor, nasty, brutish and short," with people engaged in a continuous "war of every man against every man." There will be "no place for industry . . . no culture of the earth . . . no commodious building . . . no arts; no letters; no society; and what is worst of all, continual fear and danger of violent death."[21]

Why this dramatic difference in the two accounts of life in anarchy? Part of the difference, as we shall see, is that Locke (along with others, like Rousseau, who also describes a more benign state of nature) finds in persons motivations for sociable conduct that Hobbes does not. But a bigger difference is undoubtedly that Hobbes centrally focuses on, while Locke (again with Rousseau) largely ignores, a compelling argument that at first blush appears to have as its inescapable conclusion the (prudential) *irrationality* of cooperative, peaceful conduct in anarchy. People seduced by this argument (as people in the state of nature will predictably eventually be, Hobbes thinks) will produce insecurity and war, however much they might prefer security and peace.

The basic elements of the argument are as follows.[22] Suppose (as Hobbes does) that we have in the state of nature (living together without government) a population of persons who are forward-looking, death-averse, and largely egoistic so that they all want for themselves at least a reasonable level of material well-being and security. Suppose further that these persons are roughly equal in wit and strength, all being (e.g.) vulnerable to attack while sleeping or by a group of aggressors. Finally, suppose that there is in the world a moderate scarcity of the goods these persons need or want so that conflict and competition involving those goods are inevitable. Given these conditions—conditions which characterize humankind's actual natural condition, according to Hobbes—the state of nature will, Hobbes argues, inevitably be a condition of war (of all against all). There are, in fact, three distinct reasons persons under these conditions will have for making war on others: competition (for scarce goods), diffidence (fear of attack by others), and glory (the pleasure of dominating others).[23]

Now, one might think, of course, that even given these reasons for making war, the more (prudentially) rational strategy is still to behave peacefully since all prefer the security and prosperity of peace to the horrors of war. One might try peacefully "hiding out" in the state of nature, avoiding contact with others and using force only when attacked. But those who try to hide out will have great difficulty competing with others for scarce goods, and they will be doing nothing to deter those who will want to attack them for their goods, for fun, or to force them to work as slaves or allies. Or one might pursue the strategy of cooperation, showing a willingness to disarm and settle on reasonable terms for peace with others. But pursuing this strategy, it seems, will simply make one easy prey for others, while at best creating a "peace" that merely reproduces within the "peaceful," cooperating group the same kinds of problems of distrust and insecurity that exist outside the group. In the end, Hobbes argues, "there is no way for any man to secure himself so reasonable as anticipation," where by *anticipation* Hobbes means maintaining a high defensive profile while trying "by force or wiles to master the persons of all men he can, so long 'til he sees no other power great enough to endanger him."[24]

The paradoxical aspect of this argument, of course, is that where individuals (in anarchy) pursue the prudentially rational strategy of anticipation, they will, Hobbes argues, inevitably produce the collective result of war—a result to which every individual rationally prefers a state of peace. It might seem, then, that Hobbes' argument has somehow gone off the tracks, that the rational individual strategy must be one that leads to collective peace since that is the result that all prefer. In a sense, this is Hobbes' ultimate conclusion as well. But we cannot reach that conclusion so quickly, for what is striking about Hobbes' characterization of life in the state of nature is that it seems to describe an end result—namely, peace—that all prefer to the alternatives but to which there is no individually rational path.

Hobbes' initial account of people seeking security in anarchy describes a situation that is in fact a variant of the collective action problem referred to in contemporary game theory as "the Prisoners' Dilemma." To see the logic of the problem in its purest form—and to see just how common such problems in fact are (i.e., to see that they are not confined to the predicament of separately interrogated criminals)—let us take a simple example of mutually desired exchange between two persons. I advertise my willingness to sell a particular book for $10, and you call me to express your desire to purchase it for that price. Both of us prefer that the exchange take place to a continuation of the status quo (i.e., I'd rather have your $10 than my book; you'd rather have my book than your $10), so we agree on the phone to an exchange through the mail: I'll send you the book and you'll send me $10. Then we hang up the phone and try to decide what is the (prudentially) rational course of action. I think: "What if I send the book and you *don't* send the money? Then I'll have nothing. If I instead *don't* send the book, I may end up with *both* the book and the money; and, at worst, I'll still have my book. I'm better off not sending the book no matter which choice you make." So reneging on our agreement (what we can call "defecting") looks more rational for me than honoring it (which we can call "cooperating"). You, meanwhile, are reasoning in precisely the same way (positions reversed). As a result, if both of us are rational, neither of us will do as we agreed to do. The mutually desired exchange will not take place (no matter how many subsequent phone calls and new promises are made), and we will have produced a result that both of us regard as worse than the result where we both honor our telephone agreement. But, it seems, we are unable to rationally bring about the result we both prefer.

The results ("payoffs") for this "game" can be represented schematically as follows in Matrix A (with my payoffs for the four possible conjunctions of actions in the lower left corners of the four boxes and yours in the upper right corners):

A	You	
	Defect	Cooperate

	Defect	Cooperate
Defect	Money / Book	Neither / Both
Cooperate	Both / Neither	Book / Money

(A label "Me" appears to the left of the rows.)

Each of us is better off defecting (reneging on our agreement) than cooperating (honoring it), regardless of what the other player does—or, to use the language of game theory, the strategy of defecting *dominates* that of cooperating. This can be seen even more clearly if we rank the preferred outcomes for each player, as in Matrix B:

B		You	
		Defect	Cooperate
Me	Defect	3 / 3	4 / 1
	Cooperate	1 / 4	2 / 2

My favorite outcome (1) is where I end up with both my book and your money; my second favorite (2) is where I have your money only; my third favorite (3) is where I have my book only; and my least favorite (4) is where I end up with neither. (Your preferences mirror mine but favor having the book only over having the money only.) If you defect, I will get either my preference 3 (if I also defect) or preference 4 (if I cooperate), so I prefer to defect as well. If you cooperate, I get either 1 (if I defect) or 2 (if I also cooperate), so I prefer to defect. In either case, then, I fare better by defecting and, by parity of reasoning, so do you. But if both of us behave rationally and defect, each of us will get only preference 3 (namely, the status quo before our agreement), when there is another outcome (namely, where we have both cooperated and the exchange takes place) that we both prefer to that since it gives each of us preference 2 instead. The opportunity to take advantage of another's cooperative behavior along with the need to guard against being taken advantage of oneself combine to make pursuit of the mutually preferred outcome irrational.

It should be easy now to see the similarities between this case of promised exchange and the Hobbesian case of persons in anarchy, despite the difference that ours is only a simple, two-player game, where Hobbes' state of nature is a more complex $1 + n$–player game. In both cases, unilateral cooperative behavior leaves one vulnerable to the worst possible outcome, while uncooperative behavior (if all are rational) merely preserves an undesirable status quo. What seems out of reach for (prudentially) rational persons is the outcome that is mutually preferred to the status quo (peace in Hobbes' case, beneficial exchange in ours). But it should be easy as well now to think of ways in which the stories can be altered slightly so that the mutually preferred outcome could rationally be reached. Suppose, for example, that the players had rational grounds for trusting one another not to take advantage, as they might if they were friends, say, or if both were well known to be principled keepers of agreements. Wouldn't this make it rational for both to cooperate? Well, you might respond, if I were sure that the other player were going to behave cooperatively (i.e., behave peacefully, keep our agreement), that would give me no reason at all to cooperate myself and settle for my preference 2; it would instead give me even more reason to defect and take advantage, securing my first preference among the possible outcomes.

To be sure, this response seems to betray a certain misunderstanding of what it is to be a friend or to have principles. But to be fair to Hobbes' argument, it is surely true that in a well-populated state of nature, one will be dealing primarily with people who are not one's friends and who are not of knowably flawless reputation, so that the rational general strategic stance will still have to be uncooperative anticipation, producing war (even leaving aside the unlikelihood of friendships or principles or trust flourishing in the conditions Hobbes describes). It should, however, still be noted that if we could identify specific motivations in most persons that antecedently inclined them to favor cooperation with all other persons—and not just with a tiny minority (e.g., friends, family, the principled) of those with whom they will need to deal—then this would alter the payoffs (and preference rankings) in a way that could dissolve the dilemma and make rational a cooperative play. The principal reason that other prominent state of nature theorists did not follow the Hobbesian (Prisoners' Dilemma) analysis of the state of nature, I think, is precisely that they did see (where Hobbes did not) antecedent motivations for cooperation as natural in humankind. In Locke (and in the writings of "communitarian" or communist anarchists like Kropotkin[25] and Marx), for instance, the motivation in question is a natural *sociability,* a desire to live with and be in concord with one's fellows. In Rousseau, the motivation is *sympathy* (empathy, compassion) for the suffering of others and the consequent unwillingness to unnecessarily harm them. Either motivation, when allowed to modify the predominantly egoistic motivational structure of Hobbesian persons, is capable of altering the payoffs (and changing the preference rankings) in our game to favor cooperative play so that the state of nature is no longer adequately modeled by the Prisoners' Dilemma. Successful advantage taking is no longer ranked higher than successful cooperation, so noncooperation (defection) ceases to be the dominant state of nature strategy.

How else (besides new "cooperative motives") could the mutually preferred outcome be rationally reached by Hobbesian persons in anarchy? Another obvious solution might be to simply introduce into the game a reliable *enforcer* of agreements, who punishes those who renege (or, in the state of nature case, who punishes those who don't behave peacefully). The enforcer's punishments could reduce the payoff for successful advantage taking sufficiently to make the payoff for mutual cooperation the first preference for both players, again dissolving the dilemma. In a political society, of course, it is routinely the job of the legal system to play precisely this role of enforcer (though individual conscience and the threat of social sanctions like ostracism also play part of this role). The addition of an enforcer to the game is in fact ultimately a part of Hobbes' solution to the problem of life in the state of nature. That enforcer is Hobbes' *sovereign,* a person or body sufficiently powerful and sufficiently motivated to keep the peace by the threat of punishment for warlike behavior. The creation of a sovereign (and of the political society ruled by the sovereign) is what Hobbes believes is necessary to end the war of all against all, and the best sovereign is the one (an absolute monarch, in Hobbes' view) least likely to allow a collapse back into the horrors of the state of nature. Hobbes thus plainly believes that the state is justified as the best form of social life for us, however difficult it might be for us to reach it.

This difficulty of achievement, however, means that it is not enough for Hobbes to simply say that people in the state of nature should come together and create a sovereign to solve their problems. For coming together in that way requires precisely the same kind of trust and cooperation—and produces the same opportunities for and vulnerability to advantage taking—that characterized their initial dilemma. While all might prefer to have a sovereign enforcer and the peace this would bring, nobody can rationally lower his or her defenses long enough to help create one (by, e.g., laying down arms, assisting in the creation of armies, police, fortresses, prisons, etc.).[26] So Hobbes still needs to explain how rational cooperation in the creation of a state (with its sovereign enforcer) is possible in the state of nature.

Hobbes' ultimate explanation is found in his reply to *Leviathan*'s "foole,"[27] a fool who reasons in just the way that our "prudentially rational" defectors reasoned. This explanation points to three necessary additions to our Prisoners' Dilemma model of the state of nature. First, our discussion thus far has concerned only "one-shot" (or single-play) Prisoners' Dilemmas, where the players are concerned solely with maximizing their immediate payoffs from the game. But typical social conditions, including interaction in a state of nature, will involve not one Prisoners' Dilemma–style situation but a long series (or iteration) of such situations, in which players will regularly confront again those with whom they have previously played or those who have witnessed or heard about their performances in previous games. I might succeed, for instance, in taking advantage of your cooperative behavior (if, say, you send your money while I keep my book) in our first game; but I will then simply be excluded from all subsequent games by you (and by those who know about my conduct), and I will thus lose any chance of gaining from future mutually beneficial exchanges (or, for that matter, from future advantage taking). Many game theorists have argued that in iterated Prisoners' Dilemmas (or, at least, in iterated dilemmas with an indefinite number of plays), as well as in iterated games with more than two players, the individually rational strategy is in fact not defection (i.e., noncooperation) but, rather, one like "tit-for-tat" (in which a player cooperates until the opponent defects and then mirrors the opponent's plays).[28]

Second, one might imagine in response to this worry that all that is really needed in order to benefit most from defection is a bit more cleverness and selectivity in one's advantage taking. One needs to operate more like Thrasymachus' unjust man,[29] preying selectively and secretly on the foolish cooperators around one, eliminating witnesses where necessary, but carefully preserving a (false) reputation for justice so that one will not be excluded from future opportunities for beneficial cooperation. To this sort of fool Hobbes says it is irrational to in this way rest your chances for future happiness on the stupidity and inattention of others, relying on good luck to avoid being branded an unreliable or dangerous associate. This is particularly irrational in light of the fact that (third) the potential payoff for successful cooperation in the state of nature is so substantial and the potential payoff for single-play advantage taking is so limited. When people succeed in cooperating together, they reap both immediate advantages as well as longer-term benefits in opportunities for future cooperation. But above all, when people are known to be good cooperators (reneging or being warlike only where others do so first), they will be regarded by others as good candidates for inclusion in any *political* associations that might be forged. And successful cooperation in that endeavor will give to all the enormous benefits of peace and security. By contrast, those excluded from the association (by virtue of their warlike, noncooperative records) are condemned to live out their short, miserable lives in a state of war with each other (a prospect not that much better than death at the hands of a defecting advantage taker).

We could represent these facts schematically (in Matrix C) by adding cardinal payoffs (representing dollars, units of happiness, or the like) to the ordinal preference rankings (the numbers in parentheses) and allowing the cardinal payoffs to represent the expected gains or losses from a long iteration of Prisoners' Dilemma–style interactions (turning it into what is sometimes called an "assurance game").

C

	You	
	Defect	Cooperate
Defect	$0 (3) $0 (3)	$–50 (4) $50 (2)
Cooperate	$50 (2) $–50 (4)	$5000 (1) $5000 (1)

(Me on the left; Defect/Cooperate rows)

Notice that Matrix C no longer represents the noncooperative strategy (defection) as dominant since each player does (much) better by cooperating when the other cooperates as well. Defection is the best choice only when the other player also defects. Successful advantage taking still offers significant benefits (over the status quo and over being taken advantage of), but these benefits pale before the benefits of successful cooperation. Not only, then, is defection no longer dominant, but the relative gain from playing cooperatively is so great that cooperation now looks like the rational play (i.e., for someone trying to maximize the expected payoff).

  The true representation of the Hobbesian state of nature, then, once the reply to the "foole" is taken into account, actually resembles Matrix C more than it does our earlier Matrix B. In Matrix D below, I have substituted the specific Hobbesian state of nature payoffs for the cardinal numbers in Matrix C. In Matrix D, mutual defection merely continues the state of war, while mutual cooperation achieves peace. Being taken advantage of gets one loss or even death, while successful advantage taking reaps one the gain taken and the glory of triumph over others. But remember, gain and glory are "enjoyed" (given these assumptions) only while one continues to exist in a state of war with others. This means that the payoff for successful advantage taking includes the payoff of a war of all against all since only by fabulous good luck will a defector be included (or, once luckily included, retained) in a political society at peace. But this included cost does not hold for the payoff for being taken advantage of, for one who incurs only loss (avoiding death) is still a realistic candidate for being included in the enjoyment of civil peace. Defection can only be the dominant strategy in Matrix D if the payoff "Gain/Glory" is preferred by both players to the payoff "Peace." But given the huge value of peace and the enormous disvalue of war (which is included in the payoff "Gain/Glory"), this cannot be the case.

D

		You	
		Defect	Cooperate
Me	**Defect**	War War	Loss/Death Gain/Glory
	Cooperate	Gain/Glory Loss/Death	Peace Peace

Hobbes' final position, then, is (to use contemporary language) that the state of nature only seems to be structured like a single-play Prisoners' Dilemma because of the seductive attractiveness of the immediate benefits that can be reaped by successful advantage taking. In fact, however, any such immediate benefits are vastly outweighed by the lost opportunity (to enter with others into a peaceful political society) which such advantage taking reliably costs. It is, Hobbes argues, in fact prudentially rational to join with others to create states where none exist and to behave cooperatively so as to preserve states where they do exist. States are better for us than the state of nature, and prudence permits (indeed requires) us to pursue them, even should we find ourselves in a state of nature. This, for Hobbes—and for the many who find his arguments persuasive—constitutes a solid prudential justification of the state.

2.4. Anarchist Doubts

But if it is prudentially rational to act peacefully in creating a state from the state of nature, the anarchist replies, why isn't it prudentially rational to just act peacefully, without a state being involved? Surely the logic of the argument remains the same: in an ongoing state of nature, uninterrupted by the creation of a state, each person continues to face a series of Prisoners' Dilemmas, great difficulties in concealing noncooperative conduct, and a huge loss if not included in future cooperative ventures. Peaceful conduct thus continues to look rational. So why isn't security just as available to rational beings in a state of nature as in a state?

The answer may be that it is just as available to people in a state of nature who behave in a reliably rational way. The problem is that people are not reliably rational. Even those who are typically rational will, without additional incentives for cooperation, occasionally give in to the temptation to take advantage, seduced by the prospect of immediate gain or by the fear of being taken advantage of themselves. Some who are less rational are moved regularly by barely controlled noncooperative passions, while others positively revel in causing injury to their fellows. Wherever rational cooperation prevails for a time, it is constantly threatened by irrationality, both from within the cooperating group and from without. The state's role is to counter such irrationality with a force sufficient to preserve the peace, by threatening and (where necessary) employing punishments for noncooperation. Even if (contra Hobbes) people are motivated by such natural cooperative sentiments as sociability, compassion, or squeamishness about violence, it is still hard to believe that these sentiments are powerful enough in all or most of us to bolster our rationality sufficiently to make peaceful, cooperative conduct the rule—without the rule of law to stiffen our resolve.

It is, of course, not only as an enforcer that the state can play an important role in countering the problems of life in the state of nature. As Locke emphasized, the (limited) state will not only restrain and punish deliberate wrongdoers better than comparatively weak individuals but also serve as a neutral, impartial judge in the inevitable disputes between individuals who genuinely intend to act rightly (but who are led into conflict by differing perceptions and biases). And the state can serve to supply *coordination* points where persons disagree about the best solutions to (or where their free choices otherwise fail to resolve) problems that all really want to cooperate in solving. For instance, where persons disagree about which side of the road to drive on or where their private charitable acts inefficiently distribute aid to the needy, governments can mandate solutions where individual action would be incapable of solving (or unlikely to solve) the problem.

Further, even in its role as enforcer, the state functions as much to *assure* as to *threaten*. There are, remember, two (prudentially rational) motives one might have for defection: the desire to reap the added benefits of noncooperative advantage taking and the desire to avoid the losses incurred by being taken advantage of while cooperating. In threatening defectors with punishment for noncooperative advantage taking, the state can at the same time solve the assurance problem of those who, but for their fear of being taken advantage of, would happily cooperate.[30] It can thus motivate peaceful, cooperative conduct on all sides, making the state's potential role in the provision of security (and other collective goods) a substantial one indeed.

The anarchist, of course, might just concede (though many do not) that the state can perform all of these functions—and thus provide these significant benefits—in a way that no individual person can provide for herself or himself. The anarchist believes, however, that individuals can interact with others to provide these benefits for themselves without help from states and at lower (prudential and moral) cost than when they are provided by states. Let us focus for a moment on the good of security, the chief benefit of which governments are alleged to be the sole possible source. Why cannot nonaggressive individuals in the state of nature simply band together with others (whom they determine to be reliable cooperators) to provide security for themselves? Where two people have a cooperative security agreement, they can watch each other's back, and one can stand guard while the other sleeps or labors for both; and two bodies are obviously better for deterring aggression than one. Admittedly, each risks (possibly fatal) defection by the other. But the prospects for solitary survival (and certainly for comfortable solitary survival) in the state of nature are so poor to begin with and the potential benefits of ongoing cooperation are so great that rational persons will accept such risks. And, of course, the benefits of cooperation—and the attractiveness of membership—increase dramatically as additional reliable people are accepted into the defensive cooperative, while the risks of being fatally taken advantage of decline. As numbers increase, some can patrol in shifts against aggressors, while the others sleep, eat, build defenses, produce food, recreate, and so on. Indeed, it would be natural for those who were especially skilled in defending against aggression to join together and offer their security services to others (less skilled in this area) for a price. These "protective agencies"[31] could then guard against (and possibly punish) aggression from without and defection (i.e., noncooperative advantage taking) from within, thus providing efficient security arrangements within a state of nature and offering their services to all of the (cooperatively qualified) clients they could attract and realistically protect.

The state thus seems unnecessary as a substitute for multiple voluntary security cooperatives.

Defenders of states commonly make either of two kinds of replies to this sort of anarchist argument. The first, well known from Robert Nozick's defense of the minimal state, is that competition between protective agencies in a state of nature will naturally produce a *dominant* protective agency, which will in turn naturally and legitimately evolve into a state.[32] State of nature security arrangements are thus inherently unstable. The second response is that wherever defensive cooperatives are sufficiently stable and successful to provide real security—so that productive labor, rest, and recreation are possible within their protective scope—those defensive cooperatives *are* states.[33]

These replies are difficult to assess precisely because (as we've seen) concepts like "political society" and "state" are so inherently vague. But to the second response, it is surely fair to reply that while a stable, successful defensive cooperative might qualify as some kind of political society, it is surely not by its nature a state in the modern sense. For it need neither be territorial (in the sense of claiming rights of control over a fixed geographical area) nor claim rights of sovereignty (in either lawgiving or external independence). Indeed, it is not at all obvious to me that a stable, successful defensive cooperative need even qualify as a political entity, given my doubts that the kinds of understandings or rules necessary simply for defensive cooperation constitute "laws" or "government." Perhaps it would be enough to allow that such a cooperative is necessarily "quasi-political" in nature but could easily lack most of the distinctive features of states.

With this understanding, we can reply to Nozick's argument in a fashion more direct and less qualified. Nozick himself rightly maintains that a dominant protective agency is not itself a state; rather, he argues only that it is morally obligated to turn itself into a state.[34] Even without questioning this line of argument—and it is in fact the most questionable aspect of Nozick's main argument in Part I of his book[35]—the anarchist can still win the argument (about whether it is possible for security to be efficiently provided in a state of nature). For efficient dominant protective agencies are, even in Nozick's account, only *obligated to become* states. They can plainly continue to function efficiently without discharging that obligation and actually becoming states.

Admittedly, this would involve conceding that security could be provided in the state of nature only at a moral cost (namely, the cost of the agency's ignoring its obligations to independents). But anarchists, of course, charge states with providing security only at a much higher (moral and prudential) cost.[36] States, anarchists charge, impose enormous and unnecessary limitations on individual and group liberty, inflicting massive violations of rights or serious diminutions of genuine human expression in the process. States break down our sociable and cooperative inclinations by taking over the coercive enforcement of cooperation. Uncoerced cooperation between persons is remarkably still very much in evidence, even in modern states; but states tend to undermine such efforts, setting persons against one another in order to make them dependent on the state for everything. States necessarily involve hierarchies of power and other substantial and unhealthy inequalities between persons. States teach us to act for the wrong kinds of reasons (e.g., out of fear of punishment or blind loyalty) and to substitute the judgment of others for our own. And, perhaps worst of all, states involve concentrations of massive, largely unchecked power, providing outstanding opportunities for oppression, exploitation, and slaughter. The record of the modern state has not been very encouraging in this regard. In light of such costs and risks, anarchists maintain, if we can have anything like adequate comfort and security against aggression without the state (and we can, anarchists contend), we should leap at the chance. The state lacks both prudential and moral justification, being neither the ideal form of social life for us nor even preferable to the sole alternative (i.e., the state of nature) traditionally considered.

Even if we remain skeptical (as most of us surely will) about this strong anarchist conclusion, most of us probably accept enough of the anarchist's worries about the state to accept a much weaker, but related, conclusion: that it is morally permissible (and perhaps not even wildly imprudent) for persons to try to live together without a state (if only they can find some unowned territory on which to do it) or to withdraw from the states in which they live for this purpose (if only they can find somewhere to withdraw to). The voluntary anarchist community on Mars probably seems OK to most of us. But it seems unlikely that many will find the anarchists' case sufficiently compelling to conclude with them that we all ought to work actively to dismantle our states, by force if necessary (as it almost certainly would be necessary). After all, history does not offer us much encouragement about the prospects for life in a state of nature either.[37] And groups that actually succeeded in dismantling their political institutions (without then immediately departing for Mars) would seem likely to just face coerced subjection to some nearby acquisitive state.[38]

Yet, at another level, it seems unfair to the anarchist case to dismiss it in this way on the grounds of a historical record and practical obstacles that include the existence of states. Anarchists (following Godwin's famous case) often argue that political societies have largely created the problems—of dependence, power seeking, and acquisitiveness—that would make it impossible now for persons to cooperate peacefully in a state of nature. After all, the history of the world thus far has almost exclusively consisted of the history of savagery plus the history of political society. We have little evidence bearing on how civilized people, but people free of the influences of political life and free of threats from surrounding political societies, would fare. There is a reason why Marx tells us so little about the stateless, "higher communist" society that will allegedly inevitably follow the proletarian revolution.[39] Of course, a political philosophy that denied justification to even decent, limited states on the basis of speculation—that a much better form of nonpolitical life will be available once the unwholesome influence of states subsides—would have to be charged with objectionable utopianism. But the anarchist case is surely suggestive and potent enough that it would be just as unreasonable to insist that political society is the only acceptable (i.e., morally permissible and prudentially rational) form of social life.

We have in this chapter to this point considered only the comparative advantages of the modern state and the state of nature. But there are, of course, other possibilities we could consider here. One is that the state itself may be fine or best as a form of social life for us, but only when states are collectively ordered differently from the way they have been in modern political history (e.g., with a larger number of smaller states or a smaller number [perhaps as small as one] of larger states). The second possibility is that the state itself is inferior to some nonstate form of political society.

I cannot here address these possibilities at any length. But on the first, consider this: does it not seem likely that the size and number of states in the world matter vastly less to their justification than do their individual character and organization—that is, how they treat their own subjects and the subjects of other states? The best kind of state is the kind that satisfies the guidelines explored in the remainder of this book. And the best world of states is one composed of that best kind, not a world with a certain size or number of states. The only really theoretically intriguing possibility in terms of size and number seems to me to be that of a *world-state*, whose potential moral and prudential attractions are hard to miss. Most prominently, of course, by eliminating the possibility of violent conflict between states—and, consequently, by eliminating untold costs both in human happiness and in resources expended conducting and preparing for war—the world-state would seem to promise both peace and much enhanced prosperity for all. I am myself inclined to think that characterizing a world-state as the best form of social life for us constitutes too utopian an ideal for a reasonable political philosophy. But I recognize that readers may judge differently (and I invite them to reconsider this question in the context of our discussion of international issues in Chapter 6).

As for the second possibility (that some nonstate political society may be superior to the state), I must be even briefer. The modern state's distinctive characteristics—its fixed territory and its (limited) sovereignty—seem directly related to its ability to deliver to its subjects those important goods on which the justification of political life appears to rest. So even without considering the wide variety of possible nonstate polities, it seems plausible to conclude that any political society that lacks either fixed territory or genuine sovereignty—that is, any nonstate—will be seriously hampered in its ability to deliver the goods that could justify its existence. It will not be until later—most particularly in Chapter 6—that we will be in a position to clearly see some of the principal reasons for questioning this preliminary verdict in favor of the modern state.

Suggested Reading

Gregory Kavka, *Hobbesian Moral and Political Theory* (Princeton: Princeton University Press, 1986).

Christopher Morris, *An Essay on the Modern State* (Cambridge: Cambridge University Press, 1998).

John Sanders and Jan Narveson, eds., *For and Against the State* (Lanham, MD: Rowman & Littlefield, 1996).

David Schmidtz, *The Limits of Government* (Boulder: Westview, 1991).

Michael Taylor, *The Possibility of Cooperation* (Cambridge: Cambridge University Press, 1987).

CHAPTER 3

Obligations

3.1. The Problem of Political Obligation

Each of us has at some time—and some of us have frequently—thought about disobeying the law. When we do, one question we almost always confront is "Can I get away with it?" But another question that occurs to most of us on at least some of these occasions is "Would it really be wrong so to act?" Is legal disobedience just a matter of risking punishment, or is it a moral failing, perhaps because in disobeying we fail to discharge some obligation that binds us? Much of what the law prohibits, of course, seems morally wrong quite apart from its legal prohibition, as in the cases of murder, assault, and rape.[1] But legal disobedience often seems wrong to many, even where what the law requires is not so obviously independently required by morality (because others are not so directly harmed by our conduct), such as cheating on our taxes, evading jury duty, using illegal substances, or failing to register for the military draft. One way to explain this appearance would be to argue for the existence of a quite general moral requirement of legal obedience, a requirement not premised on the independent moral standing of the acts and forbearances that law requires. "Political obligations," as these are normally understood by philosophers, are such general moral requirements to obey the laws and support the political institutions of our states or governments, requirements that are usually thought to bind (nearly all) citizens (and other subjects) of (nearly all) modern states.[2] It is the breach of these political obligations that would most naturally explain why legal disobedience *per se* seems at least *prima facie* wrong. The "problem of political obligation" is the problem of providing a philosophical justification for our belief that we citizens in fact stand under such general moral requirements of obedience and support.

This is a philosophical problem to which most nonphilosophers can immediately relate, bearing as it does on their practical concerns about daily conduct. While we all know, of course, that much of our obedience to law and support for political institutions is a function of childhood training, simple habit, or fear of sanctions, we also know that most people believe as well that disobedience to law would in most instances be wrong. People's beliefs on this subject are not uncomplicated, however. As strongly as we may believe in the wrongness of disobedience, most of us recognize as well that at least sometimes it is legal *obedience* that would be wrong (or, at least, that disobedience would be permissible). It is, for instance, hard to resist the case that can be made on behalf of Thoreau's refusal to pay his legally required taxes or in support of the illegal acts of American abolitionists running the underground railway, the rescuers of Jews in Nazi-occupied Europe, the civilly disobedient campaigns of Gandhi or Martin Luther King. So if one attempts a defense of the general requirements of political obligation, it seems necessary to provide as well an account of the *limits* of these obligations.

The problem of political obligation has been one of the central problems of political philosophy throughout its history, though it has, like all such problems, gone in and out of fashion over the centuries. Plato's *Crito,* one of the earliest recorded philosophical treatments of any subject, deals directly with the problem of political obligation. Late medieval and early modern political philosophers were preoccupied with the problem. And it has again come into focus in the last half of the twentieth century. Between those periods, the problem was largely ignored; but during those times when philosophers were not especially worried about justifying political obligations, this seems to have been the case mostly because they took the fact of such obligations to be so obvious as to require little real defense. After all, general obedience to law and general support for government seem essential to political stability, and stability is an end of central importance to all of us. Indeed, even when political philosophers have concentrated on the problem of political obligation, their stance has typically been "conservative"—that is, their concern has been (exclusively or principally) with how to justify political obligation, not with whether it can be justified. But while our conservative feelings on this subject may be strong, it is important to remember that they are not self-justifying. People can plainly feel obligated when they are not (as when the housewife feels obligated to utterly give up on her own goals in life in order to facilitate her husband's) or feel free of obligation where obligations exist. Marx referred to such feelings as elements of "false consciousness," a phenomenon very much to be expected where power relations are at issue (since it is very important to those who have or want power over others that those others be brought to regard themselves as obligated to comply). So the political philosopher's job in this area must be to critically evaluate our strong feelings, not just to accept them as pointing to the truth—to search for rational justifications of political obligation where they exist and to be prepared to acknowledge the limits of conservative feelings on the subject where they do not.

How, we might well ask, does the political philosopher's task here—the task of resolving the problem of political obligation—relate to the task we just explored in Chapter 2, where we discussed possible justifications of political society? As we saw in Chapter 2, section 2.1, it is one thing to argue that political society (or some particular form of political society, like the modern state) is the best or an acceptable form of social life for us and quite another to argue that each of us must work to create such soci-eties where they don't exist and to support them where they do. Arrangements can be good (or even ideal) of their kind without being entitled to our allegiance or support, and nonvoluntary imposition on us of those arrangements can wrong us, perhaps by violating our rights. The scientist who develops reliably beneficial serums still wrongs me when he craftily injects me with them against my will. The perfectly ordered and run bank or insurance company is not entitled to require me to be a customer, however good it may be that such businesses exist. In general, it seems, the right to coerce compliance with beneficial arrangements requires significantly more of a defense than merely pointing to the virtues of those arrangements or the benefits that flow from them; it requires arguments that have as conclusions the existence of an independent duty or obligation of compliance on the part of those forced to comply.

Political societies, of course, are major players in the coercion business. Supposing, then, that political societies (or states) actually are good for us, it seems we will need to distinguish our account of their virtues and the benefits that flow from them from our account of their *author-ity* over us (or their *legitimacy* with respect to us) and our obligations to them (to comply with them, support them, or create them). These two dimensions—the general "justification" of political society and its specific "legitimacy" with respect to us—are, in my view, quite independent dimensions along which a political society can be morally evaluated.[3] Justified societies can be illegitimate with respect to some of their members (as when otherwise good societies coercively impose membership on unwilling persons), and unjustified societies can be legitimate (since we may freely undertake obligations to support arrangements that in fact have few real virtues, that provide few substantial benefits for us, or that are worse than others of their kind). My concern in this chapter will be with questions of legitimacy, authority, and (especially) obligation. Indeed, as we will see, this chapter will be concerned, even more narrowly, with only one aspect of political legitimacy or authority: namely, the *internal* legitimacy of states and governments. Questions about justification we have already begun to address in Chapter 2 and will continue to explore throughout the remainder of the book, with the question of the general justification of political society having already been examined in Chapter 2 and questions about the more specific virtues of states (i.e., what makes one state better than another) to follow.

Now it may seem, of course, that my claims about the independence of justification and legitimacy have the appearance of truth (if they do) only by virtue of falling into (either or both of) two kinds of seductive confusions: the first involving running together two quite different ways in which political societies can be "justified" and the second involving ignoring the differences between political and nonpolitical arrangements. First, one might say, you are right that the fact that an arrangement merely benefits us (more than would alternative arrangements) is not in itself sufficient to establish general obligations or duties to support and comply with such arrangements. But other of an arrangement's possible virtues—that it is *just,* say, or that it is *democratic*—are sufficient to argue for an obligation of support and compliance, perhaps by virtue of simply undermining the bases of objections about coercion. Second, it could be claimed, the principles that determine our obligations to political arrangements are simply quite different from those that determine our obligations to nonpolitical ones. Political arrangements have a centrality or necessity in our lives and, more generally, govern our lives in ways that make them quite different from other kinds of arrangements. So it will serve our purpose not at all to appeal to intuitions about our obligations to businesses, benefactors, or clubs (etc.), there being no principles of obligation that apply uniformly to all kinds of social arrangements.

We will, of course, be discussing justice and democracy in Chapters 4 and 5, thus putting considerably more flesh on the bare skeleton of these ideas that will be utilized in this chapter. But we must here consider, along with all of the other popular lines of argument purporting to justify political obligation, at least the basic outlines of accounts of political obligation that claim to derive it directly from the virtues or general qualities of the political societies in question or from the special character of political arrangements. So I hope to show in this chapter (specifically, at the end of section 3.3), even before our more detailed examination of justice and democracy, that the distinction between the justifying qualities of a state and that state's legitimacy with respect to any given person, far from being based on any seductive confusion, must be maintained as a central distinction in political philosophy.

Before we can begin our examination of the various defenses of political obligation, however, just a bit more must be said about the basic concepts our examination will employ and the relations between them. I have thus far used terms like *obligation, duty, authority,* and *legitimacy* without making much of an effort to explain what I mean when I do so. Let us try briefly to be clearer, beginning with *obligation* and *duty,* then turning to *legitimacy.* Obligations and duties have often been distinguished by saying that *obligations* are those moral requirements we have because of some voluntary performance on our part (e.g., the obligations we acquire when we make a promise or deliberately and wrongfully injure another person), while *duties* are those that fall on us nonvoluntarily, by virtue of our occupying some nonvoluntary role or status (e.g., the duties not to murder or assault others that attach to the nonvoluntary role of "person").[4] On the face of it, there seems to be no reason why our political obligations have to be "obligations" in this technical sense, rather than "duties"; both could be suitably general moral requirements with the right kind of content.

But it will prove helpful to be slightly more precise than this in our characterization of the categories of moral requirements into which our political obligations might fall. In addition to this distinction between voluntary and nonvoluntary requirements, we can distinguish between "special" and "general" moral requirements, with special requirements being those that arise out of special relationships we have with specific persons or groups and general requirements being those that bind persons regardless of their special relationships, acts, or roles. This distinction is worth noting because, as we will see, there are certain advantages to accounts of political obligation that make that "obligation" a special moral requirement. But while voluntary requirements are all special (by definition), special moral requirements need not all be voluntary. It is a perfectly common feature of our moral lives to acknowledge the requirements we owe to our parents, family members, friends, or neighbors; these requirements are plainly special in that they depend on our special roles or relationships (those with no friends, e.g., owe no duties of friendship), but they may just as plainly seem to arise nonvoluntarily. Whether we call such special, nonvoluntary moral requirements "obligations" or "duties" seems unimportant. What is important, however, is that this way of categorizing moral requirements suggests three, rather than two, basic categories—general-nonvoluntary, special-voluntary, and special-nonvoluntary requirements, rather than simply duties and obligations. And, as we will see, the three major approaches to the problem of political obligation that we will examine below differ precisely in their regarding political "obligations" as falling respectively into the three different categories of moral requirement we have just identified.

The ideas of authority and legitimacy with which we shall be here concerned relate them closely to the moral requirements we have been discussing. Legitimacy, according to standard dictionary definitions, concerns conformity to law, to other rules or principles, or to established procedures. It is in virtue of such conformity to rules that legitimacy is achieved or conferred. But the *payoff* for legitimacy is routinely in the currency of *rights,* and it is its connection to these rights that makes legitimacy an interesting property. Legitimacy is conformity to rules or principles that confer important rights. The rules and principles, of course, as well as the rights conferred by qualifying under them, can be either legal or moral, for we have both legal and moral conceptions of legitimacy. Our concern here will be with conceptions of moral legitimacy and with their connections to our moral obligations or duties.

One common understanding of a state's political authority or legitimacy sees it as conferring the state's moral right to act in those ways that are central to the conduct of actual decent states.[5] In particular, the right in question is often said to be a "right to rule,"[6] that is, a right to perform unimpeded the major executive and legislative functions of typical states.[7] But decent states are usually thought to possess more than just a right to make and coercively enforce law. They are thought to possess as well the right to be obeyed (and assisted) by their citizens in the exercise of their rights to rule. When political authority and legitimacy are seen as conferring these rights, a state's authority or legitimacy must be understood as (at least in part) conferring a right which is just a logical correlate of its subjects' political obligations. It is political obligations in this sense—obligations that correlate with important aspects of the rights conferred by a state's legitimacy or authority—for which we will seek possible justifications in this chapter.

As we have seen (in Chapter 2, section 2.1), states claim not only obedience from their subjects but also rights to geographical territories and "sovereignty." Rights to territory and to *external* legitimacy and sovereignty (i.e., to independence from outside control) correlate (at least primarily) not with the political obligations of citizens but with the obligations of outsiders to refrain from interfering with the state's central functions.[8] It is instead the state's claimed rights to obedience (and support) and to *internal* legitimacy and sovereignty (i.e., to being the "final authority" within its territory) that correlate with citizens' political obligations. There are many political philosophers who insist that state legitimacy is not to be understood in this way as conferring rights that correlate with subjects' (or others') obligations but only as conferring a *liberty* (or permission) to rule, which correlates with no obligations. We might thus, in such a view, provide an account of state legitimacy and the moral rights it confers while saying nothing at all about the moral obligations of citizens. Even if citizens altogether lacked political obligations, states might still be legitimate, enjoying a moral liberty to rule.

To this view I will say only that it seems overwhelmingly clear that, even remaining agnostic on the connection between state legitimacy and our obligations to obey, we take ourselves at the very least to be bound not only to respect the sovereignty of other legitimate states but also to refrain from *competing* with our own states in their efforts to rule (e.g., by vigilantism, setting up our own rival legal systems, etc.). Weaker notions of legitimacy than that can have no claim to the name. If so, however, at least some of the rights conferred by state legitimacy or authority are straightforwardly rights that correlate at least with these requirements of noncompetition. But moral obligations of noncompetition of this sort appear to require the same kinds of defenses as would more general obligations of support and obedience. The problem to be addressed in both cases is why persons should regard themselves as morally bound to respect or support the state's rule over its particular claimed territories and subjects, rather than acting according to their own judgments of what is best. If we can answer this question for the noncompetition case, I think, we can answer it for the obedience case. But if that is true, then there is no point in trying to separate questions about political legitimacy from questions about our correlative moral obligations as citizens. Every plausible candidate account of political legitimacy will tie that property of states to some correlative moral obligation of citizenship, an obligation that will require a defense employing the same kinds of considerations that have traditionally been utilized to try to show the existence of political obligations.[9] So, while we will return to additional questions about legitimacy later (in Chapter 6), it is to those considerations and the obligations on which they bear that we should turn now.

3.2. Justifying Obligation

Aristotle famously claimed in his *Politics* that "every state exists by nature" and that man is "by nature a political animal."[10] This text was the principal source of a long tradition of *political naturalism*: the view that it is part of the natural order of things for persons to be politically organized, with some subject to the political authority of others. While there were many versions of secular naturalism, the forms of political naturalism that were most influential during the Middle Ages and much of the early modern period were varieties of religious naturalism, according to which the political authority of monarchs (emperors, pope) was taken to be naturally bestowed on those persons by God. Often, the defense of such religious naturalism appealed to the doctrine of St. Paul: "there is no authority except from God, and those that exist have been instituted by God. Therefore he who resists the authorities resists what God has appointed, and those who resist will incur judgment."[11] Subjects' obligations to obey and support their political authorities were, in this model, ultimately derived from their obligation to respect the Creator's choices (in his conferrals of authority on particular humans). Established authorities were sometimes said to rule as "little Gods" (to use James I's memorable phrase) and by "divine right," a right that correlated with subjects' obligations of passive obedience. Perhaps the most ambitious theory of this sort was the "patriarchalist" theory of Robert Filmer, advanced in his *Patriarcha* (and famously attacked in Locke's *First Treatise*), in which Filmer attempted to derive the authority of the Stuart monarchs (through repeated instances of inheritance of authority down through the ages) from the authority over the world originally granted by God to Adam.

Related (secular) theories of similar antiquity maintained that the ability to rule demonstrated by established authorities evidences a "natural" superiority in rulers that should be respected by those who find themselves subject to their power. Our obligations, in this view, are to follow nature's dictates, which in the case of our political lives largely mandate obedience to the stable powers that be. What this theory has in common with divine right views, of course, is that both take the fact of sustained subjection to stable political power as evidence for claims of *rightful* subjection (i.e., claims of political legitimacy and political obligation).

A more modern, but similarly "naturalistic," account of political obligation utilizes a so-called sanction theory of obligation, according to which to be under an obligation to do A is simply to be subject to a reasonable likelihood of being punished for failing to do A. Such sanction theories are frequently ascribed to Hobbes and Bentham (among others), but the clearest historical instance of the view is in the writings of the positivist jurist John Austin. Since being subject to political power routinely involves being liable to punishment for the failure to comply with applicable law, sanction theories again seem to make the fact of political subjection the basis for claims of justified subjection.[12]

Few readers today will find any of these forms of "political naturalism" convincing as attempts to justify political obligation. Quite apart from any doubts that contemporary readers might have about God's existence or about God's willingness to directly manage human affairs by conferrals of authority on particular persons, even contemporary monarchs are unlikely to share James I's view that monarchs are accountable for their conduct only to God and that obedience (or, at least, nonresistance) is every subject's mandatory course. Similarly, history hardly seems to bear out the claim that the stable possession of political power indicates any natural superiority (either intellectual or moral) or even any special suitability for ruling. Finally, as Hart has famously argued,[13] sanction theories seem to quite implausibly conflate being "obliged" to do something (i.e., having no real choice because of the threat of a sanction for failure) with actually being obligated to act. Genuine obligation (which is what we are interested in here) plainly has no necessary connection with threats of harm for nonperformance, as can be seen in the many common instances in which failures to discharge clear obligations meet with no real likelihood of negative consequences at all. We will, accordingly, spend no further time on these (or other) varieties of political naturalism, concentrating here instead on theories of political obligation that make that obligation contingent on the state's actual provision of key goods, on its moral quality, or on the actions or relations of the obligated subjects.

How, more precisely, might we try to defend or justify the claim that most citizens in most modern states are morally obligated to obey their laws and support their political institutions? Surprisingly, perhaps, we can find at least hints of almost the full range of strategies we might wish to consider in that most ancient of treatments of our subject, Plato's *Crito*.[14] *Crito* is Plato's (probably largely factual) account of the reasons Socrates gave (and perhaps subscribed to) for remaining in an Athenian prison (from which he might easily have escaped) to face his unjust death sentence. Some of Socrates' reasons, of course, are largely personal ones (concerning, e.g., the welfare of his children and friends) and need not concern us here, insofar as they lack the generality we seek. But in his imagined conversation with the Laws of Athens (in the second half of the dialogue), Socrates also outlines a series of quite different arguments for obedience to his state's commands, arguments that seem both much more generally applicable and straightforwardly moral in character—thus, on both grounds, making the arguments good candidates for justifying political obligation.

At one point (51e) Socrates, summarizing his case, has the Laws declare that "one who disobeys does wrong in three ways."[15] The first is that the state and the Laws are like a parent to Socrates: "we have given you birth" (51c); and parents, Socrates claims, must either be persuaded to change their commands or be obeyed. The second way in which legal disobedience is a wrong is that the Laws are like a guardian, having "brought [Socrates] up" and "given [him] and all other citizens a share of all the good things

[they] could" (51e,d). Disobedience in the face of such a history would, we can assume, at the very least constitute a wrong of ingratitude. Finally, the Laws maintain that by remaining in Athens without protest, after reaching manhood and seeing how the Laws "manage the city," Socrates has "in fact come to an agreement with us to obey our instructions" (51e). And agreements, we know, ground obligations to act as one has agreed to act.

Socrates, then, seems to be insisting that he is morally bound to obedience for at least three different reasons. And there is more, for there appears to be at least one additional argument for obedience presented by the Laws, beyond the three that are explicitly summarized. The Laws in fact begin their case against Crito's proposal that Socrates run away (and in so doing disobey the law) by proclaiming "Do you not by this action you are attempting intend to destroy us, the laws. . . . Or do you think it possible for a city not to be destroyed if the verdicts of its courts have no force but are . . . set at naught by private individuals?" (50a,b). The argument here is unclear, but it appears to be that Socrates would do a serious moral wrong (were he to escape) either (1) by causing great unhappiness, (2) by acting in a way that would cause great unhappiness were many others to do the same, or (3) by destroying (or attempting to destroy) something of great value—a good or just city and legal system (as Socrates concedes Athens and its Laws to be [54b,c]).

Sorting through Plato's arguments in this way allows us to discern three general strategies for justifying a claim to be bound by political obligations, strategies that involve appealing respectively to the existence of each of the three different kinds of moral requirements distinguished above in section 3.1. And these argumentative strategies can plainly be generalized far beyond the special circumstances of Socrates' situation, making them strategies that can be (and have regularly been) appealed to in attempts to justify *our own* political obligations.

Socrates' reference to his (unchosen) standing as a "child of the State" seems to employ the idea of special, nonvoluntary moral requirements, those that bind us simply because we occupy some (unchosen but requirement-laden) role, status, or position. Since such requirements are often called "associative duties (or obligations)," let us call accounts of political obligation that employ them (i.e., that explain our political "obligations" as being moral requirements of this kind) "associative accounts." When Socrates appeals instead to the benefits his state has provided him or to his agreement/promise to obey the laws, he is pointing not to a role or position he occupies but rather to some specific transactions or interactions with the state that gave rise to new moral obligations (i.e., obligations to reciprocate for benefits received or to keep a promise). While some of these obligations could in principle be special, nonvoluntary requirements—since one can be benefited nonvoluntarily—they will normally be special *voluntary* requirements, such as the requirements to keep promises, to reciprocate for benefits actively sought, or to do one's fair share in supporting a cooperative scheme from which one voluntarily takes benefits. Let us call accounts of political obligation that utilize such requirements "transactional accounts." Finally, when Socrates points to the unhappiness that would be caused by (his own or others') escape and disobedience or to the consequences of such actions for good or just institutions, he seems to be employing in his argument some idea of a general, nonvoluntary moral requirement that binds us all, such as a duty to promote (or to not diminish) utility/happiness or a duty to promote (or to not lessen or undermine) justice or goodness. Since such general nonvoluntary moral duties are often called "natural duties" (falling on us as they do "naturally," not by virtue of our actions or particular relationships), we can call accounts of political obligation that employ such requirements "natural duty accounts."

I am not familiar with any serious proposal for justifying general political obligations that does not fall under one of these three headings: associative, transactional, or natural duty. There will obviously be significant differences between competing accounts even within these strategic groups, such as the differences between a utilitarian theory of political obligation and one (like that defended by the antiutilitarian John Rawls) that derives political "obligations" from the "natural duty of justice," both of which, these differences notwithstanding, count in my classifications as natural duty accounts. But, as we will see, the accounts within each of these categories also share certain properties that are important to their prospects for argumentative success.

3.3. Associations, Transactions, and Natural Duties

Associative theories of political obligation, I have said, understand our political obligations as a kind of associative moral requirement, as a kind of special, nonvoluntary requirement that attaches to an unchosen role or status—in this case, the role of citizen (member, resident, subject). Socrates likened this political role to that of a child who owes associative filial duties to its parents. Others might cite the Aristotelian idea of "civic friendship," with citizens understood as owing to their fellow citizens the kinds of duties we take ourselves to owe to our friends. Those who defend associative theories today are often inspired by precisely these historical analogies, as well as by the later versions advanced in Burke, Hegel, and Wittgenstein. Other contemporary associative theorists—for instance, Ronald Dworkin[16]—seem pushed to associativism more by the apparent failure of alternative (i.e., transactional and natural duty) defenses of political obligation. What they all seem to share is a view of the world as replete with morally laden relationships in which we regularly just find ourselves, without ever having chosen to be in them, but binding us nonetheless to the people and the social arrangements that structure our lives. In the world so envisioned, family members, friends, neighbors, coworkers, and members of political, religious, social, ethnic, racial, or gender groups are all bound together in a vast web of mutual obligation.

Those, like myself, who find associative accounts unconvincing have challenged not only the associativists' claims about the moral dimensions of our nonpolitical relationships—to which our political ones are allegedly analogous—but also the associativists' insistence that there is an interesting analogy between political and these nonpolitical relationships.[17] Beginning with the first of these challenges, we can raise questions both about whether some of the claimed associative moral duties even exist and about how associativists have chosen to characterize those duties that do seem to exist. For instance, in the first place, some of the claimed associative duties (which are not, by any means, named by all associativists) seem only implausibly identified as real moral duties at all. Take the alleged associative obligations of ethnic, racial, or gender groups. Virtually nobody seems prepared to claim that I owe associative obligations of special regard toward my fellow male Caucasians of Anglo/Scottish and German heritage, despite our common race, gender, and ethnicity. Claims of special obligation are more commonly made in the case of minority or persecuted groups, such as women, African Americans, or Jews. But surely the claim here is most plausibly construed not as a claim of special obligation based on shared gender (etc.) but rather one based on shared persecution (which is why the claim seems silly in my own, completely unpersecuted case), perhaps because fellow (or potential) victims of persecution ought to be specially aware of or sensitive to their duties to assist or show solidarity with the oppressed.

Even leaving aside such questionable cases, however, doubts should surely remain about the exact nature even of those associative duties that seem relatively uncontroversial, such as those owed to family, friends, neighbors, or coworkers. First, of course, nobody seems to be able to say with much confidence or precision—or with anything remotely like a consensus—just what the *content* of these supposedly uncontroversial duties might be. Just what do siblings owe each other morally, simply by virtue of their blood relationship? Or neighbors? Or even friends or parents or children? The intuitive answers people give seem to vary with the *quality* of their personal experiences with these types of relationships, rather than being uniform across all such experiences. Interestingly, attempting to answer such questions more systematically and with more precision seems inevitably to push the associativist into an even more untenable position. For attempting to answer carefully (rather than just intuitively) questions about the content of the duties requires one to examine the justifications, or grounds, of the duties. And the most plausible analyses of the grounds of these allegedly associative duties seem routinely to reveal that they are much more like those of familiar transactional duties than associativists appear to have acknowledged, threatening to render associative accounts nothing more than elaborately costumed transactional accounts.

All of the special relationships that we can most confidently claim to come laden with associated duties seem, on careful consideration, to involve strong transactional elements—either voluntary undertakings of some sort or the exchange of significant benefits, both of which have moral significance independent of the further associative relationships in which they might take place. Friendship is, at least where it seems most clearly to have moral weight, a matter of mutual voluntary dependence and commitment. The ties to neighbors and coworkers that seem most clearly morally significant are the ones that are most like the voluntary ties of friendship. Spouses take explicit vows (and other kinds of long-term partners undertake at least implicit commitments) to one another. Parents virtually always make voluntary decisions to perform the acts that are intended to have, or are at least known to be capable of having, consequences of great moral moment—namely, the creation of their children, who will come desperately needy and incompetent into the world. Children typically benefit from their parents' care and tuition in myriad ways, so much so that it is perfectly common to suppose that the extent of filial duties is determined by the extent of parental care or benefaction. In short, the supposed paradigms of associative duties—the paradigms that serve as the *model* for associative accounts of political obligation—seem either vague and unconvincing or so shot through with transactional elements that associativists are no longer able to meaningfully distinguish their own accounts from those of their rivals.

Worse, even were their paradigm nonpolitical associative duties capable of convincing characterization in nontransactional terms, the supposed analogy between these nonpolitical bonds and political obligations is simply unsustainable. For whatever else we may say about the relationships on which associativists rely in their accounts, these relationships typically involve or arise from interactions with persons that are personal and local, not connections that are remote, impersonal, and geographical, like the connections of citizens in a modern nation-state. Nor does mere political comembership seem to generate the bonds of sympathy or concern for all of our compatriots that might seem to promise to give rise to a different sort of genuinely associative duty. For in even the best states with which we are familiar, the significant antipathy between citizens generated by different religion, race, ethnicity, political party, education, economic class, and so on prevent mere common nationality from looking like a good candidate for a source of associative duties based in mutual emotional ties. Even in reasonably just and virtuous modern states, then, "civic friendship" between citizens is just not sufficiently like serious personal friendship to use the latter in explaining the political obligations that are supposed to arise from the former.

Let us turn, then, to the transactional accounts into which attempts at associativism seem mostly to collapse. *Transactional accounts,* remember, are those that identify as the source of our political obligations some specific transactions or interactions with the state (or with our fellow citizens), those specific (or repeated) historical events being what give rise to the moral obligations of citizenship. Many of the most familiar and compelling accounts of political obligation in the history of political thought have been transactional in character, especially those defended in the social contract tradition.[18] Further, these transactional views have been extremely influential in actual political life, guiding the foundational documents of many countries (such as the United States' Declaration of Independence). This is presumably because transactional accounts capture much commonsense thought on the subject of political obligation. If asked why he is morally bound to his state, a citizen of a modern state is unlikely to answer "Because my state is like a parent to me" or "Because my compatriots are my friends." He is far more likely, I think, to answer that his obligations to his state derive from all that his state has given him (or made possible for him) or from all of the ways in which he has committed himself to a life as a citizen of that state. In short, his answers will point, however vaguely, to transactional explanations of his obligations.

Transactional accounts of political obligation are virtually all either *consent* theories—which base the obligation on a voluntary undertaking of obligation, like a promise, contract, or consent—or *reciprocation* theories—which see the obligation as one of reciprocation for benefits received or accepted. The greatest strength of both kinds of transactional accounts lies precisely in (what we have seen is) the area of greatest weakness for associative accounts: transactional accounts rely on, where associative accounts do not, kinds of obligations that are nearly universally acknowledged and whose contents seem capable of something like precise delineation. Most people accept the idea that when others go out of their way to benevolently benefit us, we ought to reciprocate in a measure that is responsive to the extent of the benefit provided. And virtually everyone accepts as perhaps the very clearest example of a special moral obligation the obligation to keep our promises and honor our agreements. So universal is this recognition that even warring countries and criminal gangs, which may ignore nearly all other moral prohibitions, often feel bound to honor voluntary pacts and agreements.

Let us begin, then, with consent theory, which characterizes our political obligations as belonging to this universally recognized class of special obligation. Its most influential historical defense was given by Locke, but each consent theory will take its specific character from the variety of consent to which it assimilates the ground of political obligation. The most obvious sort of consent on which to concentrate in a consent theory of political obligation is actual, personal consent. Our political obligations, in this version of the theory, arise in the same way as do our nonpolitical promissory, contractual, or consensual obligations. Since such obligations can be undertaken either directly and expressly (as in most oaths and promises, where we use words whose primary point is to convey such undertakings) or tacitly and implicitly (where our actions or inactions convey our consent only by virtue of the specific context in which they occur), consent theories (like Locke's) that concentrate on actual, personal consent will consider both express and tacit performances as possible grounds of political obligation. Either one would do the job.

But political philosophers who at least appear to be consent theorists and who use much of the language of consent theory often try to explain political obligation in terms of *nonactual* (counterfactual) consent. Most of these philosophers appeal instead to some kind of hypothetical consent— either a more personalized version of it, which derives each individual's obligations from what that particular individual would have consented to (had she been able to, had she considered doing so, had she been more rational or perceptive or less flawed, etc.), or a more idealized version of hypothetical consent, which derives all of our obligations from what a perfectly rational and motivationally basic or reasonable person would agree to. Hypothetical consent theories of these sorts are, in my view, more properly classed as natural duty accounts of political obligation than as transactional ones. They derive our obligations not from what we have actually chosen or done but, rather, from what we might have done in different circumstances or from what we ought to have done. To say that a perfectly rational person (or even just a more rational or thoughtful person than I) would have consented to the authority of some state is to concentrate not on some dateable, morally significant transaction but on the merits or qualities of that state (e.g., its justice or its utility) that would be appreciated by (and would elicit the consent of) more perfect persons. It is, however, precisely this sort of orientation that characterizes natural duty theories, which portray our political obligations as implied by our more general moral duties to advance good ends like justice or happiness.

Hypothetical consent theories, then, will have the strengths and weaknesses of natural duty theories (to which I shall turn momentarily), not of transactional theories. But actual consent theories, while genuinely transactional, face considerable and well-known difficulties of their own. The first and most obvious difficulty is that real citizens of real contemporary states seem seldom to do anything that looks much like making a voluntary promise or a contract to obey (or not compete with) their political superiors or institutions. While naturalized citizens may sometimes do this, most of the other pledges or promises that are even remotely common parts of political life (e.g., "pledges of allegiance" made by children or oaths of loyalty taken by political officeholders or soldiers) seem to be either made by too few citizens or too tainted by concerns about immaturity or duress (which would undermine their obligating power) to support claims of truly general political obligations with this origin across a nation-state. The commonplace political act performed by many real citizens that perhaps most resembles a promise or free commitment is voting in a democratic election. While, of course, only citizens of democratic states could on this basis be characterized as obligated by their actual consent, that would still constitute a significant result for a defender of political obligations. But I will argue in Chapter 5 that in fact this appearance of widespread promissory obligation in democratic societies is misleading and that democracies are not in fact *legitimated* by (or their subjects obligated by) widespread acts of direct or express (or even tacit) consent (or by anything else). The moral advantages of democracy are to be found elsewhere—in their superior justifiability, not in their superior legitimacy.

What, though, of the possibilities of less obvious, less pledge-like acts of tacit consent? Might not significant numbers of real citizens in real states be plausibly characterized as having tacitly or implicitly agreed to obey (and/or not compete with) their governments, even if they have done nothing that looks much like a direct promise? After all, in plenty of real states, few residents show much inclination to leave (i.e., to emigrate), suggesting a willing acceptance of their prescribed political roles in those states (roles which surely include obedience and non-competition). This is, in fact, Locke's famous suggestion: that most political consent is given not expressly but tacitly through continued residence in (and nonresistance to) states that we are free to leave.[19] Most citizens give their consent "with their feet," as it were. Indeed, given how infrequently our everyday lives seem to make contact with the political (except in democracies, the special case that I take up in Chapter 5), it is difficult to think of anything beyond residence and nonresistance that average citizens do that could be reasonably described in consensual language.

But Locke's suggestion faces famous and insurmountable obstacles. Acts of tacit consent, if they are to morally bind us in the way and for the reasons that express consent binds us, must be suitably voluntary and informed acts. Everyone, Locke included, accepts these general conditions on binding consent. Unfortunately for Locke's argument, however, many of the citizens who continue to reside in their states do so without any real awareness that residence constitutes a way of giving binding consent to their states' authority. There is no clear procedure that presents their options to them in a way that would make continued residence an "informed" choice. But even were such a procedure in place, it is not clear exactly what the options are for a typical resident of a typical state (i.e., even if continued residence were a suitably informed choice, it would not qualify as suitably voluntary). Most citizens have (for financial, familial, or emotional reasons) few realistic options to remaining in their states, and for most, resistance to the state is neither prudent nor likely to succeed. And nobody has the option of not living in some state or other, all of which make similar basic demands on their residents. Indeed, and even more basically, it is unclear just why states should be understood as having the authority to *compel* a choice between allegiance and emigration so that an "act" like continued residence could even be thought to count as consent to the former. Only if states are taken to have prior authority or rights over the land on which residents live and work would it seem legitimate for them to demand that residents of their claimed territories either leave that land or agree to subjection. But I will argue in Chapter 6 that the most reasonable bases for states' moral claims to territorial authority in fact rest on the idea of a prior authority over the persons who live and work on the relevant land. In short, only if citizens had *already* consented to the state's jurisdiction over the land could the state legitimately compel a choice between allegiance and emigration. The argument that continued residence gives tacit consent to state authority presupposes that the state already has authority based on consent; it cannot, then, be used to explain the source of that authority.

Consent theories, then, fail to justify assertions that most citizens in real states have political obligations. It might still be true, of course, that where citizens do consent to political authority, they are so obligated, just as the consent theorist says. Indeed, it might, for all I have said, be true (as I in fact believe it to be) that actual, personal consent is *necessary* for political obligation. But real political societies simply are not the kinds of voluntary associations that they would have to be for consent theory to explain the political obligations of real contemporary people. Or perhaps, we might argue, they *are* often adequately characterized as voluntary societies, even if we concede that their members do not count as consenters. Some transactional *reciprocation* theories have in fact made such claims, contending that at least some real political societies should be viewed as voluntary cooperative schemes, their members owing one another obligations to reciprocate for the benefits they enjoy from participation in the schemes—obligations that include obedience to the laws and support for the governments that structure those grand political schemes: in short, political obligations.

That is not, of course, the kind of claim made by Socrates in Plato's version of a transactional reciprocation theory. There, as we saw, the appeal was to a simple duty to reciprocate for important benefits received. The state supplies the benefits; its citizens (including Socrates) are bound to repay the state with obedience. No mention is made of voluntariness, cooperation, duties owed to one's fellow cooperators, etc. But simple reciprocation theories of political obligation of the Socratic sort—usually called "gratitude theories"—face obvious objections. Whatever else may be true of our ordinary understanding of debts of gratitude, it seems clear that we owe them only to persons who benefit us for certain acceptable reasons and that our benefactors are not specially privileged to simply name the return that is required of us. While benevolent (and perhaps some other kinds of) motives for benefiting us may suffice to generate obligations of gratitude, accidental, malicious, or self-interested benefaction normally does not. But what kind(s) of motive produces the benefits conferred by states? The motives of states (or governments) in supplying us with benefits seem either plainly mixed (in light of the mixed motives of legislative and executive bodies) or simply impossible to intelligibly identify (in light of the mechanical, institutional processes that produce the relevant benefits). Worse still, even were benefaction by the state capable of generating debts for citizens, these would at most be requirements to make an appropriate or fitting return for the benefits provided. They could not be requirements to do as the state demands their citizens do—namely, obey precisely the laws that the state enforces or support government in precisely the ways it specifies. Benefactors cannot simply benefit us and then name their own price.

It was no doubt in part concerns of this sort that motivated transactional reciprocation theorists in this century (e.g., Hart and the early Rawls[20]) to present their theories in the voluntaristic fashion described above, with the moral category appealed to being not that of gratitude but rather that of *fairness*. Decent, just political societies, while not literally consensual in the ways the classical social contract theorists wanted, are nonetheless voluntary and cooperative undertakings; and those who voluntarily participate in such schemes by freely accepting the benefits they supply have obligations of fairness (or fair play) to do their assigned parts in, play by the rules of, and support those schemes, obligations owed to their fellow participants. We may not "ride free" on beneficial schemes, taking advantage of the good-faith sacrifices by others that make possible benefits for all. Such an account of the political obligations of real persons, while limited to real persons in just states, seems to capture much of the intuitive appeal of consent theory (with its respect for individual freedom and the importance of voluntariness) but without having to clear the theoretical hurdle of portraying ordinary behavior in real political societies as literally (expressly or tacitly) consensual.

Unhappily, as even Rawls came to recognize, the claims made by such fairness theories simply do not accord with the conditions of contemporary political life.[21] For instance, in order to maintain the voluntaristic character of fairness theory in the face of the obvious fact that real citizens are mostly simply born into their polities, it is necessary to appeal to the voluntary nature of citizens' acceptance of the benefits with which their societies supply them. Rawls himself eventually claimed that citizens in real societies seldom count as having accepted the benefits of political life in this way, having had no real choice of declining those benefits.[22] Even if we think Rawls too quick with his own earlier view, however, in order to talk intelligently about citizens accepting benefits, we must at the very least show that we can distinguish between the free acceptance of benefits and the mere nonvoluntary receipt of benefits. And this distinction can only be convincingly drawn by noting the different psychological conditions of beneficiaries in the two cases—for instance, that those who genuinely accept benefits either go out of their way to try to get them or take the benefits they get willingly and knowingly.

But this way of drawing the distinction simply reintroduces, in new terms, the problem that concerned Rawls. While most subjects of decent states certainly receive benefits from their states' workings, it is questionable whether they can also reasonably be claimed to have accepted those benefits. The most important benefits states supply (e.g., security) simply fall on persons, independent of their choices (they are "public goods"). To count as accepting such benefits, citizens would at least have to take them "willingly and knowingly." And while many citizens might in fact take these benefits willingly, few, I think, count as taking them knowingly, understanding them as benefits flowing from a cooperative scheme and binding them to do their parts within that scheme. They mostly, I suspect, take the benefits to be supplied by government for a price (namely, their taxes), a price that is often seen as unreasonably high. Nor is this failure in any way an indication of negligence on their parts. Indeed, it is not even a failure, a lack of understanding. For the large-scale, pluralistic political societies of today simply cannot be realistically characterized as cooperative schemes in any strong (i.e., morally significant) sense at all. The massive impersonality and the coercive structure of the modern pluralistic state, with its significant divisions between (social, regional, economic, racial, ethnic, etc.) groups and the widely different goals and orientations these divisions involve, render ludicrous attempts to reveal the moral structure of the state by calling up our images of small-scale cooperative schemes, with friends or neighbors working together to accomplish shared goals. The pictures of voluntary cooperation and selfish free-riding that motivate fairness accounts of political obligation in the first place simply cannot be superimposed without serious distortion on contemporary political society.

Some fairness theorists have responded to these problems by simply eliminating from their accounts the requirement that political schemes be voluntary in order for citizens to be bound by obligations of fairness.[23] While this might distance the theory from its original, voluntaristic roots, it might still seem initially plausible to suppose that where very important benefits (like security) are at issue, it would be unfair for anyone who gets the benefit to refuse to do her "part" in society. But fairness theory cannot be saved in this way. Once one removes the requirement of voluntary acceptance of benefits from the account, while recognizing that real political societies lack the motivational structure and unity to count as genuinely cooperative schemes at all, one has lost all of what gave fairness theory its distinctive character and moral appeal. One is really left with a position that is not a fairness theory at all. The position has been transformed into either a simple reciprocation theory (like a gratitude theory), with all of its aforementioned defects, or a natural duty theory, asserting (e.g.) that each person has a natural moral duty to contribute to the provision of benefits that are essential to the security or well-being of all. The idea of ongoing fair reciprocation (or of any sort of transaction) being the source of political obligation has been left far behind. If transactional fairness theories fail to explain the political obligations of ordinary people, however, this fact, combined with the failures of gratitude and consent theories, argues that transactional accounts of political obligation simply cannot deliver the conclusions they promised.

Finally, then, let us consider natural duty accounts of political obligation, the last of our possible approaches to solving the problem positively. It will by now probably come as no surprise to readers to learn that I think this last strategic avenue for solving the problem of political obligation fails as well.[24] *Natural duty theories,* remember, argue that our political obligations (or duties) belong to or are implied by those moral duties that bind all persons naturally—duties owed by all persons to all others or duties to advance or promote some impartial moral good (e.g., justice or happiness). Thus, a natural duty account could employ some consequentialist moral duty—such as the single duty accepted by utilitarians, the duty to promote or maximize utility—or it could employ a nonconsequential duty—such as a duty of justice or mutual aid or rescue.[25] Apart from utilitarian theories of political obligation (e.g., those of Hume, Bentham, and Sidgwick[26]), the best-known natural duty accounts have utilized (following Kant) the idea of a natural duty of justice. The mature view of John Rawls, for instance, was that political "obligations" in a just state could be explained in terms of a natural duty to "comply with and do our share in just institutions when they exist and apply to us."[27] The Kantian idea at work here we have seen before (in Chapter 2): all persons are entitled to live under political institutions that enforce justice, and all persons are correlatively morally bound to help create just institutions where they do not exist and to support and comply with them where they do exist.

The greatest difficulties faced by natural duty theories are, I believe, faced by all of them—as a function of their common structures, not of their individual characters (so that theories as diverse as those of Rawls and the utilitarians share a common fate). In particular, natural duty theories face two challenges, neither of which can, I think, be met by any member of the natural duty family. The first challenge is that of showing that some plausible candidate natural moral duty really does have uniform (or, at least, regular) legal compliance as an implication (without giving the duty a question-begging formulation). The well-known difficulty for act-utilitarian theories of political obligation can serve as an illustration. Act utilitarianism directs that we promote or maximize utility. Sometimes, of course, such a utilitarian duty will require that we obey the law—namely, wherever legal obedience is utility-maximizing. But it is easy to imagine—indeed, we all confront every day—circumstances in which legal disobedience is required instead. We need not imagine deeply harmful laws or stop signs at midnight in the desert. Simply consider any of the many occasions on which legal detection is extremely unlikely, some personal benefit (i.e., utility) will flow to one from illegality, and no or smaller loss to others will be caused by the illegal act (say, minor tax fraud, private sodomy or use of illegal substances, trespass, traffic or parking violations, minor defrauding of or theft from a mega-corporation, etc.). These occasions are a sufficiently regular feature of ordinary life that nothing like a general obligation of legal compliance (or of support for government) could be derived from the act-utilitarian natural duty.

If we change the natural duty, the problem remains the same. Even if the duty in question is one of promoting justice (as the Kantian tradition maintains), no general obligation of compliance is derivable. Sometimes legal *disobedience* will best promote justice (as Rawls admits in the special case of civil disobedience to unjust law). And often it will simply make no difference to the cause of justice whether I obey the law or not. The kinds of self-benefiting, relatively harmless illegalities mentioned above are cases in point here as well. But, more generally, the single actions, legal or illegal, of single persons routinely have no effects at all on the goal of society's becoming more just or on society's ability to administer justice. The institutions in question are designed to persist through a certain amount of legal disobedience. Rawls attempts to finesse this problem by simply defining the natural duty of justice as a duty to "comply with" domestic law, rather than as a duty to promote justice. But if the duty in question is really premised on the importance of justice—and not, question-beggingly, on the importance of legal compliance—then the points just made remain persuasive.

Rawls attempts as well in his formulation of the natural duty of justice to finesse the second general problem faced by natural duty accounts of political obligation: what I have called the problem of "particularity." Rawls tells us that our natural duty binds us to comply with the requirements of those just institutions that "apply to us." But how do we know which institutions those are? The institutions to which we are bound must "apply to us" in some morally interesting way, for this is how our general duty of justice is particularized to complying with and supporting one particular just state (out of the many that might exist). So the fact that a state simply names me as someone to whom its institutions apply seems unlikely to do the job here since then states could just name anyone (or everyone) and thereby impose special duties of compliance on them (or many states could name the very same people). The "applications" implied by convention or by international law could qualify as morally interesting only if they did not exhibit a strong and irrational conservative bias (which they do) and only if they could be shown to have the moral authority to make such determinations (which, in my view, cannot be shown). So while Rawls plainly has in mind commonsense, territorial, conventional notions of which just institutions "apply to" whom—American institutions to those identified by American law (or possibly by international law) as Americans, Swedish institutions to the Swedes, etc.—he is not in fact entitled to assume that such commonsense divisions are in fact underwritten by morally significant differences.

Rawls, in effect, simply assumes an answer to the question for which he needs to argue; in fact, he assumes an answer to the very question that we have been exploring throughout this chapter—the question of whether or not a conservative stance on the issue of political obligation (i.e., an assumption that we have the political obligations our states claim we have) is warranted. Rawls asserts without argument the conservative position on the question of when political institutions apply to people. And that is simply to assert an important component of a theory of political obligation. Instead, Rawls owes us an account of why justice—which is the value with which the natural duty in question is concerned—gives institutions special authority over those who are conventionally (rather than morally) identified as subject to those institutions' demands.

And it is hard to see how such an account could be forthcoming. Justice is certainly not always, and is perhaps not even regularly, best served by focusing our attention on supporting and complying with our own (conventionally determined) domestic political institutions. People and societies abroad may have greater need for our support or our money. Indeed, justice may well in some cases be better served by setting up alternative institutions for administering justice, as when the resources of a just state are too overextended to effectively provide justice for all. Or people may have cultural needs for separate institutions of justice to which the prevailing conventions are not sensitive. The general point, however, is that domestic political obligations cannot simply be assumed to follow from—and seem unlikely to uniformly follow from—any natural duty that is genuinely based only on the moral value of justice (without conservative ambitions being covertly built into its characterization).

And this same general point will hold for the other kinds of natural duties on which natural duty accounts of political obligation might be based. The duty to promote or maximize utility cannot be particularized (except by illicit conservative additions) to the support of our own domestic political institutions. While utility may tend to be best promoted by doing our moral work close to home (because of the greater transaction costs of action at a distance), there is nothing even resembling a hard and fast rule that utility cannot be best promoted by expending our resources abroad. Indeed, this will plainly often be the case. If so, however, natural duty accounts face another apparently decisive objection, based on their inability to motivate—rather than to illicitly assume—an answer to the question of why we have special obligations to "our own," conventionally defined states. Natural duty theories may well utilize in their accounts natural moral duties that we should accept as genuine. What they cannot do, it seems, is show how any of these duties implies special political obligations to our countries of residence (or to the states or governments that claim our allegiance), above all others. They cannot, in short, justify general (i.e., widespread) political obligations.

Having exhausted the candidate strategies for explaining general political obligations in real societies, we can conclude that most people in most states have no such obligations. We are also finally in a position to respond to the concerns about "seductive confusions" in my distinction between justification and legitimacy that were raised (but never answered) in section 3.1. To the claim that, while an arrangement's being merely useful or beneficial may not obligate us to support or comply with it, an arrangement's being *just* can so obligate us, we can now see the proper reply: an institution's possessing the virtue of justice can no more particularize the natural duty of justice—that is, can no more bind any individual to that particular just arrangement that claims authority over him—than can an institution's beneficial qualities particularize persons' utilitarian duties. And to the concern that political arrangements are so central and important in our lives that they are simply completely unlike the other kinds of arrangements in the world—so that the virtues of political arrangements do ground duties to support and comply with them, where the virtues of other kinds of arrangements do not—the appropriate response is much the same: even if political arrangements are special in such a way that their virtues entail distinctively political duties, those duties could only bind a particular set of persons exclusively to one particular political society if there were something further that was morally significant about the relationship between those people and that society (such as associative or transactional ties between them). That a state simply names a people and a territory as its own (or is recognized as possessing authority by traditions or by institutions whose own authority is equally questionable) is surely not morally significant in this way. But the search for other sorts of moral significance in the relation between a particular state and a particular set of persons simply takes us back to the arguments that we have already explored in this chapter. In short, the distinction between a state's legitimacy (with its subjects' correlative obligations) and a state's virtues or justifiability remains an important one for political philosophy to acknowledge.

3.4. Anarchism Again

If there are no general political obligations and if (as I argued in section 3.1) all plausible accounts of state legitimacy rest legitimacy on the same kinds of arguments that fail in attempts to demonstrate the existence of political obligations, then the prospect of anarchism as the correct political philosophy looms once more. This time, however, the anarchist position under consideration is rather different from the view by that name that we considered in Chapter 2. For we have now distinguished, remember, between those features of states that might justify them and those properties or relations that might establish state legitimacy. The anarchist of Chapter 2—who we can call for convenience a "justificatory anarchist"—denied that the modern state could be justified, could be shown to be morally or prudentially superior to life in a state of nature. Justificatory anarchism was a position that we (hesitantly) rejected. But the view under consideration now is a form of anarchism that denies only state legitimacy (and its correlative obligations of obedience and/or noncompetition and nonusurpation). It denies neither that states can possess morally interesting virtues (and that living in states can be prudentially advantageous) nor that in light of such virtues states might merit our support (and that it might be rational to create them where they do not exist). This more limited anarchism denies only that our existing states have a right to our compliance and support (and/or to our noncompetition) and that we have correlative obligations owed to those states.

Robert Paul Wolff dubbed this less dramatic form of anarchism "philosophical anarchism,"[28] and it is a view that has since been defended by many others (myself included). Wolff's anarchism actually differs from more familiar varieties of anarchism in two ways (though he does not himself distinguish them), only one of which has been identified thus far. First, as we have seen, it is an anarchism that rejects only state legitimacy, not state justifiability. Second, however, the genuinely "philosophical" aspect of Wolff's anarchism lies in the fact that he does not take state illegitimacy to imply any moral obligation on us to oppose or eliminate states that exist (or even, apparently, to refrain from participating in the creation of new states). States may be bullies, restricting our autonomy without warrant; but they may be useful bullies, and in resisting them we may both act imprudently and harm others who rely on their states. Here, the relevant contrast is clearly not with justificatory anarchism but, instead, with what we can call "political anarchism." Political anarchists (who better fit the traditional caricature of anarchists as "bomb throwers," attacking the social order) believe that it is morally imperative that we resist and overthrow existing states, replacing them with more benign or permissible kinds of social relations. So philosophical anarchism is actually a multidimensional position: it is both nonjustificatory and nonpolitical.[29]

In questioning justificatory anarchism (in Chapter 2), we made a number of arguments that at least seem to undermine political anarchism as well. If the state can be prudentially and morally superior to nonstate social arrangements, it is hard to see why we should refrain from creating (should we desire to) those kinds of states which have these advantages or why we should try to eliminate virtuous and advantageous states (whose subjects may in fact appreciate them) as the political anarchist might seem committed to doing. Some political anarchists, of course, have simply rejected the arguments of Chapter 2, denying (as we saw there) that the state can be a virtuous or beneficial institution. Many other political anarchists, however, favored eliminating states because they saw in *existing* states no signs of (or any potential for) the kinds of justifying moral and prudential advantages that (we have said) states can in theory possess. And this contrast between what states can be in theory and what states have been (or tend to be) in practice suggests an additional complexity in understanding the anarchist position.

Anarchists can deny that states are justifiable or legitimate in either of two ways. The judgment "All states are illegitimate (or unjustifiable)" could be either an *a priori* judgment or an *a posteriori* judgment.[30] In the former case, it would amount to the claim that all *possible* states are by their very nature illegitimate, that some necessary feature of statehood made anything possessing that feature morally illegitimate. In the latter case, the judgment would be the weaker assertion that only all *existing* states are illegitimate, allowing at least the possibility that something could be both a state and legitimate but denying that this conjunction exists in the actual world of states. The stronger, *a priori* versions of both political and philosophical anarchism look difficult to defend. The strong political anarchist must argue that there could not possibly be a state that was good enough that it should not be resisted and destroyed, and that seems to involve positing an unduly strong connection between badness and state-hood. Similarly, strong, *a priori* philosophical anarchists must maintain, implausibly, that even a model state with uniformly just laws, freely con-sented to by all who are held subject to its authority, could nonetheless not count as legitimate.

Interestingly, Wolff's philosophical anarchism is presented by him in this strong, *a priori* form; but his commitment to that position seems to break down during the course of his book (apparently without any aware-ness on his part of this fact), until he finally appears to concede (fatally, inconsistently) that a "contractual democracy" is in fact legitimate and its subjects morally bound to obedience.[31] Weak, *a posteriori* philosophical anarchism, which can (e.g.) allow the legitimacy of consensual political associations (while denying that any such associations exist in fact), seems a far more plausible view; and it is that view that I have myself defended.

What, though, of a weaker *a posteriori* form of political anarchism? My own view is that some existing states clearly do enough good (and refrain sufficiently from unwarranted coercion) that they should not be opposed or undermined. Political anarchism, even in its *a posteriori* form, is for that reason false. But why, then, should we not simply embrace statism, reject-ing anarchism in all of its forms? We have already seen the most salient reasons not to reject (*a posteriori*) philosophical anarchism: the arguments that have been advanced throughout the history of philosophy in order to justify claims of political obligation and political legitimacy have uniformly failed to support their desired conclusions about existing states.

To continue to affirm state legitimacy and political obligation in the face of this manifest failure seems irrational. At its worst, such affirmation simply represents wrongful complicity in states' and governments' obvious programs of pacifying and controlling their subject populations; at its best, such affirmation represents an innocent confusion of two dimensions of institutional evaluation. That political institutions may in some (or even many) cases be valuable and important to many people simply cannot show those institutions to have legitimate authority over whichever persons they (or international conventions) identify as their subjects. No matter how just or beneficial the political institutions of the United States were to become, for example, their virtues could never entail the legitimate subjection to their authority of the residents of, say, Canada (in the event that the U.S. government [or even the United Nations] should declare that Canada would henceforth be part of the United States). Surely, only something like the (highly unlikely!) *choice* of Canadians to so subject themselves to U.S. authority or the sole provision to Canadians by the United States of important benefits could accomplish a legitimate annexation of this sort. But here we have simply returned to the familiar (in this case, transactional) arguments for political obligation and legitimacy, arguments that (we have seen) fail in even the more straightforward cases of those who are uncontroversially recognized as citizens or residents of well-defined modern states.

If rational argument cannot establish the legitimacy of existing states or the political obligations of residents of those states, then we cannot in good conscience reject anarchism entirely, embracing the state (even more or less) wholeheartedly. Anarchists are right in insisting that there is something morally untoward about modern states, even if they are wrong about just what the problem is and wrong when they insist that this moral impropriety justifies (or requires) active opposition to existing (or to all) states. States uniformly wrong us by seizing and wielding a monopoly on the use of force within their claimed territories, without ever legitimating those activities by entering into relations with their claimed subjects that could ground correlative obligations of support and compliance. This is surely not the greatest wrong that could be done to persons, particularly when the wrong is put in the balance with the many goods that states do or can provide to their claimed subjects (and to others in the world). But it leaves the modern state at best a morally ambiguous institution, and it leaves a qualified form of anarchism—specifically, *a posteriori* philosophical anarchism—as the best account of this moral ambiguity.[32]

Suggested Reading

W. A. Edmundson, ed., *The Duty to Obey the Law* (Lanham, MD: Rowman and Littlefield, 1999).

Leslie Green, *The Authority of the State* (Oxford: Oxford University Press, 1988).

John Horton, *Political Obligation* (Atlantic Highlands, NJ: Humanities Press, 1992).

George Klosko, *The Principle of Fairness and Political Obligation* (Lanham, MD: Rowman and Littlefield, 1992).

A. John Simmons, *Moral Principles and Political Obligations* (Princeton: Princeton University Press, 1979).

Christopher H. Wellman and A. John Simmons, *Is There a Duty to Obey the Law? For and Against* (Cambridge: Cambridge University Press, 2005).

CHAPTER 4

Justice

4.1. Justice in Political Philosophy

Justice, John Rawls says in his justly celebrated work on that subject, is "the first virtue of social institutions, as truth is of systems of thought."[1] Rawls is surely right that the vice of injustice taints social and political institutions and makes imperative their reform in a way or to a degree that most other institutional vices, such as simple inefficiency, do not. Whether this makes justice the *first* institutional virtue (or, for that matter, precisely what that means) is less clear. Political institutions seem to be capable of displaying other morally important properties besides justice (or injustice)—it is important, for example, that they be designed to keep those subject to their rules reliably safe and relatively comfortable, that they promote peace and welfare for those without their domain, etc. Or perhaps political institutions cannot do these things without also being just so that justice is not only the first virtue but the "master" virtue—the sum of all of the most important virtues that social institutions can manifest. Whether or not that is true will obviously depend on which substantive theory of justice we embrace, and we have thus far discussed justice without saying very much about that in which justice consists. We may be confident, say, that justice has some important connection to fairness or equality or desert (or all three of them); but we plainly need to say more about the precise nature of such connections (if any).[2]

It seems clear, at least, that justice is one of the most important justifying properties that political institutions can possess, that any account we gave of something that was not important in this way could not be an account of justice. The need for justice drives the oppressed (and their supporters) to the streets, funds revolutions and state foundings; the cause of justice is one for which people willingly risk or sacrifice prosperity and even life. What may seem at first puzzling, of course, is that justice is demanded not only by those with high and noble causes, or in the grand arenas of politics, but also by (e.g.) overpaid professional athletes and slimy criminal defendants. What unifies such apparently disparate demands, it seems, must be the connection between justice and *rights*. Rights can be legal (institutional, customary) or moral. They can be extremely important or relatively trivial. They can be possessed by the noble and virtuous and by the selfish or evil. That there is a strong connection between the satisfaction of people's rights and the (modern) idea of justice seems indisputable, as can be seen in the agreement on this point by moral thinkers as different (in period and in orientation) as John Locke, Immanuel Kant, and John Stuart Mill.[3] Domestic legal justice is done, we might say, when people's domestic legal rights are satisfied. A just war is conducted when people's moral rights (or states' international legal rights) are respected (with the understanding, analogous to the domestic legal case, that some of these rights may be limited or forfeited by the war's conduct). Perhaps "social" or "political" justice is done when social or political institutions respect or secure certain of persons' basic moral rights. The trick, it seems, lies in defending an account of exactly which rights those are.

But there are at least three ways in which we might disagree with one another about the nature of this supposed connection between justice and rights. First, some of us might think (with Locke, say) that justice is done so long as people's (natural) rights have simply been *respected,* as they could be (by and large) in a particularly peaceful, sociable version of the state of nature. Against those, others of us might think (with Kant, say) that justice is only really done when people's (provisional) rights are *secured* (and made real) by justice-administering, coercive institutions like those of the state. Second, some might think that justice consists in satisfying (primarily or exclusively) their *negative* rights to freedom or personal security, rights not to be invaded or interfered with by other people in their personal spheres. Others, disagreeing, might insist that justice requires (also or primarily) that we honor people's *positive* rights, rights to be given (or to be given the opportunity to acquire) income, say, or wealth, the means of production, or the means to survive. And third, where some, in one of the ways just described, might identify justice with the satisfaction or the securing of rights, others might insist that securing rights is just one possible conception of justice, that (e.g.) treating people as equals or giving people what they deserve are alternative, possibly superior, conceptions of justice.

The first of these disagreements, as we've seen, is part of the more general disagreement between the Lockean and the Kantian approaches to political philosophy. The second disagreement we will see played out between libertarian and nonlibertarian approaches to justice (and to political philosophy generally). The third possible disagreement is harder to superimpose on well-known debates in political philosophy. To someone wedded to the conceptual connection between rights and justice, it may seem possible to capture the force of apparently alternative conceptions by saying, to someone who insists that justice is foremost not about rights but about equal treatment, that this just amounts to claiming that persons have a (particularly basic) moral right to equal treatment (or to one who connects justice to desert, that this just means that people have a basic moral right to be treated as they deserve to be treated). The Rawls of *A Theory of Justice,* who never considers foundational, preinstitutional moral rights in connection with his theory of justice, could in this approach be taken to in fact be committed to a basic (natural?) right of all persons to equal or fair treatment.

For now, it is worth observing that while, as we have seen, we do talk and write about the rights at issue in (e.g.) doing legal justice and conducting just wars, most recent philosophical work on justice has in fact concerned (what is usually called) *social* or *distributive justice.*[4] Here, the subject is the justice of the most basic social and political institutions of a society (what Rawls calls its "basic structure"). Since institutions are complex sets of rules—and since occasional wrongdoing or wrongdoing by officials who abuse their positions within good institutions are not usually taken to discredit institutional structures—social injustice will normally be a rule-governed, systematic defect of social institutions. Further, since the principal function of society's basic institutions is the distribution of certain goods (and burdens)—wealth, security, employment, material goods, leisure, legal rights and duties (which will include things like taxes, military service, jury duty, and other requirements regarded by most as burdens), honors, opportunities and positions of power, etc.—social injustice will typically involve a defect in institutional rules that aims at or results in a morally improper distribution of basic social goods and burdens (hence the term *distributive* justice).

This focus on society's basic structure as the subject of a theory of justice is not uncontroversial. For we might well believe that justice actually has, in addition, a wider and/or a narrower[5] focus. The wider focus would introduce as a subject to be assessed in terms of its justice something larger than the structures of individual societies. The most natural such expansion would be to extend the theory of justice to the world as a whole so that any adequate theory of justice would include principles of *international* justice or *natural* (i.e., logically pre-political) justice, binding persons to one another independent of political or societal affiliation. We will explore the possibilities for a theory of international justice in Chapter 6. But note also that the focus on societies' basic structures as subject supports the idea of a discontinuity between a theory of justice and a theory of morality for individuals, the virtues and defects of social institutions seeming unlikely to have much to do with the best ways for individual persons to act or be. As we have seen (in Chapter 1, section 1.1), for theorists like Rawls this discontinuity is just part of the more general conception of political philosophy as autonomous from other parts of moral philosophy. But we should remember that this discontinuity view represents a distinctive position, not the only position, on the proper focus of a theory of justice.

For philosophers like Locke and Mill, the theory of justice was uniform in its application to individuals and societies, with private persons being conceived of as fully as capable of justice and injustice as social institutions (since both persons and institutions can respect or violate the moral rights of individuals). The same was plainly true, of course, in the theories of justice defended by the ancients. In Plato's famous discussion in *Republic,* justice is characterized as a kind of internal harmony—the proper ordering of the parts of a thing—which is a property, he tells us, that persons or states can possess (or fail to possess) equally. And in Aristotle's rather different focus on "special" or "particular" justice,[6] it is still clear that both individuals and societies can possess the virtues and vices of justice and injustice.

Aristotle's discussion of justice can in fact help us to understand some of the presuppositions of any theory of justice, regardless of whether we adopt the discontinuity view (i.e., accept a discontinuity between political and personal morality) or the continuity view. Aristotle agrees with Plato, of course, that justice involves a proper balance or proportion; but his first effort to explain this notion seems to diverge radically from Plato, making reference to the idea of equality: "what is just is equal [or fair], as seems true to everyone even without argument" (1131a). Now, the idea that a just distribution is an equal one is perfectly familiar with those who embrace this idea usually being called "egalitarians." Indeed, it is far from surprising that a Greek would make such a claim since the Greek word for equality, *isotes,* is probably closer in meaning to our word *justice* than is the Greek word whose meaning(s) Aristotle is actually exploring (i.e., *dikaiosyne*). What is surprising, perhaps, is that Aristotle should say "the just is the equal" when he is so clearly not an egalitarian. Aristotle in fact believes that just distributions are those that benefit people according to their merit or worth: "for everyone agrees that what is just in distributions must fit some sort of worth" (1131a25). While Aristotle acknowledges that people differ about the criteria for merit or worth, he and those he knows seem all to be allied in being not egalitarians but *meritarians* (justice is happiness according to virtue/merit).

Aristotle's meritarianism is probably best explained by noting that "Aristotle had in mind not only the distribution of public funds to office-holders and citizens in need, but also the distribution of benefits within clubs and other such private societies."[7] Indeed, the city-state of Athens in Aristotle's time was itself much more like a club or private association (for native-born, male freemen, with at least two-thirds of the resident population disqualified) than it was like a contemporary nation-state. And many of the goods that would have been distributed in such a context would have been conceived of as honors, prizes, or awards, for which merit or desert would have been the natural distributive criterion on which to focus. Further, even when we think just about aid for the needy, people distinguish between the "deserving poor" and others, again suggesting a merit-based standard for (or constraint on) distribution. So when Aristotle considers distributive social contexts, he may understandably be thinking of circumstances in which "everyone would agree" that merit should govern distributions. It might well be hard to secure similar agreement on meritarian principles as appropriate for the rather different context of the basic structure of a modern, large-scale, pluralistic political society.

Why, though, does Aristotle, the meritarian, say (with egalitarians) that "the just is the equal"? He says this, I think, because he is articulating an understood presupposition of any substantive theory of justice, stating what is sometimes called the "formal principle of justice": "treat equals equally and unequals unequally" (or "treat like cases alike, and different cases differently"). This is only a "formal" principle (i.e., it has only the form of an action-guiding principle) because it leaves perfectly open the proper understanding of the terms *equal* and *unequal*. Any two cases/persons/circumstances will be unequal in some respects (or they would not be two cases [etc.] but only one). And any two cases will be equal in some respects (e.g., that they exist or occur in time). Before we can actually apply the principle to our actions (or to our institutional rules), we must know "equal" and "unequal" *in what respect(s)*? The hard and interesting part of a theory of social justice will lie in answering that question by formulating certain *material* principles of justice,[8] the principles that specify which differences (if any) between persons will require, as a matter of justice, that those persons be treated differently in the distribution of basic social goods. That does not mean, of course, that the "formal principle" is completely empty (or that Aristotle was foolish in stating it). For the formal principle does state the fundamental underlying assumption of any theory of justice—namely, that there must be a *reason* that justifies differences in treatment, that arbitrary discrimination between cases is always unjust (indeed, always irrational).

Further, of course, when Aristotle says "the just is the equal," he plainly means to refer not to *strict* equality but rather to *geometrical* equality (or equality of proportion). Differences between cases do not warrant just any difference in treatment. Differences in distributive shares must be (in order to be just) proportional to the (degree of) morally relevant differences between cases. And such a principle of proportion is, I take it, yet another understood part of every theory of justice. Aristotle's meritarianism, then, is in fact presented so as to reveal the underlying "egalitarian" presumptions of even quite antiegalitarian substantive theories of justice.

The morally relevant differences between cases might, as in Aristotle, be claimed to be differences in merit (in virtue, ability, achievement, or effort, say), yielding meritarianism. Or they might be differences in the utility (happiness) that would result from conferring benefits on those persons, as utilitarian theories insist. Perhaps the only relevant differences are differences in the moral (or natural) rights to things that persons antecedently possess, as libertarians often claim. Or maybe the only differences between persons that matter, for the purpose of justice, are persons' needs for the things being distributed (as some egalitarians claim). Or, most dramatically, we could argue, with strict egalitarians, that there are no differences at all between persons that could morally justify treating them differently in distributing basic social goods, that a person's humanity or personhood (or residence or citizenship) is in each case sufficient to qualify that person for a fully equal share of what society can provide. It is to the arguments for (and against) these kinds of "material" proposals that we will now turn.

4.2. Utility and Equality

When John Rawls wrote *A Theory of Justice* (published in 1971), it is probably fair to say that work in the social sciences and (though certainly to a lesser extent) in philosophy, along with much nonacademic discussion of public policy issues, was dominated by a commitment (even if only vague and implicit) to utilitarianism. Rawls aimed to make clear the limits of utilitarianism's plausibility as (the sole normative underpinnings of) a political philosophy; and largely as a result of the enormous persuasiveness and influence of Rawls' work, little mainstream work in political philosophy is now utilitarian. But the appeal of utilitarianism to those outside of philosophy departments remains substantial—as just one of many examples, consider the powerful "law and economics" movement in legal theory (whose normative "wing" typically operates, explicitly or implicitly, with utilitarian presumptions).[9] The reason for this continuing popularity, it seems, is the considerable intuitive plausibility or the "naturalness" of utilitarianism. Utilitarianism is now typically characterized (thanks largely to G. E. Moore's influential discussion of it in *Principia Ethica*[10]) as the view that an act is morally right if and only if it produces at least as much total happiness (utility) as would any alternative act open to the actor.[11] As moral agents, we ought always to act so as to maximize utility. And our social institutions ought to be structured with this same end of maximizing utility as their sole guiding principle. The attractiveness of this view, as we saw in Chapter 1, section 1.2, lies in its identification of both a very attractive conception of what is good in the world—namely, happiness or desire satisfaction (which everyone seems to agree in finding good or desirable)—and a very natural understanding of how we ought to try to act (or to make our institutions function)—namely, to produce as much as possible of what is good in the world.

What, though, would a utilitarian say about the virtue of justice? Since utilitarians embrace only one foundational moral principle (i.e., "maximize utility"), the utilitarian would presumably have to characterize justice as, to use Mill's words, "only a particular kind or branch of general utility."[12] Doing justice will be nothing more than maximizing or promoting utility, perhaps in some special way or context. Mill recognizes, of course, that this is not the common view, that in fact people mostly think it possible to mount powerful objections to utilitarianism by pointing to the conflicting demands of utility and justice. Mill argues, however, that there is no such conflict. The realm of justice is the realm of rights ("wherever there is a right, the case is one of justice"), and to have a right is "to have something which society ought to defend me in the possession of" for "no other reason than general utility."[13] In the end (and contrary to common opinion) justice is simply "a name for certain classes of moral rules which concern the essentials of human well-being more nearly, and are therefore of more absolute obligation, than any other rules for the guidance of life."[14] We do feel more strongly about justice than about mere utility, as common opinion suggests; and ordinary folk (not to mention philosophers) think that this suggests an opposition between the two. But in fact what is only a difference of degree has come to seem to us a difference in kind. Justice is about very important utilities, not about something different from utility.

Not all utilitarians, of course, agree with Mill's argument, nor is it particularly clear exactly what the argument amounts to. But were Mill an act utilitarian, he could hardly mount such an argument (on any reasonable interpretation of it). For even if justice does name certain very important moral rules, act utilitarianism is committed to violating any rule whenever doing so will, in the circumstances, produce more utility than would following the rule. And this would suggest again possible conflicts between justice and utility. Indeed, as Mill anticipated, many of the most familiar counterexamples to act utilitarianism in the history of philosophy have appealed precisely to its apparent inability to accord rules, rights, and justice their proper moral weight. But if Mill is reasoning as a rule utilitarian[15] (or even regarding justice as a useful "rule of thumb"), we will want to know why he thinks someone who values only utility (and the more the better) also thinks we should follow any rule—even a very important one—when one can produce more utility in the specific circumstances by breaking it (which, as the "familiar counterexamples" reveal, can often be the case). Rule utilitarians seem to abandon the simple utilitarian theory of value, adding "rule following" to utility on the list of things that are intrinsically good. So Mill's arguments notwithstanding, it remains unclear just how utilitarianism can avoid sanctioning actions or policies that seem, intuitively, to be deeply unjust.

Interestingly, Rawls' case against utilitarianism does not center on this "counterintuitive results" argument. Indeed, he appears to concede that, at least "in a reasonably advanced stage of civilization," the social policies recommended by utilitarianism may not conflict with familiar, commonsense precepts of justice.[16] Rawls' actual case against utilitarianism is complicated, for a significant aspect of it is simply the failure of the utilitarian principle to be the one chosen within the special theoretical apparatus Rawls devises to test proposed principles of justice (which we will discuss later). But Rawls' most basic, intuitive, theory-neutral account of the defects of utilitarianism seems to be that it "does not take seriously the distinction between persons."[17] By treating individual persons as simply so many possible sources of the happiness or unhappiness to be summed in the utilitarian calculus, persons' individuality and the moral importance (both to them and objectively) of their particular lives and well-being seem to remain unaccounted for. What matters for the utilitarian is not where the happiness resides (as it were) but only how large a total of it the society as a whole can be conceived of as possessing.

Further, utilitarians count happiness (and unhappiness) in their calculus regardless of the source of that happiness so in (say) determining the justice of slavery, the slaveholder's pleasures (including sadistic pleasures) would have to be weighed against the slaves' pains in the calculus. Even if utilitarian calculation reliably yielded the conclusion that slavery was unjust or wrong (since the slaves' pains always outweighed the slaveholder's pleasures), utilitarianism would have reached this conclusion for the wrong reasons, overlooking the facts that the slaves' lives and happiness are not simply counters to be tossed into and weighed against others in an impersonal calculus and that the pleasure the slaveholder takes in his slaves' suffering makes that enslavement worse from the moral viewpoint, not better. "Each person possesses an inviolability founded on justice that even the welfare of society as a whole cannot override."[18] And this equal inviolability requires a very basic equality of treatment from our fellow persons and our societies.

Utilitarians, of course, also believe that persons are moral equals, each person's happiness being of equal value to any other's; as Bentham and Mill famously stressed: "everybody to count for one, nobody for more than one" in the utilitarian calculus. But Mill, of course, allowed that "the equal claim of everybody to happiness" must be understood to "bend" to the requirements of "social expediency" (i.e., utility).[19] Where utility is better served by unequal distributions of social goods, this underlying utilitarian "egalitarianism" does not require that we nonetheless treat all equally in social distributions. Rawls, though, advocates not just equal *consideration* of persons in the distribution of social goods—counting each person's happiness equally in our calculations—but something closer to equal *treatment* of persons by social institutions. Why would someone find such a strong conception of equality attractive as an ideal of distributive justice?

One plausible line of argument might proceed as follows. We generally think it unfair or unjust when people are treated differently by social institutions because of differences between them over which they have no control. This has the appearance of rewarding and punishing persons simply for what they are, rather than for what they have done or for that for which they are responsible. So discrimination on the basis of skin color, gender, parental social class or ethnicity or religion (etc.) seems wrong, at least where society's distribution of social goods is concerned. But what if all of our personal traits or characteristics were like skin color or gender, making all discrimination on the basis of such personal qualities look exactly like the paradigmatic injustices of socially enforced racism or sexism? People, surely, do not deserve good or ill for the genetic makeup with which, or the social circumstances (e.g., family, home, location) into which, they were born. But what if everything else about persons—all that they ever do or become—were determined by this initial genetic and social endowment (or, less contentiously, if we could simply never be confident that persons' qualities or actions were not so determined)? Then, we would have to regard everything about persons and their social circumstances as (or as possibly) simply a function of their good or bad luck in a "natural lottery" (to use Rawls' phrase). Some work harder, try more, do more with what they start out with, you say. But even the abilities to try harder, to work harder are (or cannot be known not to be) determined by people's initial endowments.

If one can in this way make all unequal treatment of persons look like discrimination on the basis of race or gender, one will have a powerful argument for strict equality in the distribution of basic social goods (or, at least, for a strong presumption of strict equality, requiring powerful, equality-respecting arguments to overcome the presumption). While Rawls does not really present the egalitarianism of *A Theory of Justice* in these terms, the defense offered for his theory makes clear, I think, that something very like the argument sketched above must be understood to underpin it. Now, the reason most of us reject strict (or even reasonably strict) egalitarianism is not, I think, that we reject the idea that society should not reward or punish people for what is not in their control. The reason is, rather, that we believe ourselves to have (or pretend that we have) good grounds for rejecting the genetic and social determinism (or the "epistemic skepticism" version of it) on which the argument for strict equality rests. Most of us think we are sometimes personally responsible for what we do or become, so the lazy and the wicked are not treated unjustly if they have less than the hardworking and the virtuous. Demands for strict equality will seem most plausible to most of us in "manna from heaven" contexts, where the goods we need to divide are ones to the production of which none of us contributed (e.g., as distributing the food from a carton that washes up on our desert island). But where the goods to be distributed to persons were created through very different efforts and contributions by those persons, most people seem comfortable with the ants and the grasshoppers getting very different shares.

This is not to say that common opinions about social justice do not incorporate some egalitarian elements, even where "manna from heaven" is not at issue. Many people find it easy to accept the idea that there should be some kind of equality in the distribution of social goods up to a certain point, through the maintenance of some kind of guaranteed social minimum (or "safety net") that provides at least for the satisfaction of people's most basic needs. Justice, they might say, requires that even the lazy, the wicked, and the incompetent (regardless of their responsibility for their own plights) not be left to starve while others have more than they can use. This suggests the idea of a *principle of need* as a preliminary (or highest-priority) principle of justice, dictating that at least the most basic needs of all should be equally satisfied prior to allowing those inequalities in distribution that are required or permitted by other principles of justice. Plainly, of course, satisfying people's basic needs will not always involve treating them equally in their shares of goods since persons can have quite different levels of need. Many egalitarians have argued, however, that using a set of resources to satisfy people's needs is actually a better way of realizing the idea of treating them equally than would be dividing those resources equally between them.

4.3. Rawls on Justice

John Rawls, however, believes that justice typically requires considerably more extensive equality in shares of social goods than would be accomplished simply by maintaining a social safety net. He comes to this conclusion by thinking about questions of social justice using an approach that "generalizes and carries to a higher level of abstraction the familiar theory of the social contract"—an approach that involves presenting the correct principles of justice for society's basic structure as those that would be the content of a hypothetical original agreement between society's members (to define "the fundamental terms of their association").[20] We should be careful not to be misled here by Rawls' "social contract" language. There is no bargaining or compromise in the process leading to the "agreement," nor is the "contract" he mentions an actual historical event—or even a possible historical event (since the constraints on the parties' knowledge and reasoning are not constraints to which real contractors could be subjected, except in science fiction cases[21]). Rather, the hypothetical original contract is just a particularly forceful organizing idea designed to model in a compelling way the kinds of constraints on reasoning about justice that we independently think would be warranted: "the idea . . . is simply to make vivid to ourselves the restrictions that it seems reasonable to impose on arguments for principles of justice" (p. 16).

In particular, Rawls' "generalized and abstracted" social contract approach is designed to emphasize those "restrictions on arguments" that are set by thinking of justice as importantly related to the value of fairness (indeed, he calls his theory of justice "justice as fairness"). Now, thinking of justice as a kind of "fair compromise" between the interests of the various members of society is an idea that is at least as old as Book II of Plato's *Republic*. But Rawls does not understand the connection between justice and fairness in quite that way. Justice, for Rawls, does not involve any "compromise," at least as we would ordinarily understand this, for the contractors are not in a position to press for reciprocal concessions, giving each some of what he most wants (nor, of course, is justice done simply by honoring actual compromises between real people). The fairness of Rawls' principles of justice derives instead from the fact that they flow from (i.e., they are chosen within) an initial situation that is specifically structured so as to be fair to all parties.

Rawls calls this hypothetical initial situation "the original position." In it "all are similarly situated and no one is able to design principles to favor his particular condition"; "this explains the propriety of the name 'justice as fairness': it conveys the idea that the principles of justice are agreed to in an initial situation that is fair" (p. 11). What else, besides the preclusion of such selfishly tailored principles, is necessary for a contractual setting to be fair? Rawls says "it seems reasonable and generally acceptable that no one should be advantaged or disadvantaged by natural fortune or social circumstances in the choice of principles" (p. 16). He accordingly proposes that in a fair initial situation the parties will not know about their natural fortune or social circumstances, so these facts cannot be used by them to formulate principles that would reward or punish fortune in the natural and social lottery. The parties in the original position operate under a "veil of ignorance": they do not know their race or age or gender, their strength or intelligence or psychology, their talents or handicaps or social standing, their "conception of the good" (i.e., what they regard as valuable or important in life), the nature of their particular society (or anything else that could be used to design principles that would distribute social goods according to special interests or mere fortune). The veil of ignorance, then, seems for Rawls to model both the (more procedural) idea that fairness precludes "tailoring" principles to match our special circumstances and the (more substantive) idea that it is unfair to choose principles for the organization of society that will allow us to profit or suffer as a result of facts about us that are "arbitrary from the moral point of view" (p. 274).

But surely, we might object, distributive distinctions between persons are not unjust simply because they are based on distinctive facts about those persons. After all, differences between persons such as differences in effort or productivity or achievement do not look "arbitrary from the moral point of view" (at least in the way that differences in race or gender do), so there would seem to be nothing unfair about letting contractors choose principles that discriminate between persons in those terms. It is at this point, I think, that our earlier "deterministic" argument—the argument that all of our distinctive traits are tied to our initial good or bad fortune in the genetic and social lottery—must be understood to play a role in Rawls' case.[22] There is no good reason to think that fairness requires that principles of justice be unresponsive to differences between persons unless we believe that all such differences are (or cannot be known not to be or not to be in some indeterminate measure) morally arbitrary, a simple matter of good or bad fortune. In discussing (and rejecting) meritarianism, for instance, Rawls, after asserting the moral arbitrariness of "initial endowments," says of meritarian principles like that of rewarding "conscientious effort" that "it seems clear that the effort a person is willing to make is influenced by his natural abilities and skills and the alternatives open to him" (p. 274).

So according to Rawls, the correct principles of justice will be those that would be agreed upon in a fair initial situation under a veil of ignorance by contractors concerned to advance their own interests. The correct principles will only be chosen, however, if the parties doing the choosing have one further (unrealistic) characteristic: that of "mutually disinterested rationality" (p. 125). Real people, of course, are neither mutually disinterested nor reliably rational, just as they are not ignorant of their genders or talents—emphasizing again that the "contract" at issue is not one made by people like us (as it was in the social contract theories of Hobbes or Locke) but only one designed to reflect acceptable constraints on our reasoning about justice. The requirement of (simple means–ends) rationality seems necessary if the resulting choice is to have any normative force (we would be disinclined to regard such a hypothetical choice as giving us reason to act if the choice were not a rational one); and the requirement of mutual disinterest (i.e., that the parties care only about advancing their own personal interests and are not moved by affection, hatred, envy [etc.] to try to advance or retard the well-being of others) guarantees that the resulting principles can be thought of as advancing the interests of each person separately, with nobody's interests sacrificed in order that others' interests be more effectively advanced (or, as would be true in cases of envy, in order to prevent this).

One obvious problem faced by such contractors, of course, is that it is not clear how they could go about choosing to advance their interests, given that the veil deprives them of any knowledge of what those interests are (by depriving them of knowledge of their "conception of the good," which identifies at least some of their interests). So Rawls supplies the contractors with a basis for choice by identifying a "thin" theory of "primary goods," with this conception of primary goods replacing their personal conceptions of the good and providing a basis on which they can try to advance their interests. Primary goods are "things which it is supposed a rational man wants whatever else he wants" (p. 79), a kind of "lowest common denominator" of the various "thick" conceptions of the good possessed by real people. Rawls names as primary goods rights, liberties, opportunities, income, wealth, and the social bases of self-respect. These are "all-purpose" goods that can be used to advance any conception of the good, so we can presume that if contractors choose so that they maximize their expected shares of primary goods, they will be well positioned to advance their actual interests, whatever those turn out to be. We should also notice that the theory of primary goods models the well-known liberal idea of state neutrality (between competing religious [or nonreligious] worldviews, between different personal lifestyles, etc.). By deriving the principles of justice only from a thin, rudimentary theory of the good, Rawls tries to guarantee that the state's basic structure will not be organized according to one favored, thick conception of the good (an atheistic Marxist one, say, or an Islamic fundamentalist one). No one could then complain that the basic structure was unfairly biased against her own thick conception since all thick conceptions were excluded from the reasoning that produced society's principles.

The basic justificatory approach in Rawls, then, is this: hypothetical agreement on principles of justice in a fair initial situation (where special advantages are nullified by conditions of ignorance) by rational, mutually disinterested "persons" should be understood to justify those principles, to show them to be valid for and binding on real people. A significant normative conclusion is thus derived from relatively minimal normative input (the thin notions of fairness, goodness, and rationality that are built into the original position model), with the normative significance of choice (as in the social contract tradition) apparently making up the shortfall. Rawls does complicate this justificatory picture somewhat by adding a second "leg" to the process of justification. We should also, he says, determine whether the principles that would be chosen in the original position "match" our considered, pretheoretical judgments about justice, such as those instances of social justice and injustice that we confidently and reflectively take as paradigms (where we "feel sure" that questions about justice "must be answered in a certain way" [p. 17]). These judgments are the "provisional fixed points" with which satisfactory principles of justice must square. Rawls suggests that justification for principles of justice must be reached by "going back and forth" between the hypothetical contract argument and our considered convictions about justice. We may allow the force of those convictions to dictate changes in the structure of the original position choice problem and hence in the principles that would be chosen there. Or we may allow the power of the contractarian model to force us to give up some of the convictions that we thought were firm. Ideally, by going back and forth between these two sources of justification, we can eventually reach a state of "reflective equilibrium," in which our considered judgments match up with the principles that the hypothetical contractors would choose (i.e., the principles have those judgments as implications and extend those judgments in plausible ways) (p. 18). When we achieve reflective equilibrium, we can be confident both that our considered convictions have clear, principled foundations and that our principles have no unacceptable implications.

What principles of justice would be chosen in the original position (as described by Rawls) and at the same time would fit with our considered judgments? Conveniently, we need not speculate about possible deals or compromises between the parties that might be necessary to reach consensus, for the parties have been stripped of all differences by the veil of ignorance and the "mutually disinterested rationality" condition. Each party has the same general knowledge to work with (limited to general social-scientific knowledge), no knowledge of his or her own attributes, the same psychology, the same "values" (set by the theory of primary goods). Contractors will necessarily favor the same principles of justice, so reconstructing the reasoning of a single contractor will suffice to give us the content of the "agreement." And if we try to imagine the reasoning of any single party in the original position, Rawls thinks, certain results seem *prima facie* clear. First, it seems unlikely that a contractor would select the utilitarian principle of justice, which permits the interests of some to be sacrificed where necessary to maximize overall societal utility. "Since each desires to protect his interests, his capacity to advance his conception of the good, no one has reason to acquiesce in an enduring loss for himself in order to bring about a greater net balance of satisfaction" (p. 13). Second, the most natural first position to which a contractor's reasoning would lead her would be a principle of strict equality in the distribution of primary goods. Nobody has reason to accept less than an equal share or to expect others to accept her having more than that. (Or not knowing [under the veil] what kind of person she will turn out to be when the veil is lifted, she will want to guarantee that every kind of person has as large a share as possible.)

But rational contractors will recognize further that permitting certain kinds of inequalities in society will in fact make them better off than would strict equality, even if they do not turn out to be the ones receiving the largest shares. For instance, by offering higher salaries to attract talented people to difficult jobs requiring those talents, productivity may be improved in a way that will increase the total pool of distributable resources sufficiently to make better off (than under a regime of strict equality) even those who are paid less than the talented. Only an irrational envy would make a person prefer equality to the greater well-being she would enjoy in a society that permitted some to be still better off than she. So while Rawlsian hypothetical contractors would want to continue to insure equality in (and as much as possible of) the basic liberties and opportunities that are central to their capacities to carry out diverse life plans (any one of which might, when the veil is lifted, turn out to be theirs), they would favor as well a principle that permits inequalities that benefit all (themselves included, whoever they turn out to be)—what Rawls calls "the difference principle." Rawls concludes, then, that hypothetical rational contractors, fairly positioned, would agree upon two principles of justice (and that these principles are therefore valid, binding principles for us):

> First: each person is to have an equal right to the most extensive scheme of equal basic liberties compatible with a similar scheme of liberties for others.
>
> Second: social and economic inequalities are to be arranged so that they are both (a) reasonably expected to be to everyone's advantage, and (b) attached to positions and offices open to all. (p. 53)

A society ordered by these principles, of course, will be straightforwardly *liberal* in its structure, guided by the concerns to maximize individual liberty, to guarantee real (not just formal or legal) equality, and to serve as a neutral, impartial umpire in cases of conflict.

Now, why would rational contractors be content to limit their prospects in this way—that is, to limit themselves to an equal share of social goods unless their having an unequally large share would make everyone else better off as well (would drag everyone up beneath them, "floating all boats")? Why wouldn't they want to leave open for themselves the possibility of using their talents to become fabulously wealthy or powerful, say, even if their occupying this superior position didn't benefit everyone else? First, of course, they do not know that they will have exploitable talents, rather than being the kind of person who is allowed by a society that permits extensive inequality to sink to the bottom social and economic stratum. And the veil of ignorance does not permit them enough specific information about their society (what traits it values, how those traits are distributed across the society, etc.) to even calculate the probabilities of success from taking a chance on such an arrangement (p. 134). Second (and here the idea of a "contract" plays a more substantial role), since "the original agreement is final and made in perpetuity," the contractors "cannot enter into agreements that may have consequences they cannot accept" (p. 153). The "strains of commitment" may turn out to be too great if a contractor agrees to principles that leave any probability, no matter how small, of his being unable to lead a satisfactory life (as would be the case if the principles permitted society to maintain even a tiny class of slaves or desperately poor persons).

Virtually every aspect of Rawls' theory of justice has been subjected to detailed criticism (reconstruction, defense), from the basic hypothetical contractarian approach to questions about justice to the description of the original position and the contractors and the derivation of the two principles. The argument has been condemned for simply building into the original position apparatus precisely the moral content (based on a quite controversial notion of a "fair procedure") that Rawls wishes to derive from it. The veil has been thought too thick, designed to allow through not the information that fairness requires but rather only that which will allow Rawls to derive his preferred conclusions. The account of primary goods has been attacked as too individualistic (with no provision for those genuinely collective goods that a focus on individual goods will leave society unable to achieve); the description of the parties has been attacked as too egoistic or too "masculine." The appeal to consistency with our considered judgments about justice has been thought to relativize the entire project to our local view of justice, undermining what would otherwise be the powerful justifying force of "rational choice" considerations.

All of these complaints may have merit, but I will not explore them here. The Rawls literature overflows with variations on them.[23] Here, I will mention only one further objection to the Rawlsian project, perhaps less often made, but certainly as damaging as those mentioned above. Even if we grant Rawls his entire original position approach, it simply does not appear that the two principles of justice he proposes—and particularly the difference principle—will in fact be the conclusion of the argument. Contractors concerned to protect themselves from unacceptable possible outcomes (and from unacceptably severe "strains of commitment") would focus not on an initial benchmark of equality in the division of social goods (and permit deviations from it only where all will benefit from them). Rather, they would seek a guarantee of a social minimum set sufficiently high to insure for everyone acceptable prospects, to permit each a real opportunity to realize a reasonable life plan. And I have already suggested that, at least for many people in societies like our own, the strongest egalitarian position that is part of their considered judgments about justice is a substantial social minimum, not any more strictly equal division of social goods—suggesting, of course, that when the "match" between the derived principles and our considered judgments is tested, some principle setting a substantial social minimum is again more likely to be the result. Only Rawls' more technical "maximin" arguments might seem to actually support the difference principle, though I believe that they in fact fail to do so as well.[24] In the end, then, Rawls' approach appears to point us not to his two principles but rather to some "mixed conception"—like average utility (or some alternative principle) with a substantial social minimum—a possibility that Rawls mentions but never really convincingly rejects (pp. 107, 278–79).[25] And such a mixed conception has strong intuitive appeal, resting as it does on the compelling idea that justice requires that societies insure first that the urgent requirements and basic needs of all citizens be satisfied (and that they thus be put in a position to effectively pursue a satisfactory life) before citizens are permitted to secure for themselves more luxurious lives.

Rawls' *A Theory of Justice* was certainly the most-discussed, and arguably the most important, book in political philosophy of the twentieth century. As such, it naturally attracted not only numerous disciples but criticisms from all parts of the political and philosophical spectra. I have mentioned a few of those criticisms, and we will discuss more later. Many have taken some of those criticisms to be responsible for Rawls' gradual recasting of his arguments, through a series of papers and culminating in his second book, *Political Liberalism;* but Rawls himself denied that explanation, insisting that the changes in his view were minimal and made necessary only by a revelation about what was necessary for the stability of a just regime in a modern, pluralistic society. The character of the differences between *A Theory of Justice* and *Political Liberalism* is a matter of considerable controversy, with many claiming—contrary to Rawls' own view of the matter—that the differences change utterly the nature and force of the theory of justice Rawls defends there. I am myself inclined to agree with this latter view, but I will try here to simply briefly note, with minimal commentary, the most obvious differences (between *Theory* and *Political Liberalism*) in Rawls' views (or, if you prefer, in the manner of their presentation).[26]

One of the characteristics of a just, well-ordered society, according to Rawls, is that it is stable (a condition I have not yet even stated, let alone emphasized). And in order to be genuinely stable over time, the society cannot be maintained by trickery or (merely strategic) compromise or force. The society must "generate its own support" (p. 154) from its members, which it can only do when they not only comply with but endorse its basic structure as just or best. Modern free societies, however, are inevitably *pluralistic,* their members quite reasonably (due to their differing experiences, the difficulties of moral argument, etc.) subscribing to diverse and incompatible conceptions of the good. And with such different views of what gives life value, how could all of society's members possibly endorse equally the same conception of justice? Rawls' answer (in *Political Liberalism*) is that so long as conceptions of justice are presented as they were in *Theory,* no conception—including Rawls' favored "justice as fairness"—could possibly secure such endorsement. Either, then, there can be no stable, well-ordered (modern, free) societies (and so none that are justifiable) or else it must be possible for a conception of justice to be presented in such a way that it could be consistent with commitment to any number of incompatible conceptions of the good. Rawls, of course, opts for the second disjunct.

In *Theory,* justice as fairness was presented as (an implication of) what Rawls calls a "comprehensive (moral) doctrine," a systematic doctrine of the values and virtues of life, defended as *true.* Justice as fairness was in

Theory an application of a more general moral view to the specific domain of the political (see Chapter 1, section 1.1). As such, justice as fairness was tied to a position that was in conflict with all of the rival candidates for the true moral theory—including all of the diverse, non-Rawlsian conceptions of the good embraced by citizens of pluralistic free societies. In *Political Liberalism,* by contrast, justice as fairness is presented as a "freestanding," "political" conception of justice, not derived from any more comprehensive moral (or religious) view, and defended not as true but only as *reasonable* (and lacking any "deep" philosophical foundations). It is thus supposed to constitute an autonomous political philosophy (applicable only to society's basic structure) that could be endorsed by proponents of the wide range of mutually incompatible comprehensive moral or religious (or philosophical) doctrines that are certain to arise in a free society. Because it is presented only as a reasonable conception to guide political organization, and not as the true political philosophy, justice as fairness does not conflict with the claims of truth made for those comprehensive doctrines from which it is not derivable. It can thus function as a "module" to be attached to (and endorsed by) the various comprehensive doctrines, being related to them either as "the consequence of, or continuous with" those doctrines or "as an acceptable approximation given the circumstances of the social world."[27] It can be the object of an "overlapping consensus" among the supporters of reasonable comprehensive views.

But why should we think that Kantians and utilitarians; Christians, Muslims, and atheists; Marxists and Quakers all would endorse justice as fairness as the best conception to guide the basic structure of their free society, given their wildly different comprehensive commitments? They might do so if justice as fairness were derivable from something else to which they were all likely to share a commitment. That something else is the "public political culture" of liberal democratic societies, which "comprises the political institutions of a constitutional regime and the public traditions of their interpretation . . . , as well as historic texts and documents that are common knowledge."[28] The public political culture serves "as a fund of implicitly shared ideas and principles" that inform "the educated common sense of citizens generally," reaching all of the diverse comprehensive doctrines inhabiting society's "background culture" of everyday life and "its many associations."[29] Appeals to these ideas can thus serve to structure the shared "public reason" through which institutions and policies can be justified to all.

With all their differences, then, the comprehensive doctrines of a free society can still reasonably be expected to share certain basic ideas about political society. The most basic of these ideas, Rawls thinks, is that of "society as a fair system of cooperation between free and equal persons viewed as cooperating members of a society over a complete life."[30] And while different interpretations of that organizing idea of liberal democracy are possible, Rawls proposes that the best such interpretation is justice as fairness. We can see the original position choice problem as the best way of modeling all of the central concepts in that organizing idea, and justice as fairness is the conception that would be chosen by original position contractors. Justice as fairness is thus derivable from ideas about political relationships that it is reasonable to expect will be shared even by proponents of quite incompatible comprehensive views. So it is a political conception that all reasonable persons in a liberal society could reasonably be expected to endorse, all regarding a basic structure guided by such a conception as best, despite their deep moral, religious, and philosophical differences.

While there are obviously *empirical* questions to be asked here—such as whether there are any real societies in which all of the major comprehensive doctrines are in fact equally committed to a shared core of public political ideas from which a conception of justice could be derived—the important *theoretical* implication of Rawls' new strategy is clearly this: justice as fairness is now (in *Political Liberalism*) advocated as a valid or binding (or reasonable) conception of justice only for *liberal democracies,* not for all kinds of political societies; for only in liberal democracies will the public political culture (and the comprehensive doctrines that develop in its context) be guided by ideas of which justice as fairness is the best interpretation. This limitation was certainly (at least) far less clear in *Theory,* where many thought that justice as fairness was being defended (in part, at least) in a way that made it valid for all societies (as an implication of a true comprehensive moral theory—namely, "*rightness* as fairness" [pp. 15, 95–96, my emphasis]). Much of the disappointment that surrounded the publication of *Political Liberalism* (and the papers leading up to it) concerned people's feelings of being thus deprived (as it seemed) of a powerful, critical theory to use in assessing the justice of political institutions around the globe.

While this brief summary may, I hope, have made it clear what the later Rawls regards as a (or the) defensible conception of justice for the basic structures of liberal democracies—and why he so regards it—it seems considerably less clear exactly what in Rawls' (new?) argument is actually doing the "heavy lifting"—that is, what feature of the argument is bearing the real burden of justifying this conception (even if the justification is seen as limited to the domain of liberal democracies). At least four general possibilities suggest themselves, all of which have been put forward by various of Rawls' interpreters. The first possibility is to regard

Rawls' project as essentially and straightforwardly *contractualist:* the basic structure of society is just if the restrictions it imposes on persons could be justified to each of them in terms that they could reasonably be expected to accept.[31] So what is doing the justifying work is the idea of the hypothetical acceptability of (imposed) coercive measures, as the contract portion of the argument in *A Theory of Justice* suggests. And perhaps the same standards for justification could be employed (with different results) in evaluating the basic structures of illiberal or non-democratic societies.

A second possibility is to view Rawls' project as really more Hegelian in character (where political philosophy is understood as having its starting point in existing practices, trying to understand their real and unifying point): a basic structure is just if it is guided by principles that are derivable from the best interpretation of the culture which is ordered by that structure. Here, we emphasize instead the role of the "public political culture" in Rawls' later work and the role of "considered judgments" (and paradigms of justice and injustice) in his earlier work. Or perhaps (third), this is really all about something more Hobbesian: what's really important in justifying political arrangements is that they be genuinely *stable.* It was, after all, concerns about stability that motivated Rawls' modification of his view; and one could certainly argue that the only reason it matters that coercion be justifiable to subjects in their own terms (the contractualist line) or that coercive institutions reflect the society's political culture (the Hegelian line) is that these are necessary for political institutions to be stable over the long term.

Rawls, of course, never identified one of these approaches as his real justificatory argument, and it may well be that his position would be (fourth) that all three strains are essential to the justificatory force of his arguments. "Justification is a matter of the mutual support of many considerations, of everything fitting together into one coherent view."[32] Even supposing that we find plausible (and internally consistent) such a "pluralistic" approach to justification in political philosophy, however, there is an obvious further problem with it. Given Rawls' determination to avoid appeal to any comprehensive doctrine in philosophy—to any controversial, "nonpolitical" view with deep philosophical foundations and defended as true—it is unclear just how we should understand the status of his overarching position on justification. If it is not a doctrine of justification that is defensible as true or that has real philosophical foundations, why should we—as philosophers, not as citizens of liberal democracies—be interested in it? Equally important, why should proponents of the diverse comprehensive doctrines in liberal societies (whose endorsement is crucial to the possibility of a justified basic structure) regard as interesting the fact that justice as fairness can be justified according to the demands of this pluralistic justificatory doctrine?

Rawls appears to answer that this conception of justification is also a part of the shared fund of ideas latent in the public political culture of liberal democracies. But aside from concerns about whether or not such a claim is true, we should surely have worries about whether such a claim is really relevant to issues about justification. Why should the fact that an approach to justification is widely shared in this way be thought to show that it is the best such approach? Rawls himself, like all representatives of the social contract tradition, is deeply sensitive to the difference between the mere acceptance of an arrangement and its justifiability since various forms of coercion, manipulation, and indoctrination can produce the former but not the latter. But why should we not view the influence of the public political culture itself as simply a powerful form of indoctrination, one imposed upon and distorting the true orientations of (and, indeed, in many cases actually being inconsistent with) the diverse and distinctive comprehensive doctrines embraced by the citizens in a free society? Only, I think, if we can either defend Rawls' theory of justification as true (contrary to the "new" spirit of Rawls' project) or find independently in every reasonable comprehensive doctrine "internal" grounds for embracing justice as fairness (which I think is very unlikely) should we find this defense of justice as fairness (in *Political Liberalism*) compelling, even when we think of the conception of justice as binding only on liberal democracies.

4.4. Merit and Entitlement

As we have seen, not only utilitarian but also meritarian theories of justice are rejected by Rawls, the latter because of broadly "deterministic" concerns about whether anyone really can ever (or ever be known to) deserve anything at all. Many of us are disinclined to accept such skeptical dismissals of merit- or desert-based distribution, perhaps because so many desired goods and opportunities seem in our own societies to actually be distributed according to (perceived, tested) merit.[33] But even most of those who have been favored by the system of "reward for merit" must surely harbor some nagging doubt about how much of their success was a function of happy initial genetic endowment and/or childhood social environment. After all, it seems unlikely to be just a coincidence that so many of the children of poor, unproductive parents grow up themselves to be poor and unproductive.

In general, then, I think the plausibility of meritarianism turns on the extent to which attributions of personal merit or desert can escape concerns that the possession (or occurrence) of meritorious traits (or actions) is largely or fully determined by one's genetic and social starting place in life (or that we are simply unable to identify the degree to which any such traits or actions are not so determined). And reasonable, thoughtful persons must, I believe, have serious concerns of this sort. But perhaps even if people cannot be confidently said to *deserve* to profit from their talents or contributions or achievements, they nonetheless have a *right* to do so—such that it would still be an injustice to deny them such profits. Desert claims and claims of right are very different sorts of moral claims. The former are usually claims that some beneficial action or state of affairs would be a fitting or an appropriate response to some praiseworthy quality or performance (or that some penalty is called for by what is blameworthy). Claims of right, by contrast, are merely claims that something must be done, refrained from, or permitted by others (and that for them to fail in this would be for them to wrong the rightholder). There is no necessary connection between having such claims and having done something (or being someone) especially deserving or virtuous.

One of the more interesting of Robert Nozick's criticisms of Rawls' arguments makes use of this point. Even, Nozick argues, if we accept Rawls' suggestions that no one deserves their "adult assets" (because no one deserves the initial genetic or social endowment from which their adult assets derive)—that is, even if the distribution of adult abilities and capacities is "arbitrary from the moral point of view"—it does not follow from this that a defensible theory of justice must begin (as Rawls begins) with equality as the distributive baseline from which any deviations must be specially justified. People might nonetheless be entitled to (i.e., have a moral right to) their talents and, in consequence, what is produced through their talents' employment, even if they do not deserve those talents. After all, people (arguably) have rights to or over their bodies (so that, e.g., it would be wrong for others to enslave them or to remove their bodily organs without their consent), even though they plainly had and were (possibly) entitled to their bodies long before, and in any event independent of, their having done (or been) anything virtuous on the basis of which they might base a claim to deserve a (or that particular) body. Perhaps people are entitled to some things they don't deserve (or, more weakly, perhaps it is simply permissible for people to benefit themselves differentially using some of their undeserved assets) so that it would be wrong to insist on an equal division of goods as a baseline for justice.[34]

The appeal in such arguments is typically to some notion of "self-ownership," a kind of property in oneself, possibly as strong as the property in other people claimed by chattel slaveholders.[35] Locke's was undoubtedly the most famous statement of the thesis of self-ownership: "every man has a property in his own person; this nobody has a right to but himself. The labour of his body and the work of his hands, we may say, are properly his." Locke, of course, goes on to argue that from this "great foundation" of property in ourselves can be derived natural (moral) property rights in the products of our labor (provided that we do not waste what we produce and that we leave "enough and as good for others" of the natural resources available to all for appropriation [the so-called "Lockean Proviso"]). When we labor on the external world, we "mix" with the world something that is unquestionably ours (namely, our productive labor), making wrongful anyone else's taking or use (without our consent) of the product that now "contains" what is ours.[36] We can, thus, Locke thought, give a "historical" account of people's moral rights to property—and hence offer a theory of, or at least a constraint on a theory of, justice—simply by tracking (from the starting point of self-ownership) the histories of people's productive labor and their subsequent uses and exchanges of the products of that labor.

Nozick makes use of these Lockean ideas to defend what he calls "the entitlement theory" of distributive justice (or, as he prefers, of "justice in holdings"), according to which "a distribution is just if everyone is entitled to the holdings they possess under the distribution."[37] The relevant entitlements, as in Locke, arise from satisfying the requirements of any of the three kinds of (historical) principles of entitlement: (1) principles of "justice in acquisition" tell us how we can legitimately acquire rights over (come to "own," morally) something previously unowned (e.g., by picking wild apples or tilling unowned land), (2) principles of "justice in transfer" tell us how we can come to be entitled to something to which someone else is currently entitled (e.g., by that person giving or selling it to us), and (3) principles of "justice in rectification" tell us how people can become entitled to holdings because of others' violations of the principles of justice in acquisition or transfer (e.g., by being owed compensation for another's theft of our legitimate holdings).[38]

Nozick never formally states his preferred versions of these three kinds of principles of entitlement. He appears to believe that he can defeat all rival theories of justice (using the arguments we will discuss later) without putting flesh on his own skeletal theory. But the text certainly gives us a pretty clear idea of the (commonsense Lockean) principles Nozick has in mind: (1) "taking" while satisfying "the Lockean proviso" (for acquisition), (2) consensual transfer (for transfer), and (3) making things as they would have been had the injustice not occurred (for rectification). The general idea is this: if people start out entitled to their holdings and there are no wrongful transactions along the way, it is hard to see how any moral complaint about the outcome—and, in particular, how a complaint of *injustice*—could reasonably be raised, regardless of whether the resulting holdings turn out to involve significant inequality.

Aside from various appeals to our free-market moral intuitions, Nozick's primary argument in favor of this entitlement theory of justice is actually an argument against all rival theories. To frame this argument, Nozick draws two distinctions between kinds of principles of justice, by means of which he believes we can exhaustively classify all such principles. The first is the distinction between *end-state* (or what he sometimes also calls "end-result" or "current time slice") and *historical* principles of justice. A principle of justice is historical if it can determine the justice of a current distribution only by reference to past events, actions, or circumstances (so that whether or not a current distribution is just depends at least in part on "how it came about"). It is an end-state principle, by contrast, if it identifies current distributions as just or unjust according to certain "structural" features of those distributions (independent of how they "came about"). So principles of the Lockean sort discussed above would, in this classification, count as historical (since we must know the history of acquisitions and transfers in order to know if the current set of holdings is just), while a strict egalitarian principle would, Nozick thinks, plainly count as end-state (since only current structural facts about the distribution—namely, that all shares are equal—are relevant to determinations of justice according to that principle).

To this first distinction, Nozick adds a second: that between *patterned* and *unpatterned* principles of distribution. Patterned principles are those that make the justice of a distribution vary along with some "natural dimension" (or combination of natural dimensions)—such as a principle of merit, which says the justice of distributions varies according to their success in mirroring variations in the natural dimension of personal merit. Unpatterned principles do not in this way try to identify justice with the achievement of any pattern. So, again, the Lockean account would appear to qualify as unpatterned since it is unconcerned with the "shape" of distributions; gifts, inheritances (and, more generally, people's choices), luck (and so on) can all create entitlements without tracking some "natural dimension" in the rightholder. The Lockean account, as Nozick presents it, is interested only in whether or not the procedural constraints on acquisitions and transfers were observed (and in whether violations of those constraints were rectified), not in the size of the shares that result.[39]

Dividing candidates according to these two distinctions might at first appear to yield four possible kinds of principles of justice. But the idea of an unpatterned end-state principle seems internally inconsistent (since it is hard to see how a principle could identify justice with the presence of some significant structural feature in a distribution without also tracking the corresponding pattern). If so, that will leave us with simply patterned (both historical and end-state) and unpatterned historical principles.

Nozick appears to believe (and in this I think he is correct) that there are no plausible unpatterned historical principles but those that could be used to flesh out his skeleton of an entitlement theory. That means that if patterned principles could be convincingly rejected, Nozick's entitlement theory would seem to remain as the only real contender for a defensible theory of distributive justice. Nozick, accordingly, frames his principal arguments as attacks on "patterning" in the theory of justice (i.e., attacks on what allegedly unites meritarianism, need-based and strict egalitarianism, Rawlsian egalitarianism, utilitarianism, and all other theories not equivalent to the entitlement view).

Nozick's argument against patterned principles is exceedingly simple and initially quite compelling: "liberty upsets patterns."[40] Pick your favorite patterned principle(s), Nozick says, and imagine it ordering society according to its requirements. The resulting distribution will be, *ex hypothesi,* perfectly just; and persons will thus have rights over the shares of goods conferred on them in satisfying the favored pattern. But having a right to those goods means (at least) being at liberty to use them in various ways (e.g., to consume them, give them as gifts, trade them, use them to produce other goods, etc.). And the moment that people begin exercising their liberties to use their goods in these ways, the initially just pattern of distribution will be upset. People will consume differentially, produce differentially, gift differently, make bad trades, and so on—all of which will (according to your favorite principle[s]) constitute unjust departures from the favored pattern of holdings, despite nothing having gone on that looks in any way morally untoward.

Further, in order to maintain the just pattern in the face of people's actually living their lives with their goods, society would have to either stop people from using, transferring, or creating goods in apparently perfectly innocent ways or continually take and redistribute goods as shares departed from the favored pattern. But either of these policies would in effect amount to a denial that people ever had rights to their goods in the first place and hence would undercut the hypothesis that conformity to the favored pattern really did make society just. Patterned principles require violations of even those rights that the patterned principles themselves confer. This appears to leave the entitlement theory as the only remaining candidate for a valid theory of justice. And the entitlement theory, in Nozick's view, will identify as just only the minimal, free-market political society that (nonanarchist) libertarians have long favored.

But it is important to see why this initially compelling argument is really less forceful than it seems to be. Nozick very effectively employs "micro" examples (e.g., his famous Wilt Chamberlain example[41]) to draw out our intuitions about the wrongness of interfering with free exchange.

But he uses these examples to attack (patterned) principles of justice that are intended to be applied only as principles for the basic structure of a society (i.e., at the "macro" level). Rawls' difference principle, for example, says nothing directly about whether Wilt Chamberlain ought to be allowed to keep the extra income his superior basketball talents allow him to earn (despite Nozick's insinuation that any patterned principle must recommend immediate and tyrannical redistribution). The difference principle is a principle for guiding *institutional* design, for insuring that whatever acquisitions and transfers take place do so within the context of fair background institutions. While institutions guided by the difference principle will undoubtedly heavily tax Chamberlain's extra wealth, exactly how and when they do this will presumably be relative to both the specific social context and the results of democratic political decision making.

Rawls in fact seems happy with society's permitting the "market freedoms" Nozick cherishes, provided that they are exercised against fair background conditions. The market freedoms look most imperative where we imagine all as equals with comparable resources competing in a fair marketplace. But superior initial endowments—genetic advantages (like Chamberlain's), a good home, education, business connections, inheritance—plainly make us very unequal indeed in any real unregulated free market. Rawls' arguments in effect ask us to remember that market freedoms, however important, are not all that's important to guaranteeing people a fair chance for a meaningful life. Adequate resources and genuine opportunities are just as important, and guaranteeing these inevitably means limiting market freedoms in certain ways. Opponents of Rawls' theory may well think that he goes too far in this direction, that it is not necessary to begin with a baseline of strict equality in order to give all a fair chance for a decent life. But even if that is your view—even if, say, you think that maintaining a modest social minimum is enough by way of giving everyone a fair chance—you should see that Nozick's arguments against "patterning," if adequate, would hold as much against this modest view as they would against Rawls' stricter egalitarianism. Nozick's arguments would condemn redistribution of wealth for the purpose of guaranteeing each of society's members even a $5 annual income.

It is also important to notice, I think, that Nozick's seemingly innocent refusal to flesh out and argue for specific historical principles of entitlement in fact permits him unfairly to make some very substantial and undefended assumptions. Nozick simply presupposes, for instance, the soundness of consent (i.e., free, informed exchange) as the principle of just transfer (i.e., he appears to assume that all consensual transfers are "justice-preserving"). But however plausible this principle of transfer may seem when applied to particular examples of free exchange among equals, it is a principle that also appears to have limits that will bear directly on Nozick's ability to defend his free-market, libertarian ideal. Are free transfers "justice-preserving" when they create monopolies, which allow some to control in dramatic ways the opportunities and life prospects of others? If rich white men who have inherited great wealth (by free transfer) all decide only to do business with one another, are minorities, women, and the less wealthy treated justly by a society that permits this? It seems odd for one deeply committed to the value of liberty to overlook the obvious losses of liberty such a principle of "justice" would seem to permit.

Similar problems surround Nozick's vaguely characterized principle of justice in acquisition. Without a full specification and defense, how can we know that the best historical principle of just acquisition will not (e.g.) identify serious need as entitling one to others' "holdings"—as Locke, Nozick's model, in fact believed? If that were the case, of course, the entitlement theory would in no way imply the justice of a free-market, minimal state. Further, of course, it is cavalier in the extreme for Nozick to simply assume that it is possible to adequately defend a principle of just acquisition (and natural property rights) at all, let alone a principle that will not have strongly egalitarian implications for possible rights of ownership. On the contrary, the most natural opening assumption to make in any argument for unilateral rights of acquisition would be that all persons (and all generations) are equally entitled to lay claim to portions of the earth and its resources, suggesting a natural egalitarian baseline in permissible property acquisitions (as, again, in my view Locke assumed by defending a strong "proviso," one requiring that "enough and as good" always be left for others). In other words, the argument from "self-ownership" to "world-ownership" is not one that will obviously yield antiegalitarian, free-market conclusions (or, indeed, any conclusions at all). There is in fact a long tradition, ignored by Nozick, of "left-libertarian" thought (the contemporary development of which owes much to the work of the egalitarian Marxist philosopher G. A. Cohen), a tradition that accepts self-ownership, the initial premise of the entitlement argument, but denies that unequal "world-ownership" (or external property rights) can in any simple way be inferred or derived from that premise.[42]

4.5. Critical Traditions

It is probably fair to say that the dominant "positive" traditions in modern philosophical theorizing about justice are the four we have thus far considered: utilitarian, liberal egalitarian, meritarian, and natural right libertarian theories. But there have also been a number of prominent "critical" traditions of thought about justice, some long-standing and some of more recent origin. By "critical" traditions, I mean traditions of resistance to (and criticism of) those dominant positive traditions but ones that have also been less clear or forthcoming in presenting rival positive views of their own. Perhaps the best example of such a critical tradition is Marxism, with its combination of a passionate rejection of "bourgeois justice" and a rather hazy vision of what should (or must) replace it. Karl Marx himself, of course, had good reason to emphasize the critical over the positive. He was a witness to (what he took to be) the defects of the modern view of justice in practice, but he could only really speculate about the likely shape of postrevolutionary communist society, a society that can emerge only after humans finally throw off the pervasive influences (to which Marx himself was necessarily also subject) of alienating property relations and the bourgeois ideology that rationalizes them.

Marx actually viewed himself more as a (social) scientist than as a philosopher. Philosophy, he wrote, is a symptom of social disorder, and it will disappear when class conflict is overcome. The young Marx thought that the communist revolution would "realize" philosophy—that is, it would give reality to our philosophical ideals—and so end our preoccupation (such as it is!) with philosophy. The older Marx thought that the revolution would return people to the (scientific) study of the real world, thus destroying philosophy (which by then he conceived as throughout ideological). So Marx's principal efforts were spent not on moral or political philosophy but rather on developing and presenting his scientific "historical materialism," a theory that explained all features of societies and the forms of consciousness in them in terms of the basic economic facts about those societies (their "productive forces" and the relations between the classes of persons involved in production). One of the implications of this theory, of course, was Marx's famous account of human history as a history of class struggles (based on "contradictions" in the modes of production) and revolutionary transitions to new forms of economic relations. And that account, Marx thought, showed the inevitability of the demise of capitalist economies, worldwide proletarian revolution and "dictatorial" rule, and (through a series of "phases" of increasingly socialized economic relations) eventual "higher" communist society—in which there will be no classes, no alienated labor, no private ownership of land or the means of production, no "property-like" political or familial institutions, and so on.

It has never been entirely clear to what extent Marx wanted to engage as well in political philosophy (as a branch of moral philosophy, in the way we have characterized it here). On the one hand, Marx was regularly contemptuous of moralizers, and he often dismissed moral values as simply one more tool used by society's dominant class to preserve its dominance.[43] Thus, the ideas of right, equality, and justice are said to be simply bourgeois ideas, which reflect only the bourgeoisie's interests in evading social responsibility and institutional interference. Marx's "meta-critique" of morality, religion, and philosophy (including especially moral and political philosophy) marks them all as mere means of domination (in ways of which even the dominant class may not be aware). On the other hand, it is hard to read Marx's criticisms of capitalist economic relations without immediately recognizing their moral tone, their use of the language of exploitation and alienation, their condemnation of the capitalist's "theft" of the "surplus value" that rightly belongs to the laborer. Perhaps, then, it was only the bourgeois versions of right and justice that Marx deplored, not the moral ideals themselves. And higher communist society, remember, will be guided by a (now famous) principle of distribution (or of distributive justice?): "only then can the narrow horizon of bourgeois right be crossed in its entirety and society inscribe on its banner: From each according to his ability, to each according to his needs!"[44]

Marx has often been said to be here only stating a fact about communist society, not a principle according to which communist society can be understood to be just or morally preferable (to what preceded it). In such a society, people will produce freely (no longer being shackled by the division of labor or the need to produce in order to survive) and take only what they need (since the reasons for competitive accumulation of wealth have been eliminated). But it is worth noting both that this principle is said by Marx to be one that replaces "bourgeois right"—seemingly, with a conception of right that actually reflects humans' cooperative and productive nature—and that it is to be inscribed on the "banners" of communist society, banners being a place one seldom finds statements of fact. As a principle of distributive justice, it is too vague to take us much beyond the "priority of need satisfaction" principle discussed earlier (in section 4.2). But it seems clear that it should be taken to constitute one of the most straightforward normative commitments in Marx's (and Marxist) political philosophy, properly construed.

Few contemporary Marxists accept Marx's deterministic scientific theory or its claims for the inevitability of a workers' revolution. So their focus is more naturally on the moral aspects of Marx's case against capitalism—on the wrongness of exploitation, on the moral costs of alienated labor, and on the ways in which the political institutions that arose with capitalist economies have tended to secure only anemic versions of human liberty and equality. Thus, many Marxists today stress the need for deeper social change to realize those ideals, genuine equality of opportunity and life prospects, collective control of the means of production, severe limits on rights of inheritance and bequest, and so on. Here, the work of Marxists comes into direct contact with the similar ambitions of other approaches to political philosophy that we have discussed. The recent work of the aforementioned Marxist philosopher G. A. Cohen is an excellent example of this coalescing of themes in political philosophy, his work being cited as the inspiration for work by Marxists, liberal egalitarians, and left-libertarians alike.

Another "critical" philosophical tradition, similar to Marxism in certain superficial ways, traces its emphasis on the importance of community not to Marx but instead to such philosophers as Aristotle and Hegel. "Communitarianism" names both a cluster of positions in political philosophy and a recent social and political movement (which endorses "popularized" versions of many of the positions defended by communitarian scholars).[45] Its most prominent philosophical spokespersons during the past few decades have been Alasdair MacIntyre, Michael Sandel, Charles Taylor, and Michael Walzer, though of these only Sandel ever actually identified himself as a communitarian (and even he has now rejected that self-description, preferring to characterize his views as a form of "republicanism"). As with Marxist philosophers, communitarians have always been considerably clearer (and far more nearly unanimous) about what they oppose than they have been about the positive position they favor.

In some ways, the communitarian attack on liberal political philosophy resembles that mounted by Marxists. Like Marxists, communitarians argue that liberal individualists have a flawed ("atomist," unsocialized) conception of the self and human nature. Similarly, both claim that individual rights (and conceptions of justice organized around that idea) should not be the central focus of political philosophy and that the importance of community is woefully ignored in individualist thought. And both think that the just society imagined by individualist philosophers is really nothing more than a bunch of entangled, egoistic individuals, with nothing in common but their desires to get on with their private pursuits. In this deeply impoverished view of human potential, politics is simply a matter of setting up a neutral umpire to resolve disputes and threaten punishment for particularly aggressive pursuits of private interests.

Once this criticism of liberalism concludes, however, any resemblance between Marxist and communitarian political thought ends. The Marxist critique, in effect, is that liberals don't go far enough in the direction of liberating humankind, settling for the merely formal (and class-biased) bourgeois version of freedom—a freedom which leaves the proletariat vulnerable to exploitation and all human interaction distorted by alienating property relations. The Marxist ideal is the stateless, propertyless, religionless, classless community, free of all moralizing, repressive limits on humans' social and productive capacities. The communitarian critique, by contrast, tends to be the more conservative charge that liberals go too far in that liberating direction. Communitarians believe that we need to revitalize (or create) a more definite structure of interlocking social communities, one in which people know their roles and agree on what is valuable in life. We cannot justify political arrangements except by showing that those arrangements advance genuinely shared goals, a true common good. Our ideal should not be the liberal ideal of a state that is neutral between competing conceptions of the good; rather, the state should aim to promote society's common good and to support the practices that make such a common good possible.

Communitarians do not, of course, favor coercive imposition of such arrangements by, say, benevolent despots; like both liberals and Marxists, they too believe in the importance of self-government. But true self-government, they maintain, requires communal bonds with one's fellow citizens, which makes possible shared reasoning about what's best for all. The communitarian ideal often seems to be the less pluralistic, more homogenous (often religious) communities of the past, communities that Marxists condemn as exploitative and oppressive. Communitarians find the potential for community in our own societies' shared practices and traditions (which Marxists want to overthrow), practices and traditions that are endangered by the divisive egoism permitted and indeed encouraged by liberal political institutions. If the possibility of true community is to be taken seriously, we must find it in the contingent practices of our own particular communities, just as Hegel thought it necessary to reveal the point of, and thereby to reconcile us to, our roles and duties in the concrete practices of our societies.

Because there really is no "core" or "standard" (positive) communitarian position, I can do no more here than quickly discuss a few themes that run through much work identified as communitarian. For instance, virtually all communitarians seem to want to emphasize the fact that we occupy various social roles in the overlapping communities of social life and that these roles routinely define (or help to define) our senses of self, our conceptions of the good, and our moral duties. But communitarians draw different conclusions from these facts. For Walzer, for example, these facts show why the standards of justice must be culturally relative—that is, different for different kinds of cultures (including liberal standards of justice for societies like ours). Justice is about distributing goods, but things only count as "goods" for us because of our shared understandings of their social meanings, social meanings that differ from time to time and place to place. Justice, for Walzer, is about each society's distributing each kind of good in accordance with the criteria that that society accepts as appropriate for the "sphere" in which that good belongs.[46] For MacIntyre, the social roles into which we are "drafted" constitute the only possible avenue of escape from the moral disagreement and (rationally irresolvable) conflict about value that characterize modern society. The Enlightenment robbed us of our sense of humankind's *telos* (end, purpose) and the consensus and direction that that idea gave us. For rational moral discussion (and eventual agreement) to again be possible, we must find grounds for agreement in our local traditions and practices and in the social and cultural roles that we inhabit. Only if we can remake and sustain these local sources of value can we hope to recreate consensus on a rational conception of good for all and save ourselves from the *anomie* of modernity in which we are strangers to one another.[47]

Sandel appears to accept the need for revitalizing local community, just as he appears to accept in certain ways the cultural relativity of justice.[48] But more centrally than either of these, Sandel argues that the fact of our social embeddedness requires us to accept a different view of the self from that embraced by liberal individualists (like Rawls and Nozick). Liberal individualists, Sandel says, accept a view of the self as "unencumbered," as "prior to its ends." Such selves are seen as free to choose their ends or values, and the state's job, correspondingly, is to leave us as free as possible to make these choices. But this view of the self, Sandel says, is deeply (and obviously) mistaken, as is the liberal political philosophy built on this foundation. Our selves are not "unencumbered" but rather deeply "embedded," firmly "situated" in social contexts that give us our ends. We do not so much choose as we "discover" our ends, by exploring the social roles we inhabit. Indeed, we cannot even conceive of ourselves as independent of these roles and the ends they prescribe.[49] Take the case, Sandel says, of Robert E. Lee and his unchosen obligations to his native state of Virginia, obligations arising from his social embeddedness and that outweighed his personal opposition to secession and his chosen obligations as an officer in the U.S. military. Here, we see plainly that "the liberal conception of the person is too thin to account for the full range of moral and political obligations we commonly recognize."[50]

What makes this example such a strange one for Sandel's purposes, of course, is that Lee plainly deliberated, agonized, and finally *chose* with enormous difficulty certain of his "ends" as those that were most important to his sense of who he was. He clearly did not think that the mere fact that his obligations to Virginia were "given" by his unchosen social role was what made them more important than his (also deeply important) chosen obligations to the United States. Had Lee chosen instead to abandon his ties to Virginia and remain in the U.S. military (as many southern military officers in fact did choose to do), it is not clear in what terms we could criticize his decision. Liberals have never (so far as

I know) denied the psychological fact that persons come to value things deeply by virtue of the unchosen sites where they are socially situated. But individuals are plainly capable of deliberating about, reconsidering, and even rejecting those "given" values; we see examples of this every day in our ordinary lives, as Sandel in the end admits. And the point of many of the freedoms emphasized in liberal political philosophy is precisely to insure that this kind of deliberation and thoughtful choice of ends—ends that best express the identities of those who pursue them—is possible. How any of this involves a flawed conception of the self remains obscure.

Exactly what does the communitarian prefer to these liberal freedoms? Sandel appears to say that we need less individual freedom and more support for means of finding (and ultimately more promotion of) our common good. But where in our deeply pluralistic modern political communities is this common good to be found? Liberals say that justice (equality, freedom) is all the common good that can be found in such societies, that beyond this there is only disagreement about values. The only basis for free cooperation in such societies is the toleration of diversity. Communitarians also, of course, favor diversity, often emphasizing the need for revitalizing the variety of local traditions and institutions (though this sometimes smacks of the desire to fragment society into the smallest possible perfectly homogenous groups—within which, presumably, we would never reconsider or reject our given ends). At the same time, however, communitarians often bemoan the passing of times when political societies were more like families or groups of friends, close-knit genuine communities (not loose associations) in which ends were genuinely shared.

Historical reflection reveals, of course, that such genuine political communities were frequently (and not, I think, coincidentally) ones that held slaves, treated women as property, abused those who were different, shunned and killed dissenters, and so on, so that the "common good" they advanced was actually quite selective. Sandel concedes that there have been "episodes of darkness" in the history of the kind of society favored by communitarians (and by "civic republicans")[51] but insists that such communities can be inclusive, promote self-government, and be founded on values that are genuinely shared—that, to quote one liberal critic, we can "live in Salem, but not . . . believe in witches."[52] Liberals, however, are understandably left with the suspicion that there are no such genuinely shared values on which to rely and that the real aim is to impose *majority* values on those who don't share them or to simply inculcate shared values (and overwhelm dissent and thoughtful reconsideration) through revitalized local practices.

Sandel actually appears to believe that the sort of intolerance opposed by liberals is most likely where strong traditions and local values have broken down. Indeed, a constant theme in communitarian writings has been that too much individual autonomy will (and has already begun to) break social bonds and lead to social disintegration. We need to rebuild our traditions and local community values in order to secure the liberties (and the social stability) that liberalism can only endlessly (and emptily) promise. This, I confess, seems to me not at all the lesson that history teaches. The greatest episodes of inhumanity in our history have been precisely in the name of social solidarity, to protect traditions and values from perceived threats to them. This has been especially true where the state has been enlisted to protect such values. What we need to encourage, liberals argue, is not stronger, less flexible traditions but rather the possibility of critical detachment from our cultures, traditions, and roles. The vast variety of traditions, practices, and values can be left free to flourish (or to attract what support they can from people free to choose them) but only within a political framework that secures all against the possibility of "episodes of darkness."

Not all communitarians, of course, look to the homogenous communities of the past for their political ideals. Some look forward, seeking new sources of social unity that can bring us together and stabilize our increasingly diverse societies but without restricting our choices or leaving us vulnerable to majority oppression.[53] Such a quest for social unity, bounded by familiar liberal background institutions, seems less an attack on than a friendly reminder (of the possible sources of political stability) for liberal political philosophy and so lacks much of the distinctive character of the communitarian critical tradition. But whether even so innocuous a goal as a "liberalized community" can be accepted without reservation will depend on how such socially unified societies relate to persons and groups who are not members of them (a topic to which we shall return in Chapter 6).

I will conclude this chapter with a few, again regrettably brief, words about one last, much more recent critical tradition of thought about justice—namely, feminism. There is, of course, nothing like a single philosophical methodology that all feminist theorists have in common. Nor is there one approach in moral or political philosophy to which all feminists subscribe; in fact, there are Marxist and communitarian feminists, utilitarian and meritarian feminists, libertarian and liberal egalitarian feminists. What unites these disparate views into one critical tradition of thought in political philosophy is their shared concern with the ways in which women have been oppressed and subordinated throughout the history of political societies. The more positive positions associated with this critical tradition have (as with Marxism and communitarianism) remained vague or controversial but with their general outlines being suggested by successive "schools" or "waves" of feminist theory—what are sometimes referred to as "sameness theory" (aiming at legal and political reform to achieve equal treatment for women or "sex/gender blindness," meant to be analogous to demands for legal "color blindness"), "difference theory" (aiming for genuinely equal treatment by demanding different treatment in response to sex/gender differences), and "dominance theory" (aiming at revolutionary change to correct the systematic sexual dominance of society by men).

The structure of feminist criticism (i.e., criticism of other traditions of thought about justice) has been in certain ways very similar to that of Marxist criticism. One critical strand mounts (what we have called) "meta-critiques" of the enterprise of political philosophy. For example, as we have seen (in Chapter 1, section 1.4), it is possible to structure a feminist critique of political philosophy whose logic closely follows that of Marx but with *gender* replacing *class* (as in Catherine Mackinnon's work); so traditional political philosophy (which has been, of course, throughout its history practiced almost exclusively by men) can be condemned as just another tool for rationalizing, and thereby for concealing (from all parties) and helping to preserve, the dominance of one gender over the other. Alternative forms of feminist meta-critique target not so much the entire enterprise of political philosophy but more the alleged "scope" or "authority" of its conclusions.

Thus, for instance, feminist theorists drawing on the studies of Carol Gilligan[54] (and others) can argue that traditional political philosophy draws on an "ethics of justice," a form of justification (centered on principles and rights) that tends to be favored by men in their approach to moral problems. Women, by contrast, tend to favor (or at least to emphasize as well) a quite different "ethics of care," which stresses the importance of relationships, special responsibilities, and sensitivity to the needs and feelings of others. As a consequence, the arguments offered by (male) political philosophers—and especially the justifications they offer for their particular theories of justice—while (perhaps) compelling for men, have no (or severely diminished) force and authority for women. Similarly, some feminist epistemologists have stressed the male bias in the normative dimensions of our commonsense epistemology. In telling us what knowledge is and how knowledge is possible, epistemology also tells us how we ought to go about acquiring our beliefs (since knowledge is better than mere belief), which processes lead most reliably to knowledge (e.g., scientific method beats out "intuition"). Traditional epistemology has been dominated by men (usually white, affluent, heterosexual men) who have tended to discount the quite different experiences of women (minorities, gays and lesbians, the poor, etc.) as possible sources of knowledge, treating only their own experiences as privileged in this way. Women's knowledge, some argue, being produced more cooperatively, can never count as knowledge at all in the male ideal of knowledge acquisition—that of the dispassionate, disinterested, solitary, (male) scientist accumulating objective data. Since political philosophy plainly also rests on knowledge claims—about how people and societies are, about how principles and theories can be known or justified—political philosophy's conclusions are infected by this problem. The conclusions of political philosophy, including the "positive" theories of justice we've considered in this chapter, are in reality just part of a male perspective on (reflecting male desires about) the world; they "fail" for women.

A second critical strand of feminist political philosophy, like its Marxist counterpart, defends not a meta-critique of the enterprise of political philosophy but only the need for (certain of) the established positive traditions of thought to take seriously their own substantive commitments. For instance, the ideal political societies described by philosophers ought to be the ones that are actually required by the arguments philosophers employ. Thus, communitarian feminists remind communitarians to take seriously all of women's social roles, not just those involving subordination to men, and to focus on a good that is genuinely common or shared.[55] More persuasively, I think, many liberal egalitarian feminists have emphasized important ways in which the liberal ideals of equal treatment and genuine equality of opportunity require far more dramatic changes in existing institutions and associations than have been explicitly acknowledged by male liberal philosophers.

For example, feminists have argued convincingly that arrangements that many liberals have assumed would satisfy demands for equality and opportunity in fact fail to do so, for a variety of distinct reasons. First, for instance, many of these arrangements are not sufficiently inclusive, failing to treat as matters of (in)justice the plights of the severely disabled, non-human animals, and the desperately needy abroad.[56] Second, formal legal equality for women leaves untouched a political, social, and economic structure that systematically presupposes male participants who can wholly give themselves over to their professions while another serves as caregiver to their children and caretaker of their home. Business, politics, and academia, for example, are routinely structured around such assumptions, in a world in which the primary caregivers and caretakers are overwhelmingly female. Third, one of the great sources of the devaluation and dependence of women—and one of the great sources of inequality of opportunity— is the family (along with patriarchal religions). But traditional liberal political philosophy has been extremely reluctant to embrace the idea of the state's authority extending to (or the principles of distributive justice being applicable to) the "private" realm of family and religion.[57] These and other feminist arguments show that social injustice runs rather "deeper" in our lives than we might suppose and that a defensible liberal egalitarian theory needs to address the roots not only of public, much-protested injustice but also of private, often widely accepted injustice.

Suggested Reading

Brian Barry, *Theories of Justice* (Berkeley: University of California Press, 1989).

G. A. Cohen, *Self-Ownership, Freedom, and Equality* (Cambridge: Cambridge University Press, 1995).

Will Kymlicka, *Contemporary Political Philosophy,* 2nd ed. (Oxford: Oxford University Press, 2002).

David Miller, *Principles of Social Justice* (Cambridge, MA: Harvard University Press, 2001).

Martha Nussbaum, *Frontiers of Justice* (Cambridge, MA: Harvard University Press, 2006).

Michael Walzer, *Spheres of Justice* (New York: Basic Books, 1983).

CHAPTER 5

Democracy

5.1. Justifying Democracy

Probably more now than at any time in human history people around the world appear to agree that political societies ought to be democratic. Even tyrants and dictators clearly feel obliged to at least use democratic rhetoric, and the most ardent opponents of proposed or actual democracies (who, leaving anarchists aside, seem mostly to be religious fundamentalists) regularly attack them by appealing themselves to democratic ideals—for instance, by charging that true democracy is impossible given the influences of Western or antireligious people or nations. In the face of such a consensus, it may seem that arguments purporting to "justify democracy" are otiose.

These arguments, however, can help to cast considerable light on the meaning and point of democracy. Indeed, some of the consensus on the superiority of democratic government is probably somewhat artificial. Calling something "democratic" is now virtually always to praise it, so even people who in fact are confused about or who disagree about what democracy is will probably mostly agree that democracy is good or imperative. At the most basic level, for instance, it is seldom clear whether one who praises democracy is praising a particular type of political decision procedure (i.e., a political process for resolving disagreements and reaching decisions) or praising instead some set of social policies that are characteristic of states that employ (some variant of) democratic decision procedures. The two principles that most ordinary persons would identify most closely with democracy, I suspect, are procedural in character—namely, "one person, one vote" and majority rule. But we also, of course, think of democracy in substantive (i.e., nonprocedural) terms, in terms of the basic liberties or freedoms that citizens of democracies typically enjoy, such as freedom of conscience, freedom of expression, and freedom of association. Interestingly, this is to identify democracy with what are typically the fruits of constitutional constraints on democratic lawmaking, which have thus often been characterized as antidemocratic. Still others associate democracy most closely with the economic liberties characteristic of free-market (or modestly constrained free-market) capitalism, which appear to have relatively little to do with democracy conceived of as a procedural ideal. The "consensus," then, on the virtues of democracy is not as clear as it might seem.

We know, of course, that the word *democracy* derives originally from the Greek words for "rule by/of the people." Traditionally, democracy (rule by "the many" or by all) has been opposed to *aristocracy* or *oligarchy* (rule by the few) and *monarchy* (rule by one).[1] But the "many" who did the ruling in the ancient Greek democracies were in fact a distinct minority, with women, *metics* (resident aliens), and slaves excluded from participation; so *democracy* referred there more to the (direct, nonrepresentative) decision procedures employed by those men who had inherited political privilege than it did to anything more substantial. Even modern democracies have, of course, for most of their histories employed (e.g.) economic, racial, and gender-based conditions for political participation. Just how inclusive a political system must be in order to count as "democratic" is thus unclear, as is the authority of our normal expectation that democracies will guarantee the freedoms and other goods necessary for citizens to develop and communicate informed views about the matters subject to democratic decision making (which subjects may themselves cover a wider or a more narrow range of concerns in different "democratic" political societies).

It is hardly surprising, then, that the definitions of *democracy* offered by contemporary political philosophers regularly conflict. I will not here take sides by insisting on one account of what is and is not essential to a political society's counting as a "democracy," instead simply commenting on what I take to be a constellation of broadly "democratic" political principles. Contemporary philosophers do, however, agree on one thing about democracy: they, like non-philosophers, have been nearly unanimous in praising it. It has, of course, not always been so. Readers of Plato will recall (from *Republic* VIII) that he criticizes democracy as, after only tyranny (or dictatorship), the very *worst* form of government. Part of Plato's reason for this ranking was an obvious and enduring objection to democracy: the potential for unwise decisions flowing from rule by "the mob." Democracy had only occasional friends among political philosophers between Plato and the early moderns. And even Locke, often cited as one of the most influential modern sources of democratic theory, was really more of a constitutionalist than he was a democrat. While he believed that every legitimate political society is, at root, a "perfect democracy,"[2] what Locke stresses is always the *limits* on political power (and, thus, on any democratic decision making). There is much, then, for political philosophy to sort out and explain while engaged in its enterprise of "justifying democracy."

What would it be, though, to "justify democracy"? As we saw in Chapter 2, section 2.1, to justify an arrangement is to show either that it is permissible for us (to create or live under it), that it is best (optimal) for us, or that it is mandatory for us (to support or create it). The last kind of "justification" (or, better, "legitimation") of democracy, I treat separately in section 5.2. As for the first kind, few who have believed that *states* can be justified have doubted that *democratic* states are permissible arrangements. The most familiar justifications of democracy, unsurprisingly, have instead been "optimality" justifications—that is, attempts to show that democracy is better than any other kind of political society. But even supposing that we all understand justification in this way, various attempts to justify democracy are bound to look rather different from one another. For there are a large number of "democratic" organizing principles; and even when the guiding principles of democracies are identical, there are many different specific institutional arrangements that may count as embodying those principles (perhaps to different extents). So as we examine purported justifications of democracy, we need to remember that these justifications may support differently the different sorts of possible democratic states.

The justifications of democracy that most of us would first attempt, I think, would make central reference to values like freedom and equality. By *freedom* we might have in mind the kind of freedom usually called individual "autonomy" (or "self-government").[3] Rousseau famously characterized true freedom as obedience to self-imposed law;[4] such freedom is inconsistent both with being governed by others and with being governed simply by one's own, lawless desires (it was this insight that led Kant [whose moral theory centrally employs this idea of freedom] to call Rousseau "the Newton of the moral realm").[5] To be free (in this sense) is to decide for oneself what ought to be done and to choose to act under the "constraint" of this determination. But if such freedom is morally important, surely democratic political societies must do a better job of permitting/promoting it than would societies in which law is not (in any sense) made by the governed. And perhaps the various political and economic freedoms associated with democracy can also be defended as necessary for self-government. Similarly, political equality seems both morally important (reflecting, as it does, the equal moral standing of persons, independent of inherited social or genetic advantages) and to straightforwardly motivate much of what seems central to democratic politics—for example, full inclusiveness in franchise rights ("one person, one vote") and in eligibility for political office ("open offices"), along with majority rule (which appears to give each an equal voice in political decision making).

Such appeals to democracy's respect for persons' freedom and equality, however, are only one kind of justificatory strategy that political philosophers have employed on democracy's behalf. Speaking loosely, philosophical justifications for democracy can be sorted into "intrinsic" and "instrumental" categories. *Intrinsic justifications* (the sort described above) try to show that there is something about democratic decision making that makes it in itself morally (or prudentially) desirable or authoritative (and thus superior to other political decision procedures), independent of the quality of the decisions that actually flow from democratic procedures. *Instrumental justifications* try instead to show that democratic procedures will reliably produce decisions or results that are morally (or prudentially) superior to those produced by alternative political decision procedures. One can, of course (and several schools of democratic thought do), employ instrumental and intrinsic justifications together in one theory, just as one can employ more than one kind of instrumental or intrinsic justification in a single theory. I separate the justificatory "strands" here simply for analytic clarity, not to indicate any obvious incompatibility between them.

The most widely supported intrinsic justifications of democracy argue that democratic procedures best respect the values of autonomy, fairness, or equality (equal consideration or equal respect) or best promote the development of virtue in citizens. The most prominent instrumental justifications argue that democratic procedures are the most reliable in producing outcomes/decisions that maximize social happiness, that match or reflect the common good or general will of the body politic, or that satisfy the substantive requirements of (nonprocedural) principles of justice.

I will begin here with the (conceptually simpler) instrumental justifications. Such justifications need not all be simple utilitarian defenses of democracy, but utilitarianism certainly provides us with one such argument: democratic government makes people happier (or better promotes desire satisfaction) than do other forms of government. John Stuart Mill's defense of representative democracy is the classic justification of this sort. According to Mill's "proof,"[6] a representative democracy most effectively promotes both the present well-being of citizens (using persons' existing abilities efficiently by, e.g., having them look after their own rights and interests, about which they care more than do others) and their future well-being (influencing their character development in happy directions, making them more active, educated, and sympathetic). Combined with the public discussion and scrutiny that democracy involves,[7] the result will be better decisions and laws, which in turn (along with people's tendency to more readily accept constraint and to maintain order when they feel they are "governing themselves") will produce greater overall happiness.[8]

Mill's argument is, of course, only that representative democracies *tend* to better promote happiness than do their competitor systems. They do not do so *necessarily*. And that fact may seem to render Mill's argument for democracy weaker than would be some alternative *intrinsic* justification, one that finds democracy's advantage in some feature of it (e.g., its consistency with individual autonomy) that is necessarily present in a democracy (and necessarily absent in nondemocratic states). All instrumental justifications, of course, will share this "weakness" since the outcome of democratic decision procedures can, in principle, be anything at all, good or bad. But one kind of instrumental justification that might seem to aim for something "stronger" is the Rousseauian argument that democracy most reliably yields decisions that reflect the general will of the political society in question.

Rousseau's presentation of the idea of the general will is notoriously difficult. But it can probably be discussed most clearly in the light cast by two distinctions. The first is that between a person's will (which is always for the good of the "willer") and a person's wants or desires (which may, due to inadequate information, insufficient self-control, etc., actually be for what is bad for the "wanter"). The second is Rousseau's distinction between the "particular wills" of individuals, the "will of all" in a society, and the general will.[9] Each person's particular will is simply his will that what is good for him be achieved. The will of all in any society is, Rousseau tells us, just the sum of the particular wills of the society's members. But the general will is the will for the *common* good—for the good of the body politic as a whole—which is, as it were, the particular will that the body politic would have were it a single individual. And an individual's will can be general (or participate in the general will) to the extent that it is for the common good.

Presented in this way, of course, general will talk is just a special way of talking about what is good for communities or for collections of individuals. Bodies politic do not really have wills in the way that individual persons have wills. Is Rousseau's argument, then, really just a variant of Mill's, emphasizing democracy's purely contingent instrumental advantages (but using the language of "common good" instead of that of "general happiness")? At times, Rousseau seems to take a rather stronger position on the general will, one that might appear to distance him from Mill. Sometimes he appears to say not that democratic lawmaking is the most likely to track the society's general will but rather that the general will is "declared" after counting the votes or that the decisions reached democratically will "always be good."

This stronger position, however, is either completely implausible—since there is no reason at all to think that true democracies will be *infallible* with respect to their own good—or completely empty, merely asserting without justification a very controversial idea of what "the common good" consists of (namely, whatever is democratically decided, without regard to its apparent relation to the actual well-being [as this would normally be construed] of the group or its members). And in fairness to Rousseau, the two principal occasions on which he makes such strong claims (about democracy and the general will) occur in the context of his discussions of certain restrictions on democratic lawmaking (i.e., the elimination of subsidiary groups, the provision of adequate information, asking citizens to vote with an eye to the common good),[10] restrictions that are most naturally viewed as simply increasing (even if impressively) the *likelihood* that democratically produced laws will express the general will, not *guaranteeing* that they will do so. It seems fairer, then, to read Rousseau as here asserting only that democratic lawmaking, unlike other sorts of lawmaking, can (by these restrictions) be made to reliably (but not necessarily) track the society's general will.

In the end, I think, Rousseau's defense of democracy[11] is probably best understood as coming in three pieces or stages. The portion we have been considering—that which makes central reference to the general will—is best seen as just an (instrumental) argument that democratic decisions (at least when the democratic lawmaking is subject to certain constraints) are more likely (than decisions made in other kinds of states) to be those that are good for the society as a whole. It is in the other (intrinsic) portions of Rousseau's defense that democracy is defended differently (and less contingently). These other two components (to variants of which I will turn shortly) are (1) that only democratic decisions will leave citizens autonomous[12] and (2) that only participation in democratic political life can "moralize" persons and make them virtuous.

None of this, of course, is to say that instrumental justifications of democracy lack force. To the extent that we agree with Mill that democracies are likely to have a happier citizenry than nondemocracies (or, with Rousseau, that democracies will better act on their general will)—and I think the case for at least Mill's view is reasonably compelling, both in terms of common sense and in light of the historical record—we should certainly regard this as at least contributing to an appropriate justification of democratic government. Happiness is, after all, morally important, even if it is not the only thing that is morally important. Similarly, a compelling (instrumental) case can be made for the view that democracies are the most

likely political societies to have laws that are good in nonutilitarian senses
(e.g., laws that are just or that respect individual rights).[13] In democracies,
citizens can (at least sometimes) act as watchdogs and "throw the rascals
out" when their rights are disregarded; and the public debates and deliberations on policy matters that democracies (can) include seem more likely
to converge on results that are morally satisfactory than do the decision
procedures of alternative systems.[14] And just outcomes are also, after all,
morally important, even if the means by which they were reached were
not in themselves morally exemplary. In the end, then, I think that the best
justification of democracy will be at least partly instrumental.[15]

Let us consider next what, if anything, can be added in the way of a
(stronger) intrinsic defense of democratic government. I will try here only
to introduce our discussion of the intrinsic justifications involving the values
of autonomy and equality, saving the bulk of that discussion for subsequent
sections (and I will defer altogether [until section 5.4.] discussion of the
idea that democracy most effectively promotes virtue in its citizens[16]). We
have seen already the rudiments of the autonomy and equality justifications.
These are often employed together in a "pluralistic" justification of democracy, as in the well-known arguments of Robert Dahl. The portion of Dahl's
argument that appeals to autonomy appears to be Rousseauian in its basic
premise: "To govern oneself, to obey laws that one has chosen for oneself, to
be *self-determining,* is a desireable end."[17] The obvious problem with achieving this end in a democracy, of course, is that where voting is governed by
majority rule, the losing minority appears not to be self-determining in this
sense. Only the group *as a whole* appears to be self-determining, not each
individual member. Rousseau argues (as we will see) that minorities in a
proper democracy are in fact self-determining, contrary to this appearance.
Dahl, however, simply accepts the point, arguing instead that majoritarian
democracy can be (in part) justified by the fact that it will "maximize the
opportunities for freedom by self-determination."[18]

These different responses to the problem are telling. Notice that Dahl's
argument, unlike Rousseau's, treats autonomy simply as a good to be promoted (or maximized), not as an individual right (or "side constraint") that
a legitimate state must respect in each person's case. Dahl is thus treating
"autonomy-promotion" as a *justifying* virtue of political systems (a virtue
which he, not unreasonably, takes to be possessed in greater degree by
democracies than by others[19]). Rousseau is concerned, rather, with *legitimating* democracy with respect to all persons subject to society's laws, by
describing a "form of association" into which persons can enter where
"*each* . . . renders obedience to his own will and remains as free as he was
before."[20] He thus cannot afford to admit, as Dahl cheerfully does, that
losing minorities are not self-determining.

Justificatory appeals to equality (or equal consideration) face obvious problems similar to those faced by autonomy arguments—for example, worries that permanent minorities, constantly outvoted by "tyrannous" majorities, are receiving nothing like equal consideration. But appeals to equality, like those to autonomy, can also be intended either to legitimate democracy—laws and the state being seen as legitimate with respect to and binding on all subjects of democracies in virtue of the fact that all are treated equally (or given equal consideration)—or only to justify it, by showing that democracies do a better job than other kinds of states of treating persons equally. These different (but normally unstated) objectives explain much of the disagreement and confusion in contemporary literature about the justification of democracy. And they provide a further reminder of the importance of keeping clearly in mind the distinction between the projects of justifying states (to which I return in section 5.3.) and legitimating them (to which we turn now).

5.2. Democracy and Obligation

It has sometimes been claimed that one of the things that is (morally) special about democracy is that (at least among realistic political societies) in, and only in, democracies are citizens morally obligated to obey the law, support their political institutions, and so on. In short, democracy solves—where other forms of government cannot—the problem of political obligation (which we addressed at length in Chapter 3). Democracies, then, would possess not only the justifying virtues discussed in sections 5.1 and 5.3 but also (internal) legitimacy—the "right to rule" that correlates in part with subjects' obligations to support and comply with their political authorities and institutions. This would, as we've seen, be a "justification" of democracy of a different sort.

We should, however, be clear from the start on one point about such "legitimating justifications": in order to be at all persuasive, they will need to solve the "particularity" (or "membership") problem. It is perfectly plausible to claim that it is a *necessary* condition for the legitimacy of a state that it respect its subjects' autonomy or show its subjects equal consideration (in the ways that democratic decision making are said to do). But such claims are vastly less plausible as claims about what is *sufficient* for legitimacy. Merely treating people well in a decision-making process is not adequate defense for coercing them unless (at least) those people can be shown to be (morally speaking) *subject to* that decision-making process. We cannot legitimate imposing our laws on, say, Canadians or Mexicans simply by treating those persons equally in our lawmaking process (by giving them an equal vote, etc.). They must, at the very least, accept their subjection to the results of our democratic lawmaking process. And it is this particularity problem that is regularly not addressed in theoretical attempts to legitimate (and not just justify) democracy.

Consider, for instance, not merely the "unparticularized" appeals to autonomy and equality mentioned above but also the familiar views that democracy is required as a matter of *justice* (a view defended, e.g., by Rawls[21]) or that democratic governance is a *human right,*[22] something to which all are morally entitled simply by virtue of their humanity. Even if these views are true, they do not solve the moral problem of grounding the authority of some particular state's democratic processes over any particular person (in the face, e.g., of persons' claims to be morally independent of any state's authority or to be subject to some other state's processes). Only a willingness—which I certainly do not share—to regard as morally authoritative or unchallengeable the conventional or legal assignments of persons to particular states (based on individual accidents of birth and the deplorable history of states' violent grabs for territories and peoples) would allow one to think that appeals to justice or human rights could by themselves solve the problem of democratic legitimacy.[23] Justice may demand democracy, and we may each be entitled to democratic governance. If so, perhaps all persons have a duty to help promote the end of worldwide democratic governance. But until we have some good moral account of to which state (if any) each person is subject—and until we are shown why persons may not permissibly decline democratic governance for themselves—we cannot claim to have shown that any particular state's democratically made laws are legitimate with respect to any particular set of persons.

The most natural way for an attempted legitimation of democracy to address this particularity problem, of course, is to identify some transaction whereby those said to be subject to democratic lawmaking procedures have made themselves (or been made) so subject. And it is easy to see how such an argument might proceed. The distinctive feature of democracies, we can say, is that (virtually) all of those who are subject to the laws have a right to play some role in the process that yields those laws. Active participation in the lawmaking process has the look of a kind of voluntary commitment to the political system, and voluntary commitments typically generate special moral obligations, giving us what we called (in Chapter 3, section 3.3.) a "transactional" account of political obligation (and state legitimacy). Indeed, it is hard to think of any act performed by many real citizens of real states that looks more like an obligating act than does voting in democratic elections. For that act has the look of an act of consent, the paradigm of obligation-generating transactions between persons. Or perhaps it is not any isolated act of voting that gives consent but rather ongoing political participation in democracy that gives a more temporally extended sort of consent. In either case, however, one thing that would be morally special about democracies would be that democratic governments rule with "the consent of the governed."

All of this is undeniably familiar from the rhetoric of democratic politics. But we must take care not to let such rhetoric uncritically guide our thinking. In the first place, of course, it matters whether we try to identify as consensual acts our discrete acts of voting or try to find individual consent instead in some ongoing pattern of activities. Discrete acts of voting—which in modern democracies are almost always votes for specific representatives with limited terms of office (or votes for specific political parties, policies, etc.)—do not really look much like they involve consenting to the overarching authority of state or government (particularly when the voter's preferred option fails to carry the day). Ongoing political participation, by contrast, looks more like commitment to a process or a system which has authoritative democratic government as its intended consequence, so it looks more like consenting to the authority of whatever laws or government(s) that process produces. However we choose to resolve that matter,[24] though, there remains the sticky problem of applying this model to real democracies—that is, of demonstrating the political obligations of real democratic citizens (and the legitimacy of real democracies). For most citizens of actual democracies fail to vote in at least some of their democratic elections, and many vote in none at all. Constant or committed political participation in actual democracies, if not exactly rare, is certainly nothing remotely like universal. Are those who decline to vote at all—or those whose political participation is not sufficiently steady or ongoing—thereby freed of political obligations, even in a democracy?

That, of course, is definitely not part of the rhetoric of democratic political life. And that problem has driven some to argue that it is not political acts (be they discrete or ongoing) that give obligating consent in democracies but rather possessing the *right* of political participation,[25] a property that is shared by (virtually) all citizens of (contemporary) democracies. On its face, at least, such a claim appears to confuse actually consenting with having a right to consent; and surely only the former could be understood to generate actual consensual obligations. But perhaps the position can be construed more charitably. Perhaps the idea is that citizens in democracies, in possessing the various rights of political participation, possess the powers to remove officials, change laws, alter constitutions, and so on. When they decline to do these things, they should be understood to consent to whatever political arrangements stand or come about in their societies. They "had their chance" and so can't complain.

This rendering of the position, however, seems to me to suffer from deep confusions. The most obvious are these. First, it confuses consent both with ignorant (or habitual) inactivity and with mere acquiescence, neither of which has moral consequences like those of genuine consent. Many citizens of democracies, for instance, are (non-negligently) ignorant of the full range (or the details) of laws to which they are subject and the true characters and commitments of the officials holding (or running for) public office. Their failures to act in order to change laws and officials can hardly constitute binding consent in such cases. Second, and far more important, is the obvious fact that individuals in democracies possess no rights at all to alter laws, change officials (etc.). Only democratic majorities—or "the people as a whole"—possess such rights. There is thus no sense in which *my* declining to change laws, officials, or constitutional provisions indicates *my* consent to the status quo. I have never so declined, lacking as I do (regrettably) the powers necessary to accomplish such changes. That some hypothetical majority had the power to change things appears completely uninteresting as an explanation of my consensual obligation to obey and support the powers that be.

But perhaps we can at least salvage the idea that those who do vote and participate have consented to their government's (or state's) authority over them (establishing at least widespread, even if not universal, democratic legitimacy and political obligation). Despite the initial appearance that democratic voters consent only to the very particular authority of some candidate, party, policy, or the like, we might argue that they are nonetheless freely choosing to participate in a system that is straightforwardly designed to produce results (representatives, governments, laws) that all (including the losers) are bound to accept. To those who insist that they were only expressing a preference in voting, never intending to undertake obligations to accept all that results from democratic decision procedures, the reply would be that one cannot simply freely participate in conventional practices like voting and then ignore the conventionally established significance of such participation. If not intentional consent to the democratic system and its outcomes, free participation is at least an equally binding act of "quasi-consent."[26]

But are there really clear conventions governing the moral significance of democratic participation? It does not seem to me that there are. Far worse, however, where they are clear, they do not in fact support this line of argument. Voting is regularly characterized as not just a right in democracies but a duty of citizens, and some democracies legally require citizens to vote. Declining to vote, of course, is never portrayed as sufficient to free one from any of those same obligations under which voters are said to fall. Our common understanding of the significance of democratic voting, then, in no way makes it the consensual act which grounds our political obligations or the legitimacy of our laws or governments. Our duties as citizens are represented as being logically prior to and entirely independent of any democratic participation in which we might opt to engage. Voting, in short, is simply not a clear, conventional way of undertaking political obligations or legitimizing democratically made laws or governments. The commonplace observation that democratic governments enjoy "the consent of the governed" should not be (mis)understood as showing us any simple path to a philosophically respectable account of democratic obligations or legitimacy.

Let us, then, try a different approach to these questions, this time without appealing to consent at all. We share a world together, one might argue, and we frequently disagree about how best to order our social interactions. It is necessary that we act together, even in the face of such disagreements, or our most basic interests will be set back. Further, justice requires that people be treated as equals with respect to their interests. If there were a decision-making procedure for resolving disagreements (and aggregating preferences) that was fair to and treated as an equal each affected person, that procedure's results would be legitimate with respect to each and each would be obligated to support and comply with the resulting laws, institutions, governors, etc. Democratic decision making is precisely such a fair procedure, embodying as it does (publicly manifested) respect or concern for each person as a political equal (and for each person's opinions and interests as equally important).[27]

I will leave for section 5.3 this last idea that democratic decision making is an especially fair (or equality-respecting) procedure, focusing briefly here only on the portions of this argument that precede that claim (and that must be defensible in order for that claim to have any relevance for real citizens of existing democracies). For these earlier steps in fact simply beg a series of increasingly important questions. First, such claims about the "necessity" of collective action simply paper over the obvious difficulties of determining which functions performed by modern states really are "necessary" and precisely for what and for whom they are necessary. Perhaps collective "security arrangements" of some sort are "necessary" for the minimal well-being of any person. But this is surely not true for anything like all of the kinds of "security" provided by modern democratic states. Are political solutions to other familiar social problems involving public goods—say, those involving exchange, infrastructure, health care, education, and so on—"necessary"? They are certainly necessary to certain kinds of economies and lifestyles, though plainly not to others. And that, of course, does not amount to their being necessary *simpliciter.* In short, appeals to the "necessity" of collective decision making simply disguise the need for far more careful argument, and they threaten, once plausibly fleshed out, to dramatically limit the areas of social life over which democratic procedures can claim to be authoritative.[28] Nothing remotely like the scope of authority claimed by contemporary democratic states could possibly follow from any argument beginning with a simple appeal to the necessity of collective decision making.

Even worse, however, the argument's subsequent claim that a fair decision procedure would establish the authoritative character of the results of that procedure in effect reverses the proper order of argument—and here we simply return to the arguments with which this section began. Grant for the moment that (e.g.) "one person, one vote" plus majority rule constitutes (in the abstract) a fair decision procedure. That point is surely morally relevant only after it has been shown that someone (or everyone) has the authority to require that a fair collective decision be made by a particular body of persons.[29] The abstract fairness of majority rule cannot, for instance, establish that my students (who are securely in the majority in each of my classes) can authoritatively outvote me and alter the requirements I set for my class. Those students (or someone) would first need the authority to designate my class as a body to be governed by a fair (or the fairest) rule of this sort.

The argument under consideration, then, puts the cart before the horse. It cannot appeal to the fairness of (say) majority rule to establish the authority of the majority to make collectively binding law or government. We first need an argument for authority that shows over precisely which persons majority rule can legitimately be used to make decisions. It will not do, as we have seen (and will see even more clearly in Chapter 6), to simply identify as the relevant bodies of persons those identified as compatriots by international law or common opinion. For that would be to just accept without any argument at all the conservative "solution" to the problem of political obligation.

Even, then, if we can show that some version of democratic decision procedures is fair to all, we need to be able to specify independently an "all" that is legitimately subject to *any* collective decision procedure, however fair. And such a specification requires the kinds of arguments (for political obligation and internal legitimacy) that we examined and rejected in Chapter 3. The importance of democracy, then, seems not to lie in its special ability to solve the problem of political obligation (or legitimacy). It lies rather in democracy's superior justifiability. But precisely which of the many familiar features of contemporary democracies will contribute to this superior justifiability and which might actually detract from it?

5.3. Majorities and Representatives

"Unanimous direct democracy," Robert Paul Wolff writes, "is the (frequently unexpressed) ideal which underlies a great deal of classical democratic theory. The devices of majoritarianism and representation are introduced in order to overcome obstacles which stand in the way of unanimity and direct democracy."[30] Unanimity in collective decision making appears to reconcile the authority of the resulting decisions (and their enforcement) with the autonomy of the individuals subject to those decisions.[31] And directness of democratic participation similarly removes concerns that otherwise "the many" remain unautonomous, "their" choices made for them in the decision-making process by a few representatives. Majority-rule democracy and representative democracy, in Wolff's view, both represent clear departures from the kinds of democratic procedures that could hope to legitimate their results; both involve losses of autonomy (for minorities or for those represented) and both are thus of dubious legitimacy (a problem which is compounded, of course, when they are combined, as they are in most actual democracies).

Unhappily, Wolff argues, unanimous direct democracy is itself an impracticable ideal. As Wolff describes this ideal, only those laws on which the community agrees unanimously are passed and enforced. So "every member of the society . . . is only confronted . . . with laws to which he has consented," thus "harmoniz[ing] the duty of autonomy with the commands of authority." But because unanimous direct democracy of this sort "achieves its success only by ruling out precisely the conflicts of opinion which politics is designed to resolve, it may be viewed as a limiting case of a solution rather than as itself a true example of a legitimate state."[32]

If, however, Wolff wants to condemn all instances of majority-rule democracy as involving (delegitimating) unautonomy for minorities (whose wills are not reflected in the laws imposed on them), there is something odd about his claim that unanimous direct democracy preserves the autonomy of all citizens. Suppose (as in Locke's model of a legitimate civil society) that all citizens unanimously agree to be governed by majority rule. Even then, Wolff says, in agreeing to abide by laws they vote against, citizens "have bound themselves to laws they do not will, and even laws which they vigorously reject," which "is no more than voluntary slavery."[33]

But how does having chosen to bind oneself to a procedure (majority rule) in the belief that doing so is best (while knowing that it may yield laws one opposes) differ in principle from having chosen—in a unanimous direct democracy—to bind oneself to some particular law in the belief that doing so is best (while knowing that one may come to later regard having voted for that law as a mistake)? If citizens in a unanimous direct democracy, after changing their minds about some law, are nonetheless bound to abide by it because of their prior consent, why are those who have given prior consent to a regime of majority rule not equally bound to abide by laws they vote against? If unautonomy undoes obligations to comply in the latter case, why not also in the former? But if unautonomy does undo obligations (and legitimacy) in the former case, then Wolff's unanimous direct democracy is not really a political society but only "the state of nature continued,"[34] in which all remain morally free to act according to their own moral lights. And "the state of nature continued" can hardly be the unexpressed ideal that underlies classical democratic theory, it not being properly an ideal of political society at all.

Perhaps, then, we should (with Locke) regard an individual's free, informed consent as after all capable of yielding obligations that *preserve* that individual's autonomy—as a use of, rather than a "forfeiture" of, autonomy. That point alone, however, hardly counts as a defense of majority rule and political representation since so few actual citizens do consent to those arrangements. What, then, can be said in their defense? Taking majority rule first, it is not hard to see why one might regard majority rule as practically necessary in a democratic society. The requirement of unanimity in lawmaking would utterly paralyze—by rendering hopelessly conservative—any modern nation-state (or, to be more accurate, any political society that has ever existed, none having been perfectly homogeneous in all of the ways that would be necessary for good lawmaking under a unanimity principle). But are there reasons to accept majority rule not as a regrettable practical necessity but as a morally authoritative procedural principle? We have seen, of course, that majorities are not *naturally* authoritative, it being necessary first to establish that some particular body of persons is rightly subject to a mandatory collective decision procedure before we can even begin to defend majority rule as the best such procedure. But suppose we imagine this membership problem solved, perhaps by imagining (with Locke) some perfectly voluntary political association. Does majority rule—which, once conjoined with (nearly) full inclusiveness in the franchise and in eligibility for political office,[35] is the most recognizably democratic decision procedure—then yield morally binding results? Is it the *only* decision procedure that does?

Locke, as we've seen, sees majority rule as the only natural and acceptable decision procedure for incorporated groups; so for him, any consent to membership in a group just is consent to majority rule (unless other rules are explicitly adopted instead). But his reason for this view—that groups, in order to act as one, must move "whither the greater force carries them"[36]—seems both mistaken (since groups are not mere inanimate "bodies," incapable of self-control) and insufficient to justify majority rule (since the "greater force" in a body need not lie in the majority, as the phenomenon of "intense minorities, apathetic majorities" makes clear). Rousseau, perhaps surprisingly, also thought majority rule generates authoritative results, at least in certain kinds of polities (Wolff therefore follows the letter of Rousseau's texts only in their shared opposition to representation). But Rousseau's reasons are also hard to accept (or understand). He sometimes seems to suggest that in a properly ordered democracy losing minorities can have no complaint but should see instead that they are simply *mistaken* in their votes (rather than ruled by the majority against their wills). And he hints as well at the view that majority votes are authoritative because wisdom resides in majorities, so majorities are normally correct about what is best for the whole body politic.[37]

The former reason, however, turns on the view (discussed and rejected earlier) that a majority vote *determines* the general will (so that in voting contrary to the majority stance a voter, aiming at the general will, will see that he failed to hit his target). The latter reason has suggested to some that Rousseau had in mind something like Condorcet's "jury theorem," which shows that when each voter has a better than even chance of being correct, majorities are more likely than minorities to make correct decisions (in choices between two alternatives and moreso the larger the numbers of voters involved). But the jury theorem applies only under conditions that are seldom realized in typical democratic settings. So it cannot help us (or Rousseau) here. More compelling defenses of majority rule are, however, available. An obvious instrumental consideration, of course, is that where majorities rule, more people will tend to be happy with decisions (which is valuable in itself) and societies will tend (as a result) to be more stable. That line, though, argues less for simple majority rule than for whatever form of (super?) majoritarianism will best balance happiness-producing outcomes against counterproductive conservatism (which will increase as the unanimity requirement is approached).

A more promising justification of majority rule is intrinsic in character. Making laws (and other societal decisions) according to majority rule, we can argue, best realizes the goals of political equality and fairness (when combined with democratic inclusiveness and equal power in agenda setting), for it maximizes the weight in decision making of each individual's preferences/interests while giving each equal power over outcomes.[38] It thus demonstrates equal respect for all individuals' opinions and equal concern for their interests. Contrast majority rule in these regards with, say, unanimity rule, which permits the votes of those who favor inaction to have much greater weight than the votes of those who favor any positive outcome (since those favoring inaction can unilaterally defeat all positive proposals).

This case for majority rule is, I think, quite persuasive but certainly not without qualification. Claims about the fairness of majority rule will not, of course, be equally compelling in all contexts (as we have seen) or even in all contexts in which collective decision making seems a plausible demand. The fairness of a decision rule may turn on how open or informative the process is that precedes the decision, and it may be that majority rule will seem fairer when used to decide some matters than it will in deciding others (e.g., "constitutional essentials").[39] Further, of course, if the ideal of political equality and fairness requires not just that citizens' votes have maximal (equal) weight in decision making but also that citizens' favored views at least sometimes have some realistic chance of carrying the day, majority rule will not by itself be sufficient to realize that ideal. It would in fact be better realized by a procedure involving random selection of the winning preference/vote, in which each citizen's chance of having her view carry the day would then be equal to the percentage of her fellow citizens who shared her view. While such a procedure would forfeit the obvious instrumental advantages of majority rule (since very unpopular views could carry the day), it would not, it seems, be obviously unfair or obviously treat anyone unequally. Most important, of course, such a procedure would address the one obvious, enduring difficulty with the majority-rule principle.

That problem, mentioned already (and famously recognized in De Tocqueville and in Madison's *The Federalist,* nos. 10 and 51), is the threat of a "tyranny of the majority." Where we are in the majority sometimes and in the minority others, we can accept this as just part of the necessary cost of living with others. We cannot always have our way. But where we are part of a (more or less) *permanent* minority, which is always outvoted in the matters of importance to us (and especially where the majority's preferences are far less intense), it is harder to see this position as defensible. While majoritarian democracies can do their best to insure that the permanent minorities in their citizenry are not defined by (say) race or gender or religion, permanent minorities united by values or interests are an enduring and apparently inevitable feature of all contemporary states. Constitutional constraints on the power of the majority (including constitutionally established special powers for minorities) may be able to help limit this problem (albeit in apparently nondemocratic ways), as can the kinds of broad participation and open deliberation we discuss in section 5.4. But there is no way that majoritarian democracy (even of such an impure sort) can entirely avoid it. This problem constitutes the residual and unresolvable shortfall of democracy (along with all other forms of government) in the quest for a form of political life that fully realizes the goals of citizen autonomy and equality. As such, this "outcome-based disenfranchisement" is another of the shady places in which the illegitimacy of the modern state conceals itself.

Turning next to the problem of representation, we have seen already the most common reasons advanced both against and for representative ("indirect") versions of democracy. Critiques of representation are usually "intrinsic" ones, arguing (with Rousseau and Wolff) that representation undermines the great virtues of democracy: its consistency with individual freedom (i.e., each is subject only to self-imposed law) and equality (every person counts for one, not some [representatives] counting for more). The standard case in favor of representation, by contrast, emphasizes "instrumental" concerns: direct democracy would be simply unmanageable (chaotic, inefficient) in the modern nation-state (even taking into account the potentially helpful influence of new technologies). Ancient Greek city-states, tiny Swiss cantons, or New England towns might have been able to practice or aspire to direct democracy; but modern nation-states with millions of citizens simply cannot function on this model. Further, it is sometimes claimed, the results of political decision making will inevitably be better when it is done by representatives selected for their technical or political expertise (rather than when it is done by unqualified ordinary citizens), and citizens will have more time for other productive activities when relieved of the duties discharged by their representatives.[40]

Democratic politics needn't, of course, be either direct or indirect throughout. Various mixtures are possible (as in the use in representative democracies of direct ballot measures, recall procedures, initiatives, etc.), as are variations in the focus and the kind of representation employed. Representation can vary in both the *level* at which it operates (e.g., local, state/provincial, federal/national) and the *subject* of representative action (e.g., lawmaking, executive functions). And the *kind* of representation utilized (i.e., the nature of the objects represented, how they are represented, and the consequent understanding of the duties of representatives) can vary widely as well.[41] Standardly, of course, it is groups of persons (rather than, say, lower animals) that are represented, with the groups defined either by geographical location or by some shared (nongeographical) trait or affiliation (e.g., Sunni Muslim).

Representatives can claim to "re-present" (and not just "act instead of") those groups by being "typical of" the group in terms of views or interests, by sharing with the group other salient characteristics (e.g., race, religion), by being best at perceiving or deciding how to advance the group's views/interests (e.g., by possessing certain skills or education), or by having a large stake in the group's interests (by, say, holding land in the group's territory or having long family ties to the group). Representatives conceived in these ways are probably most naturally viewed as being bound by their roles to vote according to the views or interests of those they represent (insofar as these can be determined)—an approach often called the "delegate" view of representation. Some, however (most famously Edmund Burke), have defended instead an alternative "trustee" view of representation, according to which representatives ought simply to vote their own consciences (thus mirroring what those they represent should be doing).

All of these possible differences in the kinds of political representation that could be employed in a democracy will plainly affect the kind (and the force) of justification for representation that can be offered. But none of those variations will matter much if representation turns out (contrary to appearances) to be impossible. That sometimes appears to be Rousseau's position (at least with regard to representative lawmaking): "Sovereignty cannot be represented. . . . It consists essentially of the general will, and will cannot be represented. . . . Laws which the People have not ratified in their own person are null and void. . . . The moment a People begins to act through its representatives. . . . it no longer exists."[42]

Now, it is, indeed, hard to understand what it would be for will to be represented; but that seems mostly to be due to the fact that it's hard to understand what it would be for a group to have a will in any very literal sense. But if talking about a people's general will is taken instead (as suggested) as only a way of talking about what is good for the people as a whole, it seems not difficult at all to understand how a people (or particular individuals or groups) could be represented in lawmaking. Representatives need only aim at the common good (or, in thoroughly anti-Rousseauian fashion, aim at that end as it is conceived by the individuals or groups being represented). Unless we share (as I believe we should not) Rousseau's apparent view that autonomy requires actual direct making of the laws to which one is subject—precluding, say, subjection to laws made, according to one's own specifications, by a hired lawmaker—the real problem for actual democracies is not their use of political representation. It is rather that the representatives are themselves selected by (at best) majority rule within some (at best) arbitrary and certainly nonhomogenous electoral (or other) district, guaranteeing that the views, preferences, and interests of many are not represented at all in the ultimate lawmaking process. The problems with representation, then, simply mirror and aggravate the problems inherent in majority rule (or, worse, mirror those employed in even less "democratic" systems for selecting representatives).

Despite such concerns, in the end, were there reliable safeguards (beyond mere term limits) available to insure the selection of competent and (or at least) well-intentioned representatives, the instrumental case for some forms of political representation (especially in large-scale political communities) would appear to be sufficiently strong to outweigh concerns about the (intrinsic) losses of equal standing and individual autonomy that representative government seems to necessarily involve. Assuming, then, that the justification of *some form of* democracy (as against nondemocratic government) can be established along the lines already discussed, our principal remaining concern in defending indirect democracy would seem to lie in discovering how to create such safeguards. One place that many democratic theorists have suggested we look is to a more active, involved democratic citizenry.

5.4. Participation and Deliberation

As we have seen, the contrast between direct and indirect (representative) democracy need not be drawn starkly. There are ways in which even indirect democracies can more (or less) directly involve their citizens in political affairs. Even if it means ignoring Rousseau's actual categorical opposition to legislative representation, we can still motivate such insights in a Rousseauian fashion, emphasizing instead four other themes from his discussion of democracy: (1) the need to discourage development of secondary/subsidiary interest groups standing between individual citizens and the whole, (2) the need for citizens to distance themselves from private concerns and aim instead at the common good in their public lives (e.g., in public discussion and in voting), (3) the need to eliminate large economic inequalities between citizens, and (4) the capacity of active involvement in public life to have transformative effects on individuals[43]—indeed, public life's essential role in each person's good, including each person's development of virtue.

These themes, of course, suggest the necessity of extensive direct involvement by citizens even in democracies that are inevitably representative and majoritarian. And they are central themes, of course, not only in Rousseau's political philosophy but in Aristotle's, in Renaissance civic republicanism, and in much of contemporary communitarianism. One influential approach in contemporary democratic theory—often called "participatory democracy" (or, in the case of one variant, "strong democracy")[44] theory—exploits these themes to argue that the more direct the democracy, the better. Persons should be able to participate in all of the associations that affect their lives, thus maximizing the extent of their control over their lives. Persons should be educated to be *citizens* (in a strong sense of that word), to become deeply involved in public life through agenda setting, discussion, legislation, public service, etc. This is essential, it is claimed, to both an individual's virtuous life and the health of a body politic. Active citizens will be more thoughtful, more responsible, more sympathetic, less servile, and more likely to feel free and unoppressed (in addition to being much busier!).

While some of these aims (e.g., to maximize feasible self-determination) are almost universal among theorists of democracy, others clearly are not. In particular, the "participatory democracy" approach almost always seems to rest its case on a particular—and inevitably controversial—conception of what makes a person's life good or virtuous. Sensitive to this perceived bias, an even more influential movement in democratic theory (and practice) has followed a similarly Rousseauian path[45] but (in some cases) without presupposing any particular conception of the good. "Deliberative democracy" theory,[46] most commonly associated with the work of Rawls,[47] Jürgen Habermas,[48] and Joshua Cohen,[49] argues that extensive involvement of citizens in public deliberation and decision making is essential not to their own good or to their development of a virtuous character but rather to their reaching good decisions (or reaching the truth about their common good) and/or to the justice or the legitimacy of democratic polities. The aim of democratic politics should be to find a common ground in the reasonable pluralism of a free society, to work toward a reasoned consensus.

Deliberative democracy theorists usually defend their views in contrast not just to less direct democratic ideals but rather to a completely different view (common to most analytic political theory on the subject of democracy) of what democracy is for (or what's good about it, or essential to it). In this more traditional view—often called the "aggregative" or "economic" (or "market" or "interest-based") view of democracy—democracy is essentially a procedure for aggregating individual preferences, perhaps fairly and perhaps in a fashion that is (broadly) utility-maximizing.[50] Individual citizens are portrayed as bringing to the democratic table a relatively fixed ordering of preferences. They will then cast their votes according to their private and/or group interests, in an effort to maximize their personal preference satisfaction. Voting (and the resulting distribution of political power) is thus the principal phenomenon of democratic political society and the citizen's principal (but essentially private) function,[51] and democracy yields morally defensible results in the political sphere (if one cares about such things) in much the same way that competitive markets are thought to yield them in the economic sphere.[52]

From a Rousseauian perspective, however, it will seem clear that this market view of democracy ignores what are in fact democracy's most valuable and distinctive features. For this view characterizes democratic political life as essentially about the narrow advocacy of and competition between personal (or, worse, subsidiary group) interests, and it seems perfectly compatible with the creation of a professional political class, control of the process by wealthy or powerful individuals or special interest groups, and only minimal and momentary involvement in the process by average citizens.[53] What seems to be disregarded altogether is what is essential in the Rousseauian view of democracy: cooperation (rather than competition), joint efforts at problem solving, and collective reasoning about and pursuit of common aims.[54]

Not all deliberative theorists believe that we can (or should try to) identify a "common good" (or general will) for a society (and in this they tend to be following Rawls, for whom, remember [from Chapter 4, section 4.3], just states cannot aim to advance any favored [but inherently controversial] conception of the good). For them, public deliberation is necessary so that the resulting policies/laws/governments can be just or legitimate (which they cannot be unless they are defensible in terms of reasons that all persons subject to them could accept). Public deliberation is the process through which (e.g.) laws are provided with a transparent history that includes justification in terms of *public reason*—that is, in terms all can accept. Mere voting cannot accomplish this. In the public realm, citizens should employ public, not personal or subsidiary group, reason. Other deliberative theorists (often following Habermas) hold instead (or in addition) that public deliberation tends to create the conditions (e.g., openness, impartiality, extended consideration) necessary for reaching good or true judgments about a genuinely common good. And again it seems clear that mere democratic "aggregations of preferences" shouldn't even be expected to advance any genuine common good, unless the preferences being aggregated were formed and revised through a shared process of public deliberation (which is only possible where obstructing social and economic inequalities have been removed—another of Rousseau's concerns).

The deliberative approach, of course, has its critics as well. Some complain that it privileges distinctively white, male—rationalistic, argumentative—speech, thereby excluding from democratic participation women and minorities, whose approaches to cooperative action can take other forms. And, of course, the deliberative approach does seem to rest, perhaps too optimistically, on the possibility of locating a genuinely shareable viewpoint, with its associated genuinely public reason. Finally, as we have seen, mere democracy, no matter how deliberative, cannot solve other equally fundamental problems: those of political legitimacy and political obligation, which are problems more about particularity and membership than about directness of citizen input or the possibility of "public justification."

But according to Rousseauian conceptions of democracy, democracies must be made more direct (in the ways previously discussed); otherwise, they cannot be good or just polities, they will not possess those characteristics on which democracy's superior justifiability depends. When made more direct and open, however, even representative democracies will make better decisions, will involve processes through which each person (with each person's rights and interests) is taken seriously and treated as an equal, will widen citizens' perspectives and enhance their virtue (thus promoting civic friendship and broader sympathies), and will better respect autonomy by focusing on what all can agree is best, not just on what individuals happen to want. This will be especially true in democracies that work as well to eliminate the economic (and other) domination that inhibits free deliberation. And in many of these claims it seems clear to me that some Rousseauian view must be correct. The more fully a democracy involves its citizens in the process of (e.g.) lawmaking, the more fully it will possess those virtues that make democracy a better-justified form of political society than its alternatives. Respect for autonomy and equal consideration, development of certain widely accepted and beneficial virtues in citizens, and laws which are good for the society, promote happiness, and are substantively just all seem most likely to be effectively promoted where democratic polities encourage and develop institutional structures for widespread public participation in and deliberation about citizens' lives.

Suggested Reading

Charles Beitz, *Political Equality* (Princeton: Princeton University Press, 1989).
Thomas Christiano, *The Rule of the Many* (Boulder: Westview, 1996).
Robert Dahl, *Democracy and Its Critics* (New Haven: Yale University Press, 1989).
David Estlund, ed., *Democracy* (Malden, MA: Blackwell, 2002).
William Nelson, *On Justifying Democracy* (London: Routledge & Kegan Paul, 1980).
Albert Weale, *Democracy* (New York: St. Martin's, 1999).

CHAPTER 6

The World of States

6.1. An International State of Nature?

The state of nature, we have said (in Chapter 2, section 2.2), is any condition in which people live without political society (i.e., without effective government over them). Since people can plainly live in political society with some persons (i.e., their compatriots) while living out of political society with others (i.e., foreigners), we can say more precisely that two persons are in the state of nature with respect to one another if they are not both members of the *same* political society (or, as Locke would have it, of the same *legitimate* political society).[1]

Now consider the condition of the world as a whole. What we see is a large number of autonomous states, jointly inhabiting the globe (and claiming all of its useable land) but with no two states subject to the authority (or even subjected to the power) of any higher government. The single most striking and obvious fact about the international condition is the absence of a world-state, world government, and (reliably) coercively enforced international law. That fact, together with a natural tendency to think of states as incorporated wholes that are analogous to individual persons, has suggested to political philosophers (for as long as philosophers have thought and written about international political philosophy) the idea of the international condition as a state of nature between the sovereign nations of the world, with each nation being in the state of nature with respect to every other. And with no binding law imposed by a supranational authority, individual states in such an international state of nature would then naturally be thought to be bound in their dealings with each other only by those rules (if any) that would bind individual persons in an analogous interpersonal state of nature.

While Grotius was probably the most influential modern thinker to argue that individual persons (outside of society) and states are in analogous moral positions,[2] that view is better known to contemporary readers from the work of Hobbes. For Hobbes, remember, persons in the state of nature are certain to regard the strategy of *anticipation* as the most rational course of action, inevitably leading to the degeneration of every state of nature into a condition of war. And in a condition of war, Hobbes appears to argue, the laws of nature do not bind persons to behave morally, "force and fraud" being in war the "cardinal virtues." Hobbes explicitly applies this same analysis to the international state of nature in which sovereign nations are said by him to exist: "In all times, kings and persons of sovereign authority, because of their independence, are in continual jealousy and in the state and posture of gladiators, having their weapons pointing and their eyes fixed on one another . . . which is a posture of war."[3] If we suppose that for Hobbes the condition of war is always a "moral vacuum," then it follows that individual nations owe no moral duties to alien nations or persons, being left morally free to pursue their own national interests in any fashion they think rational.

This picture of international relations as a "morality-free zone" has been attractive to those who are skeptical about the idea of moral constraints on national exercises of autonomy and sovereignty, particularly to those in the so-called realist tradition in political science.[4] Hobbes' account appears to provide a theoretical justification for such skepticism. But it is important to keep in mind that no such justification for skepticism follows simply from supposing that states are like persons and that states are in the state of nature with respect to one another. For there are, as we have seen, very different and equally influential accounts of the moral condition of persons (and of nations) in the state of nature. Locke, for instance, also supposed that states are like persons (in the rights and obligations they can have); and he agreed with Hobbes that nations (and their rulers) are all in the state of nature with respect to one another: "Where are, or ever were, there any men in such a state of nature? To which it may suffice as an answer at present: that since all princes and rulers of independent governments all through the world are in a state of nature, 'tis plain the world never was, nor ever will be, without numbers of men in that state.'"[5]

But for Locke, persons in the state of nature are fully bound by the laws of nature (which require them to respect the lives, liberties, and property of all other persons [and incorporated groups of persons], wherever situated) and persons cannot lose those moral duties simply by entering into a political society. Any political society people create must either

discharge those moral duties for them or permit them to discharge those
duties themselves. People may not rightfully create institutions that violate
natural law in their name. The Lockean state of nature, then, whether interpersonal or international, is fully moralized—due, no doubt, to Locke's
view of rational persons as capable of knowing God's law for humankind,
capable of conforming their actions to that law, and positively desiring to
live in peaceful society with other persons. Further, somewhere between
the Hobbesian and Lockean accounts of the state of nature are still others, which we can call "partly moralized" (Pufendorf's account being an
important example)—that is, accounts according to which persons in the
state of nature have some real moral duties (e.g., the duty to keep mutually
beneficial promises/contracts) but not the full range of moral duties possessed by persons in society with one another.

But even if, in the end, we accept Hobbes' own framework for discussing the international state of nature, there are still a number of good reasons for resisting the skeptical conclusion about the moral duties of states
toward one another. First, of course, Hobbes himself appears to have some
doubts about whether (and how) moral rules bind individuals in an interpersonal state of nature. Not only does he allow that certain covenants are
binding even in "the condition of mere nature" (specifically, those where
one party performs first and the other is trusted to perform later),[6] Hobbes
also states that *all* of the laws of nature "are immutable and eternal," binding us always (even in a state of nature) "*in foro interno:* that is to say, they
bind to a desire they should take place."[7] By this Hobbes appears to mean
that the laws bind us to *act* as the laws require (they bind "*in foro externo*")
when, but only when, we can do so safely, without making ourselves "a
prey to others." Since there can certainly be some such occasions, even
during a war of all against all, the laws of nature will impose on us moral
duties to treat others well in at least certain state of nature situations. Even
the Hobbesian state of nature, then, seems not to be a perfect moral vacuum. And we would do well to remember in this context that Hobbes'
reply to the "foole" (discussed in Chapter 2, section 2.3 above) seems to
suggest that peaceful cooperation with others may often be individually
rational, even in the state of nature.

But if we follow Hobbes' reasoning thus in the interpersonal case, there
seem likely to be still more extensive moral constraints on the nations in
the international state of nature. For there are several clear disanalogies
between the interpersonal and the international cases that should affect
our conclusions. The first is mentioned by Hobbes himself: the rulers of
independent nations are, to be sure, at war with one another, brandishing
their weapons, building their forts, and using their spies: "But because
they uphold thereby the industry of their subjects, there does not follow

from it that misery which accompanies the liberty of particular men."[8] In other words, because a state can be internally secure (at least relatively speaking, with its subjects safe from one another and thereby free to lead productive lives), even while that state is in a permanent condition of war with all other states, the misery of life for individuals in an interpersonal state of nature is not likely to be reproduced in the international state of nature. And because the miseries and dangers of the interpersonal state of nature are Hobbes' principal reason for denying that the laws of nature bind individuals in that state, there is every reason to believe that individuals and their states will in fact be morally bound toward aliens on a regular basis in the international state of nature.

A second clear disanalogy between the interpersonal and international cases is this: in the interpersonal state of nature, Hobbes tells us, all persons are approximate equals, none so strong or so clever as to be invulnerable to attacks by others (or groups of others).[9] It is this roughly equal vulnerability that justifies our resorting to our rights of nature and doing only what we take to be best for ourselves. But in the international case, there is not (and certainly need not be) anything like approximate equality between nations in their vulnerability to attack. Extremely powerful nations (with, say, easily defended borders, abundant and developed resources, and vastly superior military technology) are not interestingly vulnerable to dangerous attacks by even confederacies of small, primitive nations. There are surely many occasions on which such powerful nations can treat weaker nations respectfully and offer them assistance, without thereby rendering themselves "a prey" to any other states. And on such occasions the logic of Hobbes' argument compels us to conclude that powerful nations are morally bound to act as the laws of nature specify.

Indeed, it seems plausible to suppose that these kinds of differences between the interpersonal and the international cases might force as well a more general conclusion: that the international state of nature cannot in fact be reasonably characterized as a condition of *war* at all. We could accept (though, of course, we need not[10]) that the interpersonal state of nature is best characterized as a state of war, while arguing that where stable society and peaceful industry are possible, where cooperation and nonaggression are regularly individually rational (as they are in the international case), there simply is no war. If we want to resist skeptical conclusions about international morality, then, it might be unnecessary to do so by rejecting the Hobbesian framework that we've been considering, embracing instead, say, some version of just war theory, according to which robust moral constraints bind even those in a condition of (or contemplating the use of) war.[11] If states are at peace with one another, they may not, even according to Hobbes, blithely disregard (or merely *desire* compliance with) the moral constraints set by the laws of nature.

A more dramatic path to rejecting skepticism about international morality, of course, would involve dismissing not only Hobbes' specific theory of the global condition but any account of the matter that relies on the idea of an international state of nature. We could do this by rejecting from the start the analogy between the moral positions of individuals and states so that the inclination to imagine states as being like individuals in a state of nature never arises in the first place. Thus, for instance, while individual persons' rights to autonomy and self-determination might seem to dictate that we refrain from interfering in their pursuits of their life plans, we might believe that nations or states are not similarly morally immune to intervention by other states (perhaps because, lacking the unity or integrity of individual persons, we think they cannot have such autonomy rights). This might at first seem a hard position to defend. After all, neither individuals nor states seem morally entitled to noninterference when they morally *wrong* (or threaten to wrong) others. But doesn't it seem that, just as individuals have a right to non-interference where they do no wrong, so do independent states or nations?[12]

This apparently plausible answer, however, needs to be qualified by the recognition that while possible wrongs by individuals lie principally in one sphere—namely, in their interactions with other persons—possible wrongs by states can be either external or internal. Even states that do no wrong to alien states and persons—and that thus look, from the perspective of international relations, like states entitled to autonomy and self-determination—may nonetheless do great and persistent wrongs internally, to their own subjects. Thus, the first obvious disanalogy between the moral positions of persons and states: persons can rarely (if ever) do internal wrongs (i.e., to themselves) that justify intervention by outside (i.e., unwronged) parties.

Indeed, when we begin to think about why states are thought of as rightholders at all, the analogy appears less and less perfect. The idea of states as moral rightholders seems compelling most obviously when we think of states as unified or incorporated wholes, wielding the rights freely granted to those wholes by the individual persons who compose the state. Just as we should not interfere with individuals in their morally innocent activities, we should not interfere with free, incorporated groups of individuals. But as we have seen (in Chapter 3), actual states virtually never enjoy anything like the unanimous consent of their subjects, depriving this model of the state (as a voluntary association) of any purchase in the actual world of states. And if we try to think of what else (i.e., other than the unanimous consent of subjects) might lead us to believe that a state was internally legitimate (and thus entitled to noninterference by outsiders), the most natural answer would seem to be that only the *justice* of the state could play this role. But then states would not be autonomous moral rightholders in a state of nature, free to set their own ends and entitled to respect for those ends, at all; instead, their rights to non-intervention and self-determination would be entirely conditional on their satisfying both domestic and international principles of justice.[13]

But does any of this really impugn the *model* of states as like persons in a state of nature? In one sense, of course, it plainly does. Real states are not moral rightholders like real persons. Even the best real states are non-voluntary and moderately unjust, and others are quite often thoroughly vicious. So the model cannot be taken to describe the actual world of states. But surely that plain truth does no damage to the model conceived of as an ideal, as part of the ideal theory of political philosophy. To suppose that it does would be to suppose that we can persuasively criticize an ideal in political philosophy on the simple grounds that it has no real application to the actual world of states. But criticizing such an ideal—in this case, the ideal of the international condition as a state of nature between (moral rightholding) voluntary associations of persons—because it is not realized in the actual world is no more convincing than criticizing an ideal of social justice because the nations of the world are all unjust according to that ideal. Given the motivational power of considerations of self- and national interest and the seductive lure of political convenience, it would in fact be surprising if ideals of justice or legitimacy *were* approximated in the real world.

If states must be voluntary, consensual associations in order to be internally legitimate (as, e.g., Locke maintained), then legitimate states, properly understood, will be moral rightholders (holding whatever rights their subjects have freely transferred to the state and its government). And the only legitimate international condition will be one in which all states that exist are not only internally legitimate in this way but in which they do no external wrong (including wrongs of omission) to alien states or persons. That amounts to (what I believe is) a defensible international ideal: a world of states, each wielding (internally granted) moral rights to some degree of autonomy and self-determination, in a (fully moralized) state of nature with respect to all other states and persons.[14] This ideal sets the target for nonideal international political philosophy, which must reveal morally acceptable paths for moving (from our current condition) in the direction of this ideal. In the end, then, there may be good reason for the long-standing appeal of the model of states as like persons in a state of nature. It is a model for what we hope the world may be, what we want the world to approximate, not what we believe a clear view of our actual world reveals.

6.2. Legitimacy and Territoriality

State legitimacy, then, has both an internal and an external dimension. Internally, states are legitimate if they possess the "right to rule" those persons who they in fact attempt to govern (as we saw in Chapter. 3, Section 3.1). But even a state that is internally legitimate in this way may nonetheless be illegitimate by virtue of its dealings with alien persons and states. Legitimate states must have both moral rights to do what they must do in order to qualify as *states* (the conceptual core of state legitimacy) and moral rights to do whatever else they in fact do. The conceptual core moral rights in need of defense (in order to establish a state's moral legitimacy *qua* modern state) would seem to be these: a set of rights over (or against) those persons claimed as subjects of the state, a set of rights held against aliens or noncitizens, and a set of rights over a particular geographical territory.[15] All entities that we would today describe as states claim substantial and similar rights (and exercise their claimed authority) in these three areas, rights we can refer to collectively as "the right to rule." And international law confers on all entities that qualify as states legal rights in each area, rights that collectively define states' legal *sovereignty*.

Let me be a bit more specific about the kinds of rights that are claimed by all states and that would have to actually be possessed in order to legitimate the practices of any modern state.[16] The first category of rights that I mentioned—what I called the rights over or against those identified as subjects of the state—defines what is often referred to as the "internal sovereignty" of the state. Thus, states claim the right to be the exclusive imposer and/or enforcer of law on those within their jurisdictions (i.e., on their "subjects"). States also claim the right to command their subjects in less rule-like and more occasional ways. These rights are held against all possible domestic competitors in the realms of legislation, enforcement, and decrees. While such internal sovereignty need not be absolute or unlimited, the finality and exclusivity of the relevant rights is a defining feature of all modern states. States also uniformly claim the right to be obeyed by their subjects and the right to represent their subjects in international affairs.

In the second category of the rights claimed by all modern states—the rights held against aliens or noncitizens—fall the rights that collectively define states' claims to "external sovereignty." States claim, first, the right not to be directly interfered with or usurped by foreign persons, groups, or states in the exercise of their internal sovereignty (i.e., primarily, in their making and enforcing of domestic law)—what are usually called "rights to self-determination" or "autonomy." In addition, states take aliens to be bound to respect what are sometimes called their "federative" rights or power.[17] States claim the right to "do business" in the world—including, where necessary, the business of war—as an acknowledged agent or legal person, as an autonomous, equal corporate entity.

Lastly, the third kind of rights claimed by all states—rights over a particular geographical territory—include rights to control that territory in ways determined to be necessary or important to the state's integrity, security, or prosperity. Thus, for example, states routinely prohibit unencumbered private sales of land to those not subject to its laws, as well as personal or group secession with territorial rights, whether for private or political reasons. States claim the right to control movement across their territorial borders. And they claim rights to control over public resources and to regulation and taxation of privately owned resources within their territories. Some of these territorial claims are held principally or exclusively against the subjects of the state in question, while some are held (or also held) against aliens.

My view is that nothing could count as a state, in the modern sense of that term, without claiming and attempting to exercise at least modest versions of all of these kinds of rights. It follows that a morally legitimate state is one that in fact possesses at the very least moral rights to perform the various functions just described, held against claimed subjects and/or alien persons or groups. As this analysis suggests, both state legitimacy and state sovereignty require the state's possession of a complex set of these three kinds of right. A state is sovereign if it possesses reasonably extensive and exclusive (or highest-order) rights over a citizenry and territory, rights that entitle it to both internal supremacy and external independence. A state is legitimate if it actually possesses the rights to do what it does. Since the rights modern states claim and the authority they try to exercise appear to constitute state sovereignty, discussions of legitimacy and sovereignty will naturally tend to converge.[18]

As we have seen, legitimacy is often ascribed not only to states but also to governments or regimes. This may be partly a function of certain ambiguities in the term *state,* which can be used in ordinary speech to refer not only to a politically organized group of persons but also to the institutions of government that such a political organization utilizes or to the group of persons occupying positions of authority within that institutional structure (or to some combination of these elements). But even absent such ambiguities, we may still wish to ascribe the same right to rule to both states and their governments, particularly if we subscribe to one distinctive and compelling model of the relation between legitimate state and legitimate government. The conceptual model I have in mind is straightforwardly Lockean, and it is a model that I believe is correct in its essentials.

States (or civil societies or peoples or nations), according to this model, are groups of persons who are organized or incorporated for political ends. These incorporated groups, if legitimate, jointly possess the right to rule over the groups' individual members (and within particular territories) because (this aspect of) the right to rule is composed of (i.e., is nothing more than the sum of) the various individual rights transferred to the group by its members. The governments of states, in this model, hold their right to rule ("political power") in trust from the people or state.[19] So in this model, the very same right to rule might be said to have been held both by a legitimate state, as original rightholder and eventual trustor, and by its legitimate government, as its eventual trustee. States will be legitimate or not according to whether or not they satisfy the principle or standard that confers such a right to rule (in Locke's case, the principle of unanimous member consent), and governments of legitimate states will themselves be legitimate if they satisfy the principle of transfer that transmits to them this right to rule (in this case, the principle that requires that governments act in trust for the people).[20] Illegitimate states, according to this view, could not have legitimate governments, never having had in the first place a right to rule that might be entrusted to their governments. Legitimate states may have either legitimate or illegitimate governments, depending on whether the government in question actually possesses in trust the right to rule.

That, we may say, is the Lockean "conceptual framework" for discussing state and governmental legitimacy. As for the substantive Lockean account of (i.e., the Lockean statement of the actual conditions for) state legitimacy, states can acquire rights (in our first category) to control their claimed subjects (within specified limits) only if those subjects have unanimously, personally consented to membership in the state. States have rights (in the second category) to full international agency and autonomy (to nonaggression, to "do business" in the world) where they, first, hold rights over their subjects of our first sort and, second, have respected the rights of nonsubject persons and groups. Right-violating conduct by states diminishes their own rights to noninterference and respect. And, Locke holds, states have (third category) rights to control their claimed territories only where those territories are composed of the prior rightful holdings in land (sea, space?) of their subjects (partial rights over which must be transferred to the society in consenting to membership), along with any rightful acquisitions of land (etc.) by the state (as a collective entity) itself. Territorial "holdings" by subjects will count as "rightful" here only if they

(1) originate in labor on (or continuous productive use of) unowned land, (2) result from (possibly repeated) consensual transfers of property with that origin, or (3) are land not literally "held" by subjects but to which subjects have rights (in non-ideal circumstances) as morally required rectification for past wrongs done to them by others (e.g., theft of land that was rightfully held according to method [1] or [2]).[21]

We saw in Chapter 3 that not only Locke's but all plausible lines of argument for establishing state legitimacy fail to confirm the moral legitimacy of existing states. Our examination there, however, concerned only certain aspects of the question of internal legitimacy—in particular, the state's acquisition of rights (to obedience and to domestic sovereignty) in our first category. The aspect of state legitimacy at issue in our second category of rights—states' rights to autonomy or self-determination—is that of the state's relation to those outside of its claimed domain. Rights held by the state against its own subjects, of course, might not be held as well against nonsubjects. So we will explore this second aspect of state legitimacy separately in the next section. Finally, there is the question of the state's rights over a geographical territory, rights that would have to be held against all persons, both domestic and alien, in order to vindicate actual states' claims and practices with respect to territory. It is these (third category) rights that will concern us in the remainder of the present section. It may, of course, seem at first blush as if there is little to discuss. States just *have* their territories. Even if some boundaries are contested, most are not. But in speaking or thinking thus, we need to remember that we are simply presuming the authority of convention, of international law, of states' *claimed* rights and their exercises of coercive control—none of which is in fact self-justifying. So our question here is "How (if at all) can we explain why and when states' claims to territory, widely accepted or not, are *morally legitimate?*"

The Lockean account of the nature and source of these territorial rights is one answer to that question. And it is an answer that is easily misunderstood. Many critics charge, for instance, that it confuses states' territorial rights with property; and states plainly do not "own" their territories.[22] But Locke's position is not that a state's territorial "jurisdiction" (to use Locke's term) is identical to or even simply composed of the property rights in land that individual subjects previously acquired. Rather, a legitimate state's territorial rights are composed from certain parts (or "incidents") of its subjects' property (along with some of those subjects' personal liberties), the remainders of those complex rights over land staying (as diminished property) in the possession of individual subjects. So legitimate states receive from their consenting subjects (e.g.) the rights to regulate uses of their land, to tax landowners, to control the exterior boundaries of the collected holdings in land, and to prohibit sale of land to nonsubjects. At the same time, subjects retain a variety of rights with respect to their legitimate holdings in land: to use them (in legally permitted ways), to reap the income from them, to alienate them to fellow subjects, to exclude use by others, etc. So the Lockean position is not that state territorial rights constitute property. Rather, it is that the legitimate state's territorial rights and the (moral) property rights of its lawful subjects are both composed from the "full" property rights that individuals can possess outside of political society.

Even defended against such confusions, however, the Lockean account is pretty clearly one that is unlikely to legitimate the claims made by many existing states. Even if one concedes (as most political philosophers do not) that the process of territorial acquisition described by Locke looks morally legitimating, resting on plausible principles of individual property acquisition and transfer, it has to be admitted that nothing even remotely approximating that process can be appealed to with any hope of applying it (except negatively) to the territorial claims made by existing states. Not only, of course, are the bases for Lockean claims to property made by individuals often obscure and entangled, relying on historical facts about property pedigree that may be unrecoverable,[23] but, worse, no existing state makes claims to territorial sovereignty that are even intended to approximate the accumulation of individual rights based in labor or ongoing productive use that Locke imagines. It is hardly news that states' actual claimed territories are often a product of military conquest or seizure, terms of treaties and negotiations completed under duress, the extermination or removal of native inhabitants, expansion to salient or defensible geographical features as boundaries or to incorporate areas rich in resources, and the like. None of this has even the *prima facie* feel of Lockean legitimation.

Despite these obvious difficulties (i.e., of apparently delegitimating many states' territorial claims), however, I think there is something deeply intuitive about the Lockean approach to territoriality. Surely the most obviously unsuspicious of any state's territorial claims are the claims it makes to the land innocently lived on and actively used by those who freely accept their roles as members of the political society in question. And the most unsuspicious demands for changes to be made in the shape of existing state territories are those that are justified by appeal to historical wrongs of (e.g.) theft or conquest (wrongs done to the claimants themselves or to those to whom the claimants are in some way closely related). Where states' claimed territories were simply forcibly annexed, where they were appropriated without ongoing use or improvement, and where rival groups can make competing claims to rights based in labor or use, states' territorial claims look most suspicious morally. All of this is just as the Lockean theory suggests. Saying that much, of course, does not even begin to address the problems implicit in the view. But the account does, at least, specify a plausible starting point and a direction for theory. Rival accounts of the (moral) entitlements of states, I will suggest, seem to offer vastly less since they typically ignore almost altogether the historical dimension of territorial claims, largely conceding not just legal but moral legitimacy to historically wrongful and morally arbitrary territorial claims by states.

Historical accounts of territorial rights, like Locke's, at least attempt to address such issues. Are there alternative historical accounts that would serve us better than Locke's? Much international legal thought about territorial rights is historical in character, but it offers little that might plausibly be taken to help us address the *moral* dimension of territoriality. Of the traditional historical bases for legitimate territorial acquisition recognized in international law—such as accretion, cession, occupation (of *terra nullius*), prescription, conquest—some, like conquest, have been rightly rejected as conferring legitimate territorial rights even in legal terms (just as "cession," almost invariably being in fact "cession under duress," is usually of dubious legal and of no moral interest); others (like occupation) have no (terrestrial) application now and in fact very seldom had real application even in the past (in light of the sticky problem of the claims of native inhabitants); and still others (like acquisitive prescription[24]) are clearly highly suspect as grounds for moral title. Nonhistorical legal appeals to simple geographical factors as a basis for territorial entitlement—factors like contiguity, continuity, or geographical unity—have the look of mere appeals to administrative convenience, rather than attempts to fasten onto morally legitimating principles. Further, of course, the international community tends to treat the territorial claims of old, established states very differently from the claims of newer or would-be states, despite the fact that the same questions about legitimate acquisition seem to apply in both cases. Much doctrine here seems little more than a simple surrender to power, to acceptance of a rule that established power makes legal right. In short, international law largely turns a blind eye to fundamental questions about territorial moral legitimacy, in effect conceding the legitimacy of established states' territorial claims while, as a consequence of setting the bar so low for existing states, setting extremely high the bar for legitimate territorial claims by rival claimants, such as dispossessed native tribes and new would-be states.

Many have found all historical accounts of territorial rights unconvincing as a class, apparently regardless of any intuitive appeal that particular historical accounts (like Locke's) might have. Some of the worries have been purely conservative in nature—that is, they are worries that historical accounts will not vindicate the current legal order of state territories. Since we have already questioned (in Chapter 3) the legitimacy of existing states' claims to obedience (and noncompetition) from their subjects, however, additional concerns about possible illegitimacy—in this case, the possible illegitimacy of those states' claims to territory—should not deflect us here. Other objections to historical accounts of territorial rights focus on claims about their *indeterminacy:* "it is impossible [for historical accounts] to develop an adequate principle . . . to adjudicate . . . rival claims to territory: it depends on where in history one starts, and whose history one accepts."[25] But while such "indeterminacy" will no doubt be a practical problem on many occasions (though surely not on all), this does not appear to be an objection to historical accounts in principle. There is, presumably, always something like a historical "fact of the matter"—it is not literally a matter of choosing between equally sound rival "histories"—even if the facts are not known or recoverable. And even where historical territorial pedigrees are not known, it is reasonable, I think, to *presume* entitlement (in the presence of productive use) where no obvious or claimed wrongs are apparent.

Finally, one might insist that historical claims to territory cannot outweigh claims based on current inhabitation. While historical claims to land may, of course, be made precisely by the land's current occupants, this is often not the case, as when people with historical claims were "unjustly removed from the country." "Do historical ties make a difference?" in such cases, ask Avishai Margalit and Joseph Raz. They answer: "Prescription protects the interests of the current inhabitants . . . on the ground that their case now is as good as that of the wronged people or their descendants."[26] While it certainly seems true that the interests of current inhabitants (i.e., of those who inhabit and labor on land that was unjustly appropriated by others) are morally weighty, it is hard (for me, at least) to believe that those interests are likely to generate strong claims to the (stolen) land itself. If you innocently purchase and come to rely on the use of my stolen bicycle, your interests in the bicycle are morally significant; but they presumably entitle you primarily to compensation (from the thief, not from me). And surely they do not entitle you to simply keep my bicycle (once the theft is revealed), even after a significant passage of time. Legal standards for (positive and negative) prescription undoubtedly serve various social purposes and may even seem morally warranted where the violations that produce prescriptive rights go unprotested for long periods of time. But this is typically not the case with people's historical claims to territory, which are often pressed passionately (and suppressed harshly) for generations. And, in any event, from a moral viewpoint, those whose labor and whose expectations are invested, however innocently, in that to which others have prior title can never, in my view, have a "case [that] now is as good" as those whose labor and expectations established a legitimate claim to the land in the first place.

But suppose we do find such concerns about historical accounts compelling? What would be our theoretical alternative? What would a nonhistorical (but still morally plausible) theory of territorial rights look like? Two related lines of argument seem to have been the most popular among political philosophers. The first we can call the "efficient delivery" argument and the second, the "stewardship" argument. According to the *efficient delivery argument,* states require geographical territories with continuous fixed boundaries in order to efficiently deliver to their subjects the goods that they are both entitled and required to provide. To take the most obvious case, it is extremely difficult to provide for the security of state subjects (particularly from external threats) without establishing a security zone with stable and defensible boundaries. Similarly, many other public goods can be much more efficiently delivered to a fixed territory than to dispersed individuals or to those settled in discontinuous geographical areas. The state's duty to efficiently deliver such goods implies a duty to take as territory the continuous geographical area in which the state's subjects reside. According to the *stewardship argument* (as Rawls states it), "unless a definite agent is given responsibility for maintaining an asset and bears the loss for not doing so, that asset tends to deteriorate." Territories will not continue to support life unless cared for, and politically organized peoples must therefore control and maintain territories. "However arbitrary a society's boundaries may appear from a historical point of view," the need for environmental oversight and population control (etc.) shows that "in the absence of a world-state, there *must* be boundaries of some kind."[27] And, Rawls appears to infer, these might as well be the boundaries that are already widely accepted.

The obvious problem with both of these lines of argument, in my view, is that while they offer reasons why it is a good thing for states to have *some* territory (and why, were there vacant territory, states might do well to or even be obliged to occupy it), they give no reasons at all why states should have any *particular* territories—that is, why we should regard as morally interesting the particular, historically arbitrary boundaries claimed and accepted by existing states. Neither efficient delivery of goods to subjects nor sound stewardship of nature requires that any particular territory be occupied or controlled by any particular state (or group). This problem is, perhaps, only really noticed in cases where there are rival claimants to some portion of the territory in question. Then, of course, different groups (say, an existing state and a dispossessed indigenous people) can claim equally the privilege of (or the need for) stewardship or efficient delivery, differing only on the issue of who should be performing these tasks. But the fact that states' territorial claims seem questionable only on those occasions when they are disputed hardly establishes that at other times they are unquestionable.

If existing states' legally recognized territories are acknowledged to be (at least in some measure) historically unjust or morally arbitrary, why should we simply take for granted their moral legitimacy? Why not assume instead that the moral legitimacy of territorial claims can only be established by testing them against all competing claims that can be advanced on behalf of different states, groups, or persons? While there are no doubt certain (nonhistorical) *utilitarian* moral advantages to a conservative stance on territorial claims—since the "transaction costs" associated with redrawing boundaries may amount to a significant social disutility—a seriously utilitarian approach to territorial rights would almost certainly imply (and far more counterintuitively) constantly shifting national boundaries, with boundaries tracking significant shifts in national and group needs and interests (as a result of, e.g., population increases or decreases, crop failures, natural disasters, depletion of resources, etc.).[28]

The need in political and legal philosophy for a viable moral account of territorial rights seems to me to have been largely ignored by contemporary theorists, who choose their theoretical starting points as if the account of the territorial rights of states is expected simply to fall out at the end, as a trivial consequence of the rest. But this is a dangerous assumption. We may begin our theory, if we like, by examining the conditions under which states or governments can justifiably claim authority over or the right to coerce or control a set of subjects. But states and governments must do their controlling *somewhere* in particular. No matter how just or authoritative a state or government, it plainly may not simply extend its territorial jurisdiction to cover whatever land (or sea or space) it names. Similarly, it is fine to begin by specifying the conditions under which a nation or a people has the right to self-determination (see section 6.3). But the people must have a place in which to be self-determining, and one place is quite clearly *not* as good as another. A genuinely moral theory of political legitimacy cannot leave its theory of territorial rights as an afterthought or simply concede the legitimacy of territory acquired and defended, for however long, by states' naked employment of force or deception. In the contemporary world of sovereign territorial states—a world in which existing states claim, individually or collectively, all of the world's useable spaces—new states face very serious challenges in establishing legitimate claims to territories of their own, territories that they need in order to function as viable equals.[29] Groups or peoples that attempt to break off from existing states must establish, in the face of a deep conservatism among the community of nations, claims to the territory they intend to occupy that are superior to the prior claims of existing states (and to those of any new rivals for statehood).

The Lockean theory I espouse suggests that we address the question of a group's legitimate claims to control over a specific territory by examining the complex issues concerning the claims to the land of those persons who are or have been the principal rightful users of it. A group can defend its claim to the territory by showing that its members' claims as users of the land are superior to those of others (and that these members are not also members in some other political society that makes competing claims to that same territory). I do not pretend that these standards will render simple any complicated or contested questions about territorial claims; indeed, they will not render simple the confirmation of even routine territorial claims by established states, given the bloody and complicated histories of most states' territorial acquisitions. But these Lockean standards both focus our attention on intuitively relevant moral questions about territory and avoid the trap of supposing that answers to complex questions about territory will trivially fall out of (or are strictly subsidiary to) answers to quite different kinds of questions.

6.3. Self-Determination and Secession

Suppose, however, that we come at these questions about states' territorial rights from a slightly different angle. States need (relatively stable) geographical territories, both for efficient delivery of the goods they owe their subjects (delivery of some of which being what qualifies them as states) and because other states will inevitably incorporate any vacant useable lands, leaving nowhere for a state without territory to function. There were once functioning migratory groups with quasi-political structures, but that was before modern states took as their territories all of the habitable earth—and even then, migratory groups typically needed to claim at least seasonal rights of control over traditional hunting or gathering grounds and agricultural land. So states need territories in order to function *as* states. But if, then, some group has a right to be or to become a state, does it not follow that it also has a right to a territory?

This kind of line on state territoriality has been taken by some of those who approach these difficult questions by articulating the conditions for groups (nations, peoples) to possess rights of self-determination or autonomy (our second category of the rights claimed and exercised by all legitimate states). Simplifying considerably, political philosophers have tended to select one of three kinds of (nonstate) groups as the sort that enjoys a right of political self-determination: (1) groups with certain cultural (or cultural/political) characteristics, (2) groups that face or that have suffered serious injustices, or (3) groups that choose to be (and are capable of being) politically autonomous. Not coincidentally, these three approaches to collective rights of political self-determination correspond to the three main categories of theories of justified secession that have been advanced; for if a group has (by virtue of its identifying features) a right to be politically self-determining, it possesses this right even if it is incorporated within a broader political society, from which it might wish to distance or separate itself. So secession can be seen as one possible way in which a group might exercise its right to self-determination.[30]

Consider, then, the first kind of group that might be entitled to autonomy (and entitled to secede from a larger political society). People's ethnic and cultural affiliations are undoubtedly (often) extremely important to their self-conceptions, and the well-being of their groups can (often) be integral to their own well-being and self-respect. These facts, by themselves, might seem to say something about the moral attributes of ethnic or cultural groups. But when the group in question is territorial and political—in the sense that it lives in a territory to which it is particularly attached (perhaps a traditional "homeland") and aspires to political organization and political control over that territory—its character seems particularly relevant to the political philosopher's concerns. Territorial, political groups of this sort that share a common culture are what many theorists have in mind when they speak of *nations*.[31] And the first of the three identified positions is precisely (in its most common form) that nations possess a moral right to be self-determining in some way[32] (which may, under certain conditions, amount to a right to unilaterally secede and pursue full independence and sovereignty).

Consider next those groups that have suffered serious injustices. Such groups may, of course, also count as "nations" (or as other kinds of ethnic or cultural groups). But groups certainly need not so qualify in order to have been collectively wronged, and their having been unjustly treated seems to be a possible ground of group rights to political self-determination that is quite independent of their other group characteristics. In this case, however, the group rights will be "remedial rights," rights to protection from ongoing and/or rectification of past unjust treatment. Allen Buchanan, the best-known recent defender of a "remedial rights only" theory of secession, discusses a variety of possible wrongs that might (given the satisfaction of certain further conditions) justify secession; but he emphasizes three kinds of circumstances in particular: (1) where secession remedies a prior unjust appropriation of a group's territories (as is often accomplished by unjust incorporation of the group into a larger polity),

(2) where secession is necessary for a group to defend itself against the threat of destruction by an unjust aggressor, and (3) where secession is necessary for the group to escape "discriminatory redistribution" (by which Buchanan means economic policies designed to systematically disadvantage the group).[33]

Finally, remember that there is another characteristic a group can possess, again in no way necessarily related to its ethnic or cultural character, that also seems relevant to rights of self-determination—namely, that group's wanting to be and having chosen to be self-determining. Individual persons, after all, seem to have moral rights to govern their own lives (within the constraints of morality) and to innocently associate with others. Why, then, should groups of like-minded persons (with aspirations to and capabilities for territorial political organization) not be thought to have a moral right of self-determination, quite independent of any further qualities these groups might possess? While it would, of course, be highly unusual for a group (of sufficient size to be politically viable) to be unanimous about such matters, a group *vote* would seem to be a natural and democratic solution to determining the group's orientation, as well as being a solution that accords with the (liberal) values of autonomy and equal respect that motivate the ascriptions of individual rights in the first place.[34]

Each of these accounts of collective rights of self-determination (and possible rights of secession) faces special problems of its own. But I want to concentrate here on the weaknesses that these accounts share as a group, on the ways in which they are questionable on common grounds. I will not argue, as "cosmopolitan" theorists like Charles Beitz do, that the very idea of collective rights of political self-determination rests on a false analogy between individuals and politically organized groups.[35] Consider, instead, the following shared problems. First, each of the accounts will, I think, have great difficulty defending the idea that rights of political self-determination are possessed *only* by the kind of (nonstate) group on which they focus. Even, for instance, if we agree with "national self-determination" theories (our first kind of account) that nations often have rights of self-determination, it is unclear why national groups are the only groups so privileged. Many groups not having the characteristics of nations seem to have interests in self-determination that are just as compelling as those of nations. And unless nations are believed to be mystically empowered (a view not entirely alien to nationalist traditions of thought), it surely seems crucially relevant to any defense of a right of self-determination for nations that their members share a desire (and a capability) to function as an independent (or otherwise autonomous or semiautonomous) political unit—which is, of course, what "choice" theories of self-determination emphasize, in lieu of any focus on nationality.

While nations might be especially likely to function well as political units—sharing as they do a history, culture, and associated territory and members being likely to be motivated by such ties to undertake the sacrifices political life requires—and while the political expression of national character may sometimes be important to members' sense of self-worth, such facts (if facts they are) seem relatively uninteresting in an argument for rights of self-determination if members do not actually desire and/or choose to be politically self-determining. In short, it is difficult to see why a group's possessing national characteristics should be thought to be more important to grounding rights of self-determination than is the group's desire or choice to be self-determining. Very similar concerns can be raised, I think, about "remedial rights only" theories (our second kind of account). Once again, while injustice toward a group might be thought to (under certain conditions) entitle it to be politically self-determining, it would again be hard to argue that injustice without a group desire for autonomous political status was somehow a *better* ground for a right to self-determination than would be a group desire without prior injustice. Only an extremely (and unreasonably) conservative stance with regard to the sanctity of the existing (historically arbitrary) order of states could seem likely to motivate so strong a position.

It is, however, other features these three kinds of theories share that seem to me to provide material for the most damaging kinds of objections to their common strategy of trying to defend group rights to political self-determination. Each theory must, of course, determine whether the group rights it espouses are new, "freestanding" rights, distinct from those possessed by the group's members, or only rights that are a collection or sum of (i.e., analyzable without loss into) the individual rights possessed (presently or formerly) by group members. The first option, I think, is one about which we should be deeply skeptical in the case of non-voluntary groups, for these routinely lack any of the unity and structure that characterize other obvious rightholders (like individuals or voluntary, incorporated associations). Yet it is precisely these kinds of nonvoluntary groups that are claimed to be rightholders by the "national self-determination" and "remedial rights" theories. If, however, these theories retreat to the view that group rights of self-determination are really just collections of individual members' rights, their problems are not less severe.

Defenders of each of the three theories (rightly) insist that the groups to which they ascribe rights of political self-determination must have some territorial dimension. This is what Buchanan (in discussing justifications for secession) calls "the territorial thesis": "every sound justification for secession must include a valid claim to territory."[36] Without a territorial dimension, a group would have nowhere to be politically self-determining.

But no group with a territorial dimension has ever been or could possibly hope to be perfectly homogenous. Territories will inevitably contain either nongroup members—in the case of nonvoluntary groups (e.g., national or ethnic groups or groups that have been unjustly treated)—or dissenters, who have different ambitions (desires, choices) for the territory than do most fellow group members. What then justifies the assertion that such nonhomogenous territorial groups nonetheless possess homogenous, over-arching (collective) political rights?

Defenders of all three accounts seem to appeal simply to the fact that majorities (or vast majorities) in the territories share a nationality, share a history as victims of injustice, or share the desire or choice of politi-cal autonomy. But we saw (in Chapter 5, section 5.3) that majorities are not naturally authoritative. Majorities may rightfully impose their wills on minorities only where authorized (by all involved) to do so or where they otherwise possess legitimate authority to do so. But theories about group rights of political self-determination are supposed to be theories that *explain* how groups can rightfully possess legitimate authority over a population in a territory. Such theories can hardly just *assume* the author-ity of a population's majority in explaining how that majority comes to have authority to dictate to all persons in a territory.[37] What, after all, has become of the individual rights (to self-determination) of nongroup mem-bers in the relevant territories? While those members—if they themselves constitute another separate nation, unjustly treated group, or group united by choice—might have yet another (minority) right to political self-determination, this would be true only in the highly unlikely case that they are also relatively homogenous and territorially concentrated. Short of that remedy, the minority would simply be subjected without moral warrant to the will of the greater number.

In the absence of unanimity (or unanimous group membership) within a territory, then, the case for group rights of self-determination (including rights of control over that territory and its population) seems startlingly weak. In the presence of unanimity, however, we have simply arrived back at the Lockean ideal of a unanimous, consensual political association. Rights of political self-determination for such an association are (rela-tively) unproblematic, being just the consensually conveyed collection of (certain aspects of) members' individual rights of self-determination. Majorities rule in such associations by unanimous consent to the ar-rangement.[38] Even the Lockean ideal, of course, has trouble with the presence in any remotely realistic polity of children and incompetents (whose interests are directly affected by the choices of the consenters) and subsequent generations of already situated persons. But, of course, there *are* no unanimous consensual political associations in the actual world of states. If existing political societies are illegitimate (as this, along with our previous argument, suggests)—lacking not only rights to obedience but also rights to control territories and rights to self-determination—and if nonstate groups similarly lack freestanding group rights of self-determination, then issues like the justifiability of secession must be treated simply in terms of the rights of individual persons. We must ask what choices persons (and groups of persons) are entitled to make, in light of the effects those choices will have on other persons who are equally entitled to individual autonomy.

Suppose, however, that you are unpersuaded by these objections, that you find compelling one or another theory's case for group rights of political self-determination. Recall that all three theories require of groups that they have territorial "connections" in order to have such rights. But do these "connections" obviously imply that the groups have moral *rights* over those territories, rights of the sort that they must possess in order to actually be legitimately self-determining? Defenders of all three accounts tend to refer vaguely to groups "having" a territory, to their being attached to a historical homeland, to their being concentrated in a territory. But none of this sounds much like argument for the existence of territorial (moral) rights. It sounds more like simple acceptance of the historically and morally arbitrary location of existing groups. In some cases, of course, "having" or "being attached to" a territory does look morally important: those who have had land (to which they were entitled) stolen from them (a "remedial rights" case) do look entitled to control over it; those whose historic homeland is territory on which they and their ancestors have lived and labored, without displacing others (a "national self-determination" case), do look entitled to control over it. But territorially concentrated groups can plainly be nations, have been unjustly treated, or have chosen political autonomy without having anything even remotely like such plausible-looking moral cases for control over "their" territories.

Groups, of course, need territories in order to function as states (or even as partially autonomous political entities). Again, however, it is unclear how showing that a group with political aspirations needs to have a territory—or even that a group needs a separate territory in order to survive as a group—demonstrates the existence of that group's right over any particular geographical region, in the absence of something more (typically, some historical relationship) that shows a morally significant connection of that group to precisely that territory. Showing such a particular connection requires an appeal to principles that are quite different from those that might seem to demonstrate the group's right to be independent (or to be independent of the states that claim authority over them). That these are widely regarded as separate moral questions is plain from the many real-world examples in which there is wide agreement about a group's right to be self-governing but no agreement at all about precisely where it is acceptable for it to do so. The claims of groups to particular territories within which to govern themselves will, again, look most defensible precisely where those claims conform to the requirements of the Lockean theory of state territorial rights that we sketched in section 6.2.

6.4. Intervention and Assistance

Unless we cling irrationally to the antiquated notion that every state's sovereignty is absolute, we must accept at the very least that any rights of political self-determination are limited or qualified in various ways. Even if (some) states, nations, or groups do possess moral rights to autonomously structure and pursue a political existence, there are plainly many things they may not do under this banner. They may not aggress against or otherwise ignore their responsibilities to those outside their political society. And they may not directly abuse or unnecessarily allow to suffer great deprivation their own members. This immediately suggests, of course, at least two kinds of limits to state autonomy (beyond the obvious limit on external aggression). Alien states or persons may be entitled (or required) under certain conditions to directly intervene in the purely domestic affairs of sovereign states (with these states being correlatively morally bound to permit such intervention). And states may be morally required to assist in various ways (from a distance) other states or groups or persons and so may not "autonomously" choose not to do so.

While there is not space here for a systematic treatment of either of these limits on states' sovereignty, I will concentrate my few remarks on the second limit—that set by duties of assistance—and offer (first) only a couple of organizing ideas about the limits set by rights and duties of (or with respect to) intervention. The idea of "intervention" is far from a clear one, despite the fact that many international legal documents (various charters [e.g., of the Organization of American States and, arguably, of the Uunited Nations] and declarations [e.g., the United Nations' *Declaration on Principles of International Law*]) seem to blithely prohibit any kind of intervention for any kind of reason in the "affairs" of any state. Intervention, properly understood, is a relatively discrete action or short-term policy (unlike, say, occupation or annexation); and it occurs without the full consent of at least some of the interested parties whose "affairs" are affected (unlike, say, unanimously and sincerely requested assistance).[39] Interventions, properly so-called, could involve the threat of military force (either with or without territorial encroachment) or its actual use; they could involve nonmilitary territorial encroachments; or they could involve less dramatic, typically economic, threats or actions (e.g., sanctions)—all in order to induce other states to change their (domestic or international) conduct or policies or to in some way address humanitarian crises that would otherwise go unaddressed. Theorists have sometimes contrasted "armed" intervention with "humanitarian" intervention; but given that territorial encroachments can occur without the use of arms and that armed force is sometimes necessary in order to accomplish humanitarian ends, it is not clear that such a distinction aids conceptual clarity.

The moral justifications for intervention in the "affairs" of sovereign states seem clearest when intervention is necessary to counter serious (domestic or international) aggression or to alleviate (what all would regard as) serious suffering. The case of aggression is perhaps the easier of the two, and I will not discuss it further here. "Serious suffering" may itself, of course, be a result of deliberately aggressive (or at least culpably negligent) treatment of subjects by their own governments. In such cases, mere humanitarian aid (from a distance) to states whose subjects are in dire need may be insufficient to address the crisis, and aid may be either resisted or (incompetently or corruptly) misused by the governments of those states. Direct intervention may then be permissible to avert disaster. Indeed, intervention may in such cases be obligatory, highlighting a clear limit on both states' rights of self-determination (if any). Even in clear cases of justified intervention, however, it is presumably defensible only if it is a last (or, at least, nothing like a first) resort, if it has reasonable prospects for success, if the means used in intervening are proportionate to (or otherwise appropriate for) both the seriousness of the cause and the nature of the objectives, etc. Intervention may also plainly sometimes be warranted in order to counterbalance prior, unwarranted interventions by others and thus to reestablish a morally preferable *status quo ante.* Interventions of the above sorts seem both the ones that are easiest to justify morally and the ones that an international legal system could embrace as justified with the fewest adverse consequences.

Harder cases (for both morality and law)—from the list of purported justifications often offered by actual states for intervening in the affairs of others—are those that involve preemption or paternalism. Extraordinary interventions have regularly in political history been rationalized in terms of "preempting aggression" by other states—rarely, it seems, with adequate warrant. While it is, of course, possible for a state to have information that allows it to be virtually certain that unjustified military (or economic) aggression will occur absent intervention to prevent it, actual interventions for preemptive purposes are almost never based on such information, routinely being either supported by inconclusive or speculative

vidence or undertaken with an exaggerated sense of the justifying scope
of "considerations of national security." That said, well-grounded preemp-
ive intervention does seem at least in principle morally justifiable: we
need not wait until the sword descends to defend ourselves or others. It
is probably harder to imagine circumstances in which a state could jus-
ify paternalistic intervention—that is, intervention aimed at preventing
great loss or harm that is not so regarded by those who would "suffer"
it. Perhaps this is because such justifications were regularly in the past
employed as thinly veiled rationalizations for colonial exploitation. But,
again, there seems to be no reason in principle why intervention to prevent
what all knowledgeable persons would agree was a great harm could not
be morally justified, even where those who would suffer that harm could
not be brought to see it as such. In contrast to the cases mentioned above,
however, it seems that an international legal system probably should not
accept preemptive or paternalistic justifications for intervention, in light of
the obvious temptations for abuse that such acceptance would present.

Consider now those cases in which intervention, properly so-called, cannot be justified but in which preventable but serious suffering or dire need
still exists in some of the world's nations. Suppose, for instance, that there
are significant disparities in wealth between the various sovereign states in
the world and that the serious suffering of people in poorer nations could
(in at least many cases) be significantly alleviated by assistance (from a
distance) from the wealthier, without any intervention and without unacceptable hardships for the subjects of wealthy nations. Something like this
is surely true of our actual world of states. What do such facts imply about
the obligations of wealthy nations (and the corresponding limits on their
rights to political autonomy)? It is perhaps natural to once again attempt
to illuminate the positive duties of states by first describing the positive
duties of individual persons. Individual persons, it seems, may have positive moral duties of three sorts (beyond those that they undertake voluntarily or acquire by accidentally harming or deliberately wronging others):
duties of *rescue,* owed to those they confront in occasional "emergency
situations" of dire need; duties of *charity,* to do their part in the ongoing
project of keeping the (local or worldwide) needy above some threshold of
well-being (or access to resources); and duties of *justice,* to do their part in
creating and maintaining a just state of affairs (locally or globally).

The relation between such individual positive duties and the positive
duties of states, of course, is not immediately clear. Were real states Lockean voluntary associations, states' positive duties to alien states, groups,
or persons would be a simple function of the terms of the association.
Members of such associations could, perhaps, continue to discharge their
positive duties individually, leaving their states free of any positive duties

to aliens. Or they might choose to (or, were individual action insufficien to discharge the duties, be required to) authorize and obligate their state (or some other organizing agency) to act in their steads so as to discharge their collected individual duties *en masse*.

But real states are not such associations, and no terms have been consen sually established to distribute individuals' and states' responsibilities fo discharging positive moral duties. Actual states must instead be though of simply as institutional entities that are often capable of exercising grea power and controlling great resources and whose actions and policies are the shared responsibility of those individuals or groups in positions o realistic control over them. To the extent that states' actions and policies do not (and cannot be brought to) fully discharge the collected positive duties of their subjects, those subjects must attempt to discharge their du ties individually (or collectively but nonpolitically). *De facto* political so cieties, in my view, owe to aliens what their collected subjects owe; and those subjects may discharge their duties in any way they can, including insuring that their governments discharge them or excluding governmen responsibility altogether by discharging them privately. The government of societies (conceived of as institutional structures) owe nothing to alien simply by virtue of being governments; what their policies should be de pends on exactly what their subjects are prepared to do themselves. O course, to the extent that those who control governmental policy allow the polity to coercively collect resources from subjects for the purpose o discharging positive duties to aliens, they are responsible for insuring tha that is how the resources are used. And government officials, like all per sons, may be entitled to require that their subjects (or others) in some way discharge the positive duties they owe to others. But in the end, it seems there is nothing like one simple answer to the question of what the policies of *de facto* governments should be regarding positive duties to aliens. Po litical solutions to need abroad are only one possible kind of solution; and the solution employed is the responsibility of the individuals who owe the duties (and the persons, if any, who coercively manipulate the parameter of feasible individual [and other nonpolitical] choice).

The discussion of positive political duties by political philosopher has not, by and large, been conducted in precisely these terms. Rathe (unsurprisingly), the discussion has mostly concerned the possible impli cations of theories of domestic justice for issues of international justice Of course, as we have seen, among the possible positive moral duties o individuals are duties to help create and support just arrangements. If in dividuals have such moral duties of justice—and if justice has an inter national dimension—then individuals' responsibilities toward aliens car be (at least in part) specified by determining what justice requires and what part individuals can (and must) play in helping to bring about and maintain a just world order. According to some of the theories of justice that we examined in Chapter 4, of course, the precise implications for any society's positive duties to aliens will depend on the society and the aliens in question. Meritarians will presumably let such duties be determined by the requirements of rewarding merit abroad, while for communitarians the content of international duties may depend on the historical traditions of the particular community being considered. Libertarians will mostly deny altogether the existence of the kinds of positive moral duties we have been discussing. But the dominant theory of justice in contemporary political philosophy might seem to have quite straightforward implications for a theory of states' positive duties to aliens.

The liberal egalitarian theory of justice defended by John Rawls, remember, had as one of its foundational assumptions the moral arbitrariness of persons' genetic and social starting places in life. But if our unchosen, unearned social positions within our domestic societies count as morally arbitrary (and if inequalities in benefits or burdens distributed according to these social positions count as unjust), then surely our *global* starting places—that is, our locations in the political societies within which we are born or find ourselves without real choice—are arbitrary as well. And justice would seem to require that we not be burdened or benefited unequally by political institutions simply because of the countries in which we "land." Fulfilling that requirement of justice, of course, would necessitate the creation of domestic and international institutional structures designed to eliminate inequalities in the distribution of primary social goods not only within but also between citizens of wealthy and poor nations (perhaps, following the logic of Rawls' difference principle, framing these structures to encourage only those inequalities between persons anywhere that can reasonably be expected to work to the benefit of everyone everywhere).

Or we could reason to the same egalitarian international conclusion from different aspects of Rawls' position. Societies' basic structures are the subject of principles of justice, in the Rawlsian view, at least in part because of the unavoidable and pervasive influences that these institutional structures exert over our life prospects. While social life is, of course, rife with influences, those of our "private" and "associational" lives are neither so enduring nor so unavoidable. Consequently, they need not be regulated by principles of justice in the way that the basic structure of society must be. If we consider the international condition, however, we can see that the life prospects of persons in every nation are deeply influenced by an international politicoeconomic "basic structure," analogous to the basic structures of domestic societies.[40] If this is true, though, then the world of states should be correspondingly regulated, in the name of justice, by principles analogous to those that justice requires for domestic basic structures.[41] Such a position is usually referred to as "cosmopolitan,"[42] for it accords vastly less moral significance to the existence of national boundaries than do alternative views of international positive duties.

None of this, however, is what Rawls himself concluded about states' (or peoples'[43]) duties of justice toward aliens. Rawls said very little about international matters in *A Theory of Justice*. But in *The Law of Peoples* he explicitly argued against the cosmopolitan view and in favor of a more modest duty of international assistance. One of the eight principles that "constitute the basic charter of the Law of Peoples" defines this duty: "Peoples have a duty to assist other peoples living under unfavorable conditions that prevent their having a just or decent political and social regime."[44] This duty does not have as its "target" equality of wealth or resources among peoples (or persons); rather, it aims only at eliminating those "burdens" that stand in the way of societies managing "their own affairs reasonably and rationally."[45] This more limited goal can be accomplished without making burdened societies even moderately wealthy, and it certainly does not require anything like equality of wealth between societies. Indeed, the duty of assistance looks much more like a duty on peoples to maintain a very modest "safety net" for all societies than it does like a global version of the difference principle. Rawls' position thus seems to involve "a division of moral labor between the domestic and international levels: state-level societies have the primary responsibility for the well-being of their people while the international community serves to establish and maintain background conditions in which just domestic societies can develop and flourish."[46]

While some may find Rawls' modest duty of assistance more palatable than a global difference principle, it remains difficult to understand why Rawls himself opts for the former. His arguments against the purported egalitarian, "cosmopolitan" international implications of his theory of justice seem to rest partly on empirical views that are at least questionable (including his downplaying of the importance of resources and wealth to "well-ordering" a society). More important, however, his case for the modest duty of assistance appears to involve claims that simply conflict with those to which Rawls seems committed in his reasoning about domestic justice. For example, Rawls supports the nonegalitarian duty by comparing it to the duty of "just savings" for future generations in domestic societies, arguing that this latter duty does not require insuring anything like access to equal shares of primary goods for future persons[47]—this despite the fact that generational "location" is about as perfectly morally arbitrary a feature of our "starting places" in a society as anything could be.

Rawls also tries to muster intuitive support for his view by appealing to two cases—each involving societies making different choices (with regard to industrialization and population control) that result in very unequal levels of societal wealth[48]—that look disturbingly like the kinds of cases that Nozick used to try to convince us to reject Rawls' domestic egalitarianism. If states are all responsible for their own inequality-producing choices, why (Nozick would ask) are individuals not similarly responsible in domestic cases? Why insist that justice requires society to (in effect) nullify such effects of individual choices with a fair background structure of re-equalizing institutions (i.e. institutions framed to conform to the difference principle) if one is not prepared to insist similarly that fairness and justice require international institutions to nullify the inequality-producing choices of societies? And, in any event, the supposedly clear cases of morally acceptable societal "choice" (and consequent inequality) can do little to help Rawls' case. At least when individuals make inequality-producing choices, they are (at least sometimes) the only ones who suffer or benefit from those choices. Societal choices by contrast, virtually never reflect the desires or priorities of all persons in those societies. And even were such choices miraculously unanimous, their effects would still fall heavily on others since they affect equally (and in many cases far more profoundly) the life prospects of later generations in that society, who made no choice at all. In the end, Rawls' position on states' (or peoples') positive duties to aliens looks (to me at least) as if it is motivated more than anything else by a rather constricted view of the virtue of justice as only a condition for the achievement of domestic political legitimacy. A more expansive concept of justice, suggested but never fleshed out in *A Theory of Justice,* seems to have been left behind by *The Law of Peoples.*

We should not, of course, allow this brief focus on issues of international distributive justice to cause us to forget that states or societies may owe further or different positive moral duties to aliens. Even if there are no international duties of justice *per se,* states (and/or their members) might (and do, in my view) still owe to aliens moral duties of rescue or charity—moral duties to assist (without intervention) alien persons, groups, or states in emergency situations or to help to maintain some acceptable minimum level of well-being (or resource access) in the world. Indeed, even if there are international duties of *justice* that are analogous to those in domestic society—and even if we employ genuinely Rawlsian reasoning to derive them—we might still reject the strongly egalitarian conclusions about international justice favored by cosmopolitan liberals. We might defend instead only the requirement of a more modest egalitarian "social minimum" for all people of the world, based on our suggestions (in Chapter 4, section 4.3) that no more than such a minimum can in fact be derived from the Rawlsian justificatory apparatus even in the domestic case. Rawls himself, as we have just seen, actually comes down closer to this social minimum view in the international case than he does to any more strongly egalitarian position.

Further, merely redistributing wealth or resources alone might not suffice to discharge all of our positive duties, even leaving aside possible duties of intervention abroad. It is easy to see, for instance, how liberal egalitarian reasoning might be thought to have quite radical implications for states' immigration policies (and thus for the moral status of national boundaries, setting further limits to states' rights of self-determination). If cosmopolitan egalitarians are right, national boundaries have nothing like the significance that they have traditionally been accorded in ordinary political thought (or in international law). Our national starting point is a perfectly arbitrary determinant of our life prospects. Indeed, sanctifying national boundaries is in large measure responsible for the unjust insulation of wealthy societies from their global responsibilities. Similarly, if the Lockean standards for territorial legitimacy (sketched in section 6.2) are correct, existing states cannot justifiably claim the kinds of control over land and resources on which they routinely insist. So again, the moral significance of existing national boundaries is sharply diminished (relative to ordinary understandings of their importance). States may be obligated to acknowledge this fact not only by sharing "their" wealth (etc.) with the people of poorer societies, but also by liberalizing immigration policies in order to give more nonmembers direct access to land and resources.

Even if all of that is accepted, however, it does not imply that historically and morally arbitrary national boundaries have no role at all to play in our thinking about how it is best for states and their subjects to act. The (relatively) familiar cosmopolitan call for "open borders" can still be resisted in a variety of ways. While states may not justifiably close their borders (and disallow or limit immigration from poorer societies) simply to preserve societal "purity," resist multinationality, or maximize societal wealth, there are other reasons why even illegitimate states with morally arbitrary boundaries may be justified in restricting immigration. First, and most obviously, it may be best, from an impartial perspective, that prosperous and otherwise attractive territories not be overwhelmed and destroyed by the massive immigration that opening their borders would bring about.[49] If the governments of illegitimate states are the only agents with the actual power to prevent such harms, they (or the people who empower them) may be responsible for regulating immigration in ways that produce a more gradual and less destructive sharing of prosperity. But second, even if actual states are not in fact entitled to all of the control over "their" territories that they claim, they may be entitled to control over some portions of their claimed territories. Further, individual subjects may have legitimate property rights in portions of states' territories, and groups of subjects may have collective rights to control in certain ways the benefits that flow from economic and political structures that they (or their ancestors) have created—all of which might limit in various ways the access to territory that could justifiably be made available to immigrants. Even, then, if we agree with cosmopolitans or Lockeans about the moral status of existing national boundaries, the consequences of this agreement, while perhaps dramatic, may not be so earth-shaking as they might at first appear to be.

Suggested Reading

Charles Beitz, *Political Theory and International Relations* (Princeton: Princeton University Press, 1979).

Allen Buchanan, *Justice, Legitimacy, and Self-Determination* (Oxford: Oxford University Press, 2004).

Allen Buchanan and Margaret Moore, eds., *States, Nations, and Borders* (Cambridge: Cambridge University Press, 2003).

Will Kymlicka, *Liberalism, Community, and Culture* (Oxford: Oxford University Press, 1989).

John Rawls, *The Law of Peoples* (Cambridge, MA: Harvard University Press, 1999).

Christopher Wellman, *A Theory of Secession* (Cambridge: Cambridge University Press, 2005).

Notes

Chapter 1

1. The syllogistic model is, of course, just the simplest of the models that make the principles of political philosophy a deductive consequence of the principles of some more comprehensive moral theory. I focus on the simple model only for clarity's sake.

2. This is roughly the view made popular by John Rawls, who holds (in *Political Liberalism* [New York: Columbia University Press, 1983]) that the principles of political philosophy should be derivable independently of the content of any comprehensive moral theory (the substance of which would be, in Rawls' view, too controversial among reasonable people to serve as the basis for a shared, public political philosophy).

3. Alternatively, we could follow Nagel, according to whom moral philosophy itself consists of both partial and impartial principles, with the derived political philosophy simply reflecting this divide (Thomas Nagel, *Equality and Partiality* [New York: Oxford University Press, 1991], esp. Ch. 2).

4. I will later in this chapter refer indirectly to a third much-discussed (but murkier and more controversial) division in moral philosophy—namely, that between *normative* ethics and *meta-ethics*. As this distinction is traditionally presented, normative ethics consists of first-order moral theories about what makes acts right (or character traits virtuous), along with the substantive claims (about specific duties, virtues, rights, etc.) entailed by those theories. Meta-ethics consists of second-order theories about what (if anything) moral terms mean, what we are doing when we make moral judgments, how (if at all) we could know such judgments to be true or to be reporting facts, etc.

5. Where *goodness* is defined independent of *rightness*.

6. Philosophers, of course, differ on the proper reading of Aristotle's moral theory; I mean here only to use his theory as one possible example of a *pluralistic* consequentialist theory—that is, a theory that accepts more than one basic value to be promoted by right action or virtue. A better but less familiar example of a pluralistic consequentialism might be G. E. Moore's "ideal utilitarianism." Deontological theories may also be pluralistic, by embracing multiple, non-reducible moral rules or principles, rather than defending only rules which can be derived from some common, more basic rule. Finally, moral theories can be pluralistic by incorporating both consequentialist and deontological features within a single theory—as many of the moral intuitionists attempted to do.

7. This aspect of my account needs qualification. A group could certainly have all the familiar marks of a society without lasting beyond a single generation. Imagine, for instance, a group (that we would otherwise be prepared to call a "society") that was destroyed in its first generation by disease, conquest, or natural disaster. In such cases, we might want to call a group a "society" by virtue of its multigenerational "aim" or orientation. We can, of course, also easily imagine a well-ordered group, with all the trappings of a society, that was *intended* to endure for only a single generation (or even only for a short time)—and so that failed to qualify as a "society" in my account. Since the moral and prudential problems facing such a group would, I believe, be quite different from those facing enduring societies, I would prefer to leave such marginal cases of "societies" to one side for separate study. In the case of a "politicized" group of this kind, we could reserve for it a term such as *political association*.

8. Margaret Gilbert's account of "social groups" (in Ch. 4 of *On Social Facts* [Princeton: Princeton University Press, 1989]) defends a stronger condition of this sort than the one I have in mind. She argues that members of a social group must think of themselves as constituting a "unity." I think it is sufficient that members of a society regard themselves as mutually subject to the society's norms of cooperation.

9. "A society is a more or less self-sufficient association of persons who in their relations to one another recognize certain rules of conduct as binding and who for the most part act in accordance with them." (John Rawls, *A Theory of Justice*, rev. ed. [Cambridge, MA: Harvard University Press, 1999], 4). For a far more complex and sophisticated—but basically similar—analysis of the concept of a society, see David Copp, *Morality, Normativity, and Society* (New York: Oxford University Press, 1995). Of the characteristics of societies that Copp identifies (pp. 127–28, 142), I disagree only with the idea that membership in a society cannot be a matter of choice. While typical societies are not, of course, voluntary, the idea of a voluntary society seems perfectly coherent.

10. By "subject" I mean here only "one who is held by government to be subject to the law." I suggest that a government's function can be either to make or to interpret law (or both) because some institutions of government have had as their function not the creation but only the authoritative interpretation of preexisting "natural law," divine law, church law, conventional law, common law, or historical law (etc.).

11. See Gregory Kavka, *Hobbesian Moral and Political Theory* (Princeton: Princeton University Press, 1986), 158.

12. Locke, for instance, famously argued that a society governed in a way that was genuinely arbitrary could not count as a political (or "civil") society at all (nor could its "authorities" count as a government). Rather, such societies count as being in a state of war with their "governors," which is for Locke a paradigmatically nonpolitical condition.

13. For a discussion of utopianism in political philosophy, see Nagel, *Equality and Partiality*, Ch. 3.

14. See Catherine Mackinnon, *Toward a Feminist Theory of the State* (Cambridge, MA: Harvard University Press, 1989), x. Mackinnon maintains that "the state is male in the feminist sense" (p. 16).

15. Because political philosophy is a branch of moral philosophy, all of the forms of moral skepticism, of course, will generate parallel forms of meta-philosophical skepticism about the conclusions of political philosophy. So, for instance, the truth of emotivism in moral philosophy would entail that evaluative judgments in political philosophy are mere expressions of emotion without truth-values, the truth of cultural relativism in moral philosophy would entail that these evaluative judgments are mere reflections of (possibly quite irrational) cultural standards, and so on. None of these possible sources of skeptical "meta-political philosophy" is considered here.

16. As we will see in Chapter 2, political ideals need not involve in this way any account of what is "best" (or optimal) politically. They may instead focus more minimally on

what is permissible or acceptable (as in the Lockean tradition in political philosophy), leaving questions of "the best" to one side. Such "permissibility ideals" can still function (as described below) as the "target" for non-ideal theory. I thank Andrew Altman for his suggestion that I make this point clearer here.

17. See Rawls, *The Law of Peoples* (Cambridge, MA: Harvard University Press, 1999), 6–8, 11–16. Rawls takes himself to be following Rousseau in doing political philosophy (ideal theory) by taking "men as they are" and "laws as they might be" (as Rousseau says at the start of *The Social Contract*). Rawls (with Rousseau), of course, does not mean that he intends to "take" men as they are now, living under (and perhaps corrupted by) unjust and unhappy circumstances; he means, rather, that he intends to respect in his theorizing realistic limits on human motivation (and psychology generally).

18. Rawls, *A Theory of Justice,* 215–16, 308–9; Rawls, *The Law of Peoples,* 5, 90. Alternatively, the rules of non-ideal theory could be seen not in this way as *transitional* rules (designed to get us somewhere better) but rather simply as whatever (different) rules bind us where others are not complying with the rules of ideal theory. This appears to be Liam Murphy's view of non-ideal theory (*Moral Demands in Nonideal Theory* [Oxford: Oxford University Press, 2000]).

19. Allen Buchanan, *Justice, Legitimacy, and Self-Determination* (Oxford: Oxford University Press, 2004), 62.

20. Ibid., 61. It is not entirely clear how we are meant to understand the force of Buchanan's insistence that a good ideal theory must be not only feasible but accessible. On its face, it appears to amount to a claim that, contra Rawls, ideal theory cannot proceed without first doing a fair bit of what Rawls would consider non-ideal theory (i.e., we must know a fair bit about how easy it will be to get from here to there, beyond our knowledge that "there" is consistent with human psychology and social science, before we can reasonably specify the "there" that constitutes our ideal). If this is Buchanan's intention, his view is, I think, flawed for the reason suggested below in the text. If not, Buchanan's view would appear to be no different from Rawls'.

Chapter 2

1. "The fundamental question of political philosophy, one that precedes questions about how the state should be organized, is whether there should be any state at all. Why not have anarchy?" (Robert Nozick, *Anarchy, State, and Utopia* [New York: Basic Books, 1974], 4).

2. Rationality being here understood not in a maximizing sense but, rather, in the equally familiar satisficing sense (i.e., where "rationality" is a threshold concept).

3. Commonsense morality accepts the categories of required, permissible, and forbidden acts, with the range of the permissible including actions that are better and worse from a moral viewpoint. A maximizing conception of morality—such as act utilitarianism—will not accept that a less than ideal (i.e., nonmaximizing) action can be morally justified.

4. See my "Original-Acquisition Justifications of Private Property," in *Justification and Legitimacy* (Cambridge: Cambridge University Press, 2001), 200–4, and "Justification and Legitimacy," in *Justification and Legitimacy,* 123–27.

5. See Christopher Morris, *An Essay on the Modern State* (Cambridge: Cambridge University Press, 1998), esp. Ch. 2.

6. Just as the age of the two great superpowers suggested the possibility of a world of two or three superstates, rather than a world of many smaller, less powerful states. H. G. Wells reportedly predicted in 1925 that within 100 years there would be only three

nations, collectively covering the globe: the United States of America, the United States of Europe, and the United States of China.

7. See my *On the Edge of Anarchy* (Princeton: Princeton University Press, 1993), Ch. 1.
8. Hobbes seemed plainly to have in mind that England during its civil war was in the state of nature. Locke, perhaps less plainly, seemed to be characterizing the final stages of the Stuart monarchy as involving a state of war (hence, for Locke, a state of nature) between king and subjects.
9. Some classical philosophers (e.g., Rousseau) and many contemporary ones have accused Hobbes and Locke of offering misleadingly anachronistic accounts of the state of nature—that is, of describing persons in the state of nature who in fact possess all of the attributes of their contemporaries, rather than those of genuinely "natural" persons. This criticism is misguided in two ways. First, as we have seen, Hobbes and Locke intended to characterize their contemporaries as (for a period of time) actually in the state of nature themselves. Second, the justifications of the state attempted by Hobbes and Locke were intended as justifications *for* (or to) their contemporaries, as justifications that showed the state to be best *for them,* there and then. It was thus perfectly appropriate to appeal to the problems that would be faced in a state of nature by people like their contemporaries.
10. This account is closer to Hobbes' view than to Locke's. For Hobbes, the state of nature was any condition in which people lived without a powerful sovereign to "keep them in awe." Locke, however, utilized a moralized conception of the state of nature, according to which the state of nature was the absence of *legitimate* political society, not just the absence of effective government. Thus, there could for Locke be effective government even in the state of nature, if that government was illegitimate. For a much fuller account of both views, see again my *On the Edge of Anarchy,* Ch. 1.
11. Locke's "justification of the state" (along with most others) is thus weaker or more qualified than Hobbes'. A different and deeper kind of qualification can be found in writers like Rousseau, who argues that the state is not the best form of social life for us as we are *naturally* but that a certain kind of state is the best that we can do for ourselves *now,* in our irreversibly socialized, politicized condition.
12. But see Gregory Kavka, "When Morally Perfect People Would Need Government," *Social Philosophy and Policy* 12 (1995), 1–18.
13. The distinction at work here between the moral and the prudential is, of course, somewhat misleading and is used only for clarity's sake. By a *moral advantage,* I mean only something that makes a form of life morally preferable to another (in one of the ways elaborated below in the text). By a *prudential advantage,* I mean only something that gives people more of what they want. I will not try here to further explore the complex relationship between morality and prudence.
14. John Locke, *Second Treatise,* sect. 95.
15. Ibid., sect. 6–8. My *The Lockean Theory of Rights* (Princeton: Princeton University Press, 1992), Ch. 1–3, discusses these positions in considerable detail.
16. *Second Treatise,* sect. 124–26.
17. We are obligated in Locke only to respect the rights of others directly (by obeying natural law proscriptions on harming the innocent), not to bring about the best possible state of affairs (i.e., that in which rights are maximally respected). We are permitted, but not required, to help enforce others' rights against third parties.
18. Though at least one prominent utilitarian, Godwin, was an anarchist who supported nonpolitical life on utilitarian grounds.
19. Immanuel Kant, *The Metaphysics of Morals* (Cambridge: Cambridge University Press, 1991), "General Division of Rights" and Ch. 1. For a discussion of the contrasts between Kant and Locke on these points, see my "Human Rights and World Citizenship: The Universality of Human Rights in Kant and Locke," in *Justification and Legitimacy,* 179–96.

20. There are parallel arguments in both Hobbes' *De Cive* and his *The Elements of Law.*

21. Hobbes, *Leviathan,* Ch. 13, para. 8–9.

22. This account of Hobbes' central argument draws heavily on Kavka, *Hobbesian Moral and Political Theory,* Part I.

23. *Leviathan,* Ch. 13, para. 6–7.

24. Ibid., para. 4.

25. Kropotkin writes that "sociability is as much a law of nature as mutual struggle" (*Mutual Aid* [London: Freedom Press, 1987], 24).

26. Interestingly, this is only really a problem for political societies created by agreement, those Hobbes calls "commonwealths by institution." In cases where political societies are created by conquest ("commonwealths by acquisition"), an enforcer arrives ready-made (in the form of the conqueror and horde), with no need for cooperation by subjects anywhere in the process (beyond their perfectly rational acts of doing what they are ordered by their conqueror to do at sword's point). On the two types of commonwealth, see *Leviathan,* Ch. 16, para. 14.

27. Ibid., Ch. 15, para. 4–5.

28. For clear, but much more complex and sophisticated, accounts of these issues, see Kavka, *Hobbesian Moral and Political Theory,* Ch. 4, and Morris, *An Essay on the Modern State,* sect. 3.4.

29. In Book I of Plato's *Republic.*

30. Some philosophers distinguish here between *assurance* problems and *free-rider* problems (e.g., David Schmidtz, *The Limits of Government* [Boulder: Westview, 1991], Ch. 4; Morris, *An Essay on the Modern State,* 90). I have not referred to the problem of advantage taking in terms of "free-riding" because free-riding involves defection that permits the defectors to enjoy the benefits of a cooperative scheme without contributing to their production. But free-riding of this sort is primarily an issue in large-scale, mature, stable schemes of cooperation. In small-scale or newly created schemes of cooperation, defection often just destroys the scheme, rather than permitting the defector to enjoy its benefits without cost.

31. See Nozick, *Anarchy, State, and Utopia,* Ch. 2.

32. Ibid., Ch. 5.

33. Kavka, *Hobbesian Moral and Political Theory,* sect. 4.4.

34. Nozick, *Anarchy, State, and Utopia,* 119. Because the dominant protective agency must deprive independents of their rights to enforce natural law according to their own lights, that agency is morally obligated to compensate them with the protective services it provides to its clients.

35. It seems eminently plausible to respond that a dominant protective agency is neither required nor entitled to prevent independents from exercising their rights in the first place; hence, it is under no standing obligation to compensate independents and become a "state" in the process.

36. The list of arguments that follows artificially assembles together some of the central claims made by anarchists of a variety of stripes, including Godwin, Proudhon, Bakunin, Kropotkin, Spooner, and Rothbard.

37. Though the work of social anthropologists might in some cases seem encouraging. See, e.g., Harold Barclay, *People Without Government: An Anthropology of Anarchism* (London: Kahn and Avrill, 1982).

38. These are Morris' skeptical conclusions about the anarchist case (Morris, *An Essay on the Modern State,* 98–100). It has, of course, always been a sore point in Marxist anarchist theory that without a simultaneous world revolution, the achievement of a stateless society in a particular territory seems pointless—since that society would be defenseless against the superior power of the remaining states.

39. Karl Marx, "Critique of the Gotha Program," in R. C. Tucker, ed., *The Marx–Engels Reader,* 2nd ed. (New York: Norton, 1978), 531.

Chapter 3

1. These are the acts referred to by jurists as *mala in se* (wrong in themselves), as opposed to those that are only *mala prohibita* (wrong because prohibited by law).

2. Political obligations are thus "general" moral requirements in two different senses: first, they are requirements to obey the law (and support the government) simply because it is valid law (and is the established government), not because of the more specific moral properties of particular laws or governments; second, they are "general" by virtue of applying to all (or most) citizens of typical or decent states.

3. For a much more detailed and extended defense of these claims, see my "Justification and Legitimacy," in *Justification and Legitimacy*, 122–57.

4. The most prominent use of this way of distinguishing obligations from duties is in Rawls, *A Theory of Justice*.

5. My own preferred account is slightly different. In my view, the moral standards according to which entities are determined to be legitimate (or not) are relative to the rights actually claimed by or necessary for the practices of those entities. Organizations or institutions of all kinds are legitimate just in case they possess the rights to do what they actually do (or, perhaps, the rights to do what they centrally or principally do). Nonpolitical voluntary associations will be morally legitimate, on this account, to the extent that they have freely acquired from their members (and are not otherwise morally prohibited from exercising) the rights to act as they do act. Political societies that would not qualify as states, in the modern sense—for instance, migratory, non-territorial societies or non-sovereign political organizations—can nonetheless still be characterized as legitimate or not in these same terms. States will be legitimate just in case they, first, have the rights to do those things that they must do in order to qualify as states and, second, have the rights to do whatever else they do beyond this conceptual core. More minimal states may well have a lower "legitimacy bar" to clear, by virtue of their doing less than more extensive states (and so, apparently, needing to defend their possession of fewer rights). Or moral argument might show such an appearance to be misleading. For it might turn out that more minimal states have no right to deny their subjects the services provided by more extensive states, just as more isolationist states may have no right to deny other nations or groups certain kinds of support (and so may be morally duty-bound to be more active internationally). In any event, the moral legitimacy of a particular state would turn, in this account of the matter, on whether or not moral argument could establish that the state in question possessed the moral rights to act as it in fact acts.

6. See David Copp, "The Idea of a Legitimate State," *Philosophy & Public Affairs* 28 (Winter 1999), 18.

7. One can, of course, also worry about the authority or legitimacy of governments, rather than states (as when concerns about electoral improprieties made some question the legitimacy of George W. Bush's government, though not the legitimacy of the United States itself). Since in my view governments obtain whatever moral authority or legitimacy they might possess from the moral authority of their states to empower particular governments, I will focus here on what I take to be the more basic issue of state authority or legitimacy.

8. Concerns with state territory and external legitimacy will be addressed in Chapter 6.

9. Allen Buchanan's recent account of political legitimacy, while avoiding reference to possessing a "liberty right" to rule, preferring instead to speak of "being morally justified in exercising political power," plainly falls in this camp. Buchanan sharply distinguishes his account of legitimacy from those which tie that idea to a correlative "right to be obeyed," and he professes to be puzzled about why anyone ever thought that stronger idea of legitimacy to be central to serious concerns in political philosophy (*Justice, Legitimacy, and Self-Determination*, 233–41) (see Ch. 1, n. 19).

10. Aristotle, *Politics,* I.ii.

11. Romans 13:1–2. Luther made popular early modern appeals to this Pauline text, though the "naturalist" reading of it was later famously challenged by (e.g.) George Buchanan and John Milton.

12. The sanction theory is, of course, a much more plausible view if it is taken as a theory about our "*legal* obligations"—that is, a theory simply about what our legal system holds us liable for doing (or forbearing)—rather than as a theory about our *moral* obligations, including our moral obligation to obey the law, which is what is here at issue.

13. H.L. A Hart, *The Concept of Law,* 2nd ed. (Oxford: Oxford University Press, 1994), 84–87.

14. The remainder of this section follows, in a more compact fashion, the presentation of these ideas in my "Political Obligation and Authority," in *The Blackwell Guide to Social and Political Philosophy* ed. R. L. Simon (Malden, MA: Blackwell, 2002), 17–37, and *Is There a Duty to Obey the Law? For and Against* (with C. H. Wellman) (Cambridge: Cambridge University Press, 2005), sect. 6. Both this section and the next follow some of the arguments I first made in *Moral Principles and Political Obligations* (Princeton: Princeton University Press, 1979).

15. Translations by G. M. A. Grube, from Plato, *The Trial and Death of Socrates* (Indianapolis: Hackett, 1975).

16. Ronald Dworkin, *Law's Empire* (Cambridge, MA: Harvard University Press, 1986), 195–215. See also John Horton, *Political Obligation* (Atlantic Highlands, NJ: Humanities, 1992), Ch. 6.

17. Much more extensive and careful discussion and critiques of associativism can be found in my "Associative Political Obligations" and "External Justifications and Institutional Roles," both in *Justification and Legitimacy.* 65–101. For other skeptical views, see C. H. Wellman, "Associative Allegiances and Political Obligations," *Social Theory and Practice* 23 (1997) 181–204, and Leslie Green, "Associative Obligations and the State," in J. Burley (ed.), *Dworkin and His Critics* (Malden, MA: Blackwell, 2004), 267–84.

18. This is not to say, of course, that mere use of the idea of a social contract places a theorist in the transactional camp. Where the "social contract" at issue is seen as more implicit or traditional than as involving specific dateable undertakings by individuals or groups (as in Burke or in the work of the contemporary theorist Michael Walzer), the resulting theory will probably belong in the associativist camp. And where the "social contract" in question is hypothetical only (as in Kant and John Rawls), the theory of political obligation that results will most likely be (as we will see) a disguised natural duty account. It is appeals to *actual* contracts or consent, dateable events (or series of events) from which political obligations arise, that make accounts in the social contract tradition transactional. My own (by no means universally shared) readings of the texts make Hobbes, Locke, and Rousseau the most famous defenders of such transactional accounts.

19. Locke, *Second Treatise,* sect. 117–22.

20. See H.L.A. Hart, "Are There any Natural Rights?" *Philosophical Review* 64 (1955), 175–91; John Rawls, "Legal Obligation and the Duty of Fair Play," in *John Rawls: Collected Papers,* ed. S. Freeman (Cambridge, MA: Harvard University Press, 1999) 117–29.

21. The paragraphs below quickly summarize arguments I have made much more carefully in "The Principle of Fair Play" and "Fair Play and Political Obligation: Twenty Years Later," both in my *Justification and Legitimacy* 1–42.

22. Rawls, *A Theory of Justice,* 97–98, 295–96.

23. See, e.g., George Klosko, *The Principle of Fairness and Political Obligation* (Lanham, MD: Rowman and Littlefield, 1992).

24. Here, I summarize only a few of the many arguments (and describe only a few of the many natural duty accounts) that I consider in *Is There a Duty to Obey the Law?* 121–88.

25. On this last idea (of political obligation as implied by a duty of rescue), see Ch. 1 and 2 of C. H. Wellman's contribution to, and my reply in Ch. 7 of, *Is There a Duty to Obey the Law?*

26. See Hume's theory of "allegiance" in *A Treatise of Human Nature*, III, 2; Bentham, *A Fragment on Government*, Ch. I, sect. 36–48; Henry Sidgwick, *The Methods of Ethics*, III, iv, 3–5; IV, iii, 4.

27. Rawls, *A Theory of Justice*, 293. See also Jeremy Waldron, "Special Ties and Natural Duties," in *The Duty to Obey the Law*, ed. W. A. Edmundson (Lanham, MD: Rowman and Littlefield, 1999), and Allen Buchanan, *Justice, Legitimacy, and Self-Determination*, esp. 85–98.

28. Robert Paul Wolff, *In Defense of Anarchism* (New York: Harper & Row, 1970), 19.

29. Justificatory anarchism could, in principle, share with philosophical anarchism its opposition to the conclusions of political anarchism; this would be an unusual, but not an internally inconsistent, conjunction of views.

30. For more discussion of this classificatory point, along with many other aspects of the possible defenses of philosophical anarchism, see my "Philosophical Anarchism," in *Justification and Legitimacy*, 102–21.

31. For the *a priori* defense of philosophical anarchism, see Wolff, *In Defense of Anarchism*, 18–19, 71. The fatal admission about contractual democracies appears first on pp. 41–42 and is repeated on pp. 69–70 (just before Wolff paradoxically again states his inconsistent commitment to the *a priori* version of the argument).

32. So in deciding how she should act in the real social world, each citizen must consider her circumstances in light of the requirements and options of morality. She must, for instance, weigh the variable extent of the wrong done in consequence of her own state's illegitimacy against the good her state does and the support it merits–good that many states do (e.g., relieving their subjects of the burdens of providing security) and good that only some states do (e.g., promoting peace and justice, relieving need in the world). Her practical conclusions might range from a policy of prudent conformity to law to violent resistance or revolutionary activity aimed at undermining the state. I do not pretend to be able to provide a clear method that citizens might employ in balancing the wrongs of right-violation against the good states do–that is, an easy way of deriving practical conclusions from the complex interactions of our two dimensions of institutional evaluation, justification and legitimacy.

Chapter 4

1. Rawls, *A Theory of Justice*, 3 (see ch. 1, n.9).

2. For representative general discussions of justice, see James Sterba, *The Demands of Justice* (Notre Dame: University of Notre Dame Press, 1980); Brian Barry, *Theories of Justice*, vol. 2 (Berkeley: University of California Press, 1989); David Miller, *Principles of Social Justice* (Cambridge, MA: Harvard University Press, 2001).

3. See Kant, *Political Writings*, (Cambridge: Cambridge University Press, 1970) 137–38, 165. Mill defends the idea of the realm of justice being coextensive with that of rights (and their correlative "duties of perfect obligation") in *Utilitarianism*, Ch. 5. For the texts (and the interpretive arguments) that yield this same reading of Locke on justice, see my *The Lockean Theory of Rights*, sect. 6.2 (see ch.2, n.15).

4. There has also, of course, been much recent work (in non-ideal theory) by philosophers of law on *rectificatory justice*—that is, on *retributive justice* (the justice of punishment) and *compensatory justice* (the justice of compensation for injuries done to others). I will not explore here these subjects or the nature of the relations between the principles of distributive justice and those of rectificatory justice, though we can, I think, in order

to have some view of these matters in mind, assume that rectificatory justice will (as Aristotle famously observed) involve "restoring" the just state of affairs that the principles of distributive justice define.

5. Friedrich Hayek, for example, argued that justice is a property only of *individual* actions, so talk of *social* justice is nonsense. See, e.g., *The Constitution of Liberty* (South Bend, IN: Gateway, 1960), 231–33.

6. Aristotle, *Nicomachean Ethics* V, 1130–35. Subsequent references will be in the text, by standard pagination in parentheses.

7. Miller, *Principles of Social Justice,* 2.

8. On the distinction between formal and material principles of justice, see Feinberg, *Social Philosophy,* (Englewood Cliffs, NJ: Prentice-Hall, 1973), 99–102.

9. Many contemporary practitioners of law and economics, of course, make only the factual claim that the law (in certain or in all areas) is best understood/interpreted as a device for maximizing social utility (or social wealth).

10. Cambridge: Cambridge University Press, 1968, ch.3. None of the classical utilitarians—Bentham, Mill, Sidgwick, et al.—seems to ever have stated utilitarianism in precisely this form.

11. This is the standard formulation of so-called *act* utilitarianism. *Rule* utilitarianism, to give it the parallel formulation, would be the view that an act is right if and only if it complies with one of that set of rules, general conformity to which would produce at least as much total happiness as would general conformity to any available alternative set of rules.

12. Mill, *Utilitarianism,* Ch. 5, para. 2.

13. Ibid., para. 15, 25.

14. Ibid., para. 32.

15. See David Lyons, "Mill's Theory of Justice," in his *Rights, Welfare, and Mill's Moral Theory* (New York: Oxford University Press, 1994), 67–88.

16. Rawls, *A Theory of Justice,* 23.

17. Ibid., 24.

18. Ibid., 3.

19. Mill, *Utilitarianism,* Ch. 5, para. 36.

20. Rawls, *A Theory of Justice,* 10. Subsequent references to this text in this section will be by page numbers in parentheses.

21. We can, Rawls says, imaginatively subject ourselves to these constraints, thinking about justice *as if* we were really agents so constrained (p. 17).

22. Will Kymlicka presents a truncated variant of this argument—which he calls Rawls' "intuitive equality of opportunity argument"—as one of Rawls' two principal arguments for justice as fairness (*Contemporary Political Philosophy,* 2nd ed. [Oxford: Oxford University Press, 2002], 57–60). Kymlicka takes the argument to fail: "what if I was not born into a privileged social group, and was not born with any special talents, and yet by my own choices and effort have managed to secure a larger income than others?" (p. 60). I believe that Rawls at least vaguely intends (and is certainly committed to defending) the stronger "deterministic" argument—that not only initial genetic and social endowment but all subsequent distinguishing traits of persons are (or cannot in any determinate measure be known not to be) "morally arbitrary" products of mere good or bad fortune.

23. See, e.g., N. Daniels, ed., *Reading Rawls* (New York: Basic Books, 1975); H. Richardson and P. Weithman, eds., *The Philosophy of Rawls,* 5 vols.(New York: Garland, 1999); S. Freeman, ed., *The Cambridge Companion to Rawls* (Cambridge: Cambridge University Press, 2003). Freeman contains an excellent Rawls bibliography.

24. In arguing that the two principles are the "maximin solution" to the choice problem in the original position, Rawls summarizes the three conditions that must be satisfied for the maximin rule to be a "suitable guide": (1) the chooser's knowledge of likelihoods must be impossible or very insecure, (2) the chooser cares little for what he could gain above what

the proposed principle guarantees him, and (3) the rejected principles have unacceptable possible outcomes (p. 134). While (1) is arguably satisfied in the original position, I see no reason to suppose that (2) or (3) would be, when the difference principle is proposed as an alternative to a mixed conception with a substantial and secure social minimum.

25. Rawls' principal objection seems to be that such a mixed conception would leave indeterminate the idea of a "substantial" minimum, whereas the difference principle offers a clear test for the permissibility of inequality. But given that Rawls' own maximin arguments for the two principles make use of concepts like "unacceptable" outcomes, it is hard to see why appeals to an "acceptable" (i.e., "substantial") social minimum should be disqualifying. And notions like "acceptable" or "substantial" can presumably be further fixed by appeal to ideas like persons' "basic needs" and/or the goods necessary to advance successfully any of a variety of reasonable life plans.

26. The following summary of the core argument of *Political Liberalism* is extremely brief and general, ignoring most of the book's complexities. Because all of the arguments that I summarize are so central (and easy to find) in the text, I footnote only direct quotations.

27. Rawls *Political Liberalism,* xix (see Ch.1, n. 2).

28. Ibid., 13–14.

29. Ibid., 14.

30. Ibid., 9.

31. Rawls' "liberal principle of legitimacy" says "our exercise of political power is fully proper only when it is exercised in accordance with a constitution the essentials of which all citizens as free and equal may reasonably be expected to endorse in the light of principles and ideals acceptable to their common human reason" (ibid., 137).

32. Rawls, *A Theory of Justice,* 19.

33. Utilitarians might argue, of course, that directing resources to the productive, the talented, and the achievers (as we do in our societies) is less a policy of rewarding desert than it is a policy of efficient use of resources (i.e., of maximizing utility in the distribution of social goods).

34. Nozick, *Anarchy, State, and Utopia,* 224–27 (see Ch. 2, n.1).

35. On the idea of self-ownership, see G. A. Cohen's insightful discussions in *Self-Ownership, Freedom, and Equality* (Cambridge: Cambridge University Press, 1995).

36. Locke, *Second Treatise,* sect. 27. This "mixing argument" is only one of many arguments for natural property rights that scholars have attributed to Locke. See my *The Lockean Theory of Rights,* Ch. 5 (see Ch. 2, n.15).

37. Nozick, *Anarchy, State, and Utopia,* 151.

38. Ibid., 150–53.

39. The two preceding paragraphs summarize *Anarchy, State, and Utopia,* 153–60.

40. Ibid, 160–64.

41. Ibid., 160–63.

42. See Michael Otsuka, *Libertarianism Without Inequality* (Oxford: Oxford University Press, 2003), and P. Vallentyne and H. Steiner, eds., *Left-Libertarianism and Its Critics* (Houndmills, UK: Palgrave, 2000).

43. See Friedrich Engels' explicit statement of this view in *Anti-Duhring,* in the section titled "On Morality," in *The Marx-Engels Reader,* 725–27 (see Ch. 2, n. 39).

44. From Marx, *Critique of the Gotha Program* (1875), in ibid., 531.

45. See A. Etzioni, ed., "The Responsive Communitarian Platform: Rights and Responsibilities," in *The Essential Communitarian Reader* (Lanham, MD: Rowman and Littlefield, 1998).

46. See Michael Walzer, *Spheres of Justice* (New York: Basic Books, 1983), esp. Ch. 1, 13.

47. See Alasdair MacIntyre, *After Virtue* (Notre Dame: University of Notre Dame Press, 1981), esp. Ch. 5, 6, 15–17, and "The Privatization of Good: An Inaugural Lecture," *Review of Politics* 42 (Summer 1990), 344–61.

48. Sometimes Sandel appears to say that an emphasis on justice is inappropriate or unnecessary for certain kinds of communities. See, *Liberalism and the Limits of Justice* (Cambridge: Cambridge University Press, 1982), 31–35. At other times, however, he writes as if the standards of justice are simply relative to the kind of community in question.

49. Ibid., 47–65. See also Sandel, *Democracy's Discontent* (Cambridge, MA: Harvard University Press, 1996), 11–19.

50. Sandel, *Democracy's Discontent, 16.*

51. Ibid., 6.

52. Amy Gutmann, "Communitarian Critics of Liberalism," *Philosophy and Public Affairs* 14 (Summer 1985), 319.

53. Kymlicka, *Contemporary Political Philosophy,* 271–73.

54. See Carol Gilligan, *In a Different Voice* (Cambridge, MA: Harvard University Press, 1982).

55. My own belief is that feminists ought not to be communitarians (at least in any very strict sense of the term). If feminism has any guiding principle, it must surely be that we are not obligated to accept whatever role or lifestyle in which we happen to find ourselves "embedded" or "situated." Feminism has always been motivated by questioning and often rejecting communities' norms for women, not by "discovering" that those norms are their own.

56. See Martha Nussbaum, *Frontiers of Justice* (Cambridge, MA: Harvard University Press, 2006).

57. On the second and third points, see Susan Moller Okin, *Justice, Gender, and the Family* (New York: Basic Books, 1989), esp. Ch. 1.

Chapter 5

1. In Aristotle's influential classification of political constitutions (*Politics,* III.vii.), he distinguishes the form of each of these three types that is correct (by virtue of aiming at the common good) from its "deviation" (which aims at satisfying narrower interests): so rule by the many is either "polity" (correct) or democracy (deviation); rule by the few is either aristocracy or oligarchy; and rule by one, either kingship or tyranny.

2. Locke, *Second Treatise,* sect. 132. For Locke, the legitimacy of political society rests on the unanimity of its subjects' consent to membership. And consent to membership, he believes, implies consent to majority rule (sect. 96–99). Thus, each legitimate polity is at base a majoritarian democracy. While the people typically entrust their political power to a government—which may be a democracy, an oligarchy, or a hereditary or elective monarchy (sect. 132)—should that trust be breached by government, political power returns to the people as a whole (sect. 243), who then wield it as a majoritarian democracy.

3. We are here discussing only individual autonomy. The autonomy of groups within political communities and the autonomy of political societies (from outside control) will be dealt with separately in Chapter 6.

4. Rousseau, *Social Contract,* I.vi (para. 4), I.viii (para. 3).

5. Cited in Kant, *Political Writings,* 4.

6. John Stuart Mill, *Considerations on Representative Government,* Ch. 3.

7. William Nelson emphasizes this aspect of Mill's case in *On Justifying Democracy* (London: Routledge & Kegan Paul, 1980), 114–18.

8. A full utilitarian case for democracy, of course, would have to consider as well the likely effects of democracy on the happiness of persons *outside* the society in question (who count equally in the utilitarian calculus).

9. Rousseau, *Social Contract,* I.vii (para. 7) and II.iii (para. 1, 2).

10. In *Social Contract,* II.iii (para. 3), Rousseau observes that were there adequate information, minimal communication between voters, and no subsidiary "intriguing groups" (whose members would try to promote their groups' own "partial" goods, rather than the common good), "the general will would result" from democratic votes. And in IV.ii (para. 8), he notes that the general will is declared not after citizens are asked to approve or reject a proposal but rather after they are asked whether it conforms with the general will. This latter passage is complicated, and we shall return to it in section 5.3.

11. Rousseau, to be clear, defends only "legislative democracy," not "democratic government." Laws in a legitimate state must be democratically *made.* But the *execution* of those laws by government is best done nondemocratically.

12. Rousseau appears to say two kinds of things on this subject, only the second of which seems plausible. First, he suggests (roughly) that since each person wills the good of the society which includes him, when a person is constrained only by laws that express the general will, he is subject only to constraints which he himself wills as laws—hence, he is autonomous, subject only to laws he in fact wills. On that line, however, we would seem to be left autonomous by subjection to any law that is good for the society, no matter who made it. So the requirement of democratic lawmaking would lack defense (unless only democratically made laws can express the general will—the view we considered and rejected [as either implausible or empty] above). Second, and more plausibly, Rousseau suggests that one who engages in democratic lawmaking actually imposes the resulting laws on herself, thus remaining autonomous. That is the version of the autonomy defense of democracy we consider later.

13. This is, in effect, Nelson's "variation" on Mill's argument for democracy. See especially *On Justifying Democracy,* Ch. VI.

14. The obvious competitor here would be a virtuous and competent monarch or aristocracy (of the sort often advocated in the political philosophy of the ancients and of Renaissance "civic republicanism"). And the obvious problems with such an ideal are the absence of checks on the use of power, the limited perspective of the ruler(s), and the paternalistic neglect (and consequent nondevelopment) of citizens' deliberative and political capabilities.

15. Most critiques of instrumental justifications of democracy are really only complaints that they fail to capture all that is morally important (or what is most important) about democracy, not that instrumental benefits are irrelevant. See, e.g., Charles Beitz's criticisms of (what he calls) "best result" theories in *Political Equality* (Princeton: Princeton University Press, 1989), 40–46.

16. Put this way, of course, the "virtue" argument for democracy looks instrumental, not intrinsic. But in the sense of these terms described above, a virtue argument counts as instrumental only if a virtuous citizenry is valued solely for its tendency to make good decisions or laws. It will count as an intrinsic argument if the virtue born of democracy is viewed as valuable in itself, independent of the ultimate "products" of this virtue.

17. Robert Dahl, *Democracy and Its Critics* (New Haven: Yale University Press, 1989), 89.

18. Ibid., 90 (my emphasis).

19. Dahl notices, correctly, that this style of justification in fact works better as the size of the majority required for passage increases, with a unanimity rule being the obvious ideal. We must thus explore the defenses of majority rule before we can reach any conclusion about the kind of democratic procedure justified by appeals to autonomy. A unanimity rule appears at first blush also to be (as we will see) what is required by arguments from autonomy that purport not just to justify but to *legitimate* democracy.

20. Rousseau, *Social Contract,* I.vi (para. 4) (my emphasis).

21. Rawls, *A Theory of Justice,* e.g., sect. 36.

22. See, e.g., article 21 of the Universal Declaration of Human Rights and Buchanan, *Justice, Legitimacy, and Self-Determination,* 145–47 (see Ch. 1, n. 19).

23. Buchanan believes that his account does in fact solve the particularity problem (ibid., 254–56). But Buchanan argues only that democratic authorities have been chosen by "*our* democratic processes" and that failing to comply with democratically made laws (in normal conditions) shows a lack of equal regard for "*our* fellow citizens" (255, my emphasis). It is thus *our* democracy's laws, not some other's, with which we are bound to comply. But Buchanan's arguments simply assume (falsely, in my view) that the conventional/legal assignment of persons to particular states makes the authorities and citizens of those states *ours* in some morally interesting sense.

24. John Plamenatz appeared to argue both that any act of voting for a candidate in a democratic election counts as political consent and that ongoing participation (or even having the right to participate) so counts. See his *Consent, Freedom, and Political Obligation,* 2nd ed. (Oxford: Oxford University Press, 1968), 167–72, and *Man and Society* (London: Longmans, Green, 1963), vol. 1, 239–41. I return later to the "consensual appearance" of voting. Some of my arguments in this section follow those in my *On the Edge of Anarchy,* sect. 8.1 (see Ch. 2, n. 7).

25. See, e.g., Alan Gewirth, "Political Justice," in *Social Justice,* ed. R.B. Brandt (Englewood Cliffs, NJ: Prentice Hall, 1972), 138, and D. D. Raphael, *Problems of Political Philosophy* (London: Macmillan, 1976), 112–13.

26. Peter Singer, *Democracy and Disobedience* (Oxford: Oxford University Press, 1973), 51–52.

27. Thomas Christiano, *The Rule of the Many* (Boulder: Westview, 1996), Ch. 2, and sect. 7 of "Authority," in *Stanford Encyclopedia of Philosophy (Fall 2004 Edition),* ed. Edward N. Zalta, http://plato.stanford.edu/archives/fall2004/entries/authority/#7. See also Albert Weale, *Democracy* (New York: St. Martin's, 1999), 197.

28. On the dubious force of appeals to "necessity" in arguments for political authority generally, see my *Is There a Duty to Obey the Law?,* 121–42 (see Ch. 3, n. 14).

29. Dahl, *Democracy and Its Critics,* 147; Brian Barry, "Is Democracy Special?" in *Philosophy, Politics, and Society,* 5th series, ed. P. Laslett, J. Fishkin (New Haven: Yale University Press, 1979), 155–96.

30. Wolff, *In Defense of Anarchism,* 27 (see Ch. 3, n. 28).

31. See, e.g., James Buchanan and Gordon Tullock, *The Calculus of Consent* (Ann Arbor: University of Michigan Press, 1962), 90. They argue for majoritarian alternatives on the basis of the transaction costs of achieving unanimity.

32. Ibid., 23, 69.

33. Ibid., 42.

34. Locke argues (in *Second Treatise,* sect. 97) that agreeing to political membership without agreeing to be governed by majority rule "would signify nothing," leaving each person "as great a liberty as . . . anyone . . . in the state of nature has."

35. I have not yet discussed issues of democratic inclusiveness, beyond noting that the more fully inclusive a democratic society is, the more plainly justifiable it will be in terms of the values of autonomy and equality. Such values seem clearly to argue against any qualification requirements that appeal to such characteristics as wealth, gender, race, ethnicity, or sexual orientation. On the other hand, few believe that there is anything wrong with excluding from (e.g.) voting rights young children, those who are severely mentally or emotionally disabled, perhaps various categories of criminals, etc. But these cases do suggest the following obvious question: if exclusion from the franchise for incompetence or immorality is acceptable, why would it not also be acceptable to offer *plural* votes to those who are especially competent or moral (as in Mill's famous plural voting proposal [*Considerations on Representative Government,* Ch. 8])? The answer, I think, must be that those who fail to reach some threshold level of (say) competence would not in fact be made autonomous or treated as equals by a system that granted them the right to vote (so the values that argue for inclusiveness do not in fact argue for this kind of inclusion). But political autonomy and equality are not further advanced (beyond the extent to which they are advanced by *equal* [near-]universal

franchise)—indeed, they are frustrated—by granting to some a privilege of plural votes. The only case for plural voting is purely instrumental (which is, as we've seen, how Mill approaches these questions), and even that case seems weak. But in this instance, any instrumental case for plural voting is in fact opposed by stronger intrinsic arguments against it.

36. Locke, *Second Treatise,* sect. 96.

37. Rousseau, *Social Contract,* II.iii (para. 1–3), IV.ii (para. 6, 7).

38. Christiano, *The Rule of the Many,* 88; Jeremy Waldron, *Law and Disagreement* (Oxford: Oxford University Press, 1999), 113–16.

39. Beitz, *Political Equality,* 65.

40. Schumpeter prefers to emphasize the negative side of this kind of instrumental calculation, noting the incompetence and irrationality of average citizens, their susceptibility to special interests, etc. (in Joseph Schumpeter, *Capitalism, Socialism, and Democracy,* 3rd ed. [New York: Harper & Row, 1975]).

41. On these issues, see Hanna Pitkin, *The Concept of Representation* (Berkeley: University of California Press, 1967); Gerald MacCallum, *Political Philosophy* (Englewood Cliffs, NJ: Prentice Hall, 1987), Ch. 10; Bernard Manin, *The Principles of Representative Government* (Cambridge: Cambridge University Press, 1997); Weale, *Democracy,* Ch. 6.

42. Rousseau, *Social Contract,* III.xv (para. 5, 11).

43. Living in a democratic civil society changes one "from a limited and stupid animal into an intelligent being and a man" (Ibid., I.viii [para. 1]).

44. See, e.g., Carole Pateman, *Participation and Democratic Theory* (Cambridge: Cambridge University Press, 1970), and Benjamin Barber, *Strong Democracy* (Berkeley: University of California Press, 1984).

45. Some will find any emphasis on the need for public deliberation to be distinctly anti-Rousseauian, in light of Rousseau's occasional suggestions that a citizen's deliberations should be private. I do not, for I think that such a restriction on deliberation is ill-conceived in light of Rousseau's overall position.

46. See, e.g., James Bohman and William Rehg, eds., *Deliberative Democracy* (Cambridge, MA: MIT Press, 1997); Jon Elster, ed., *Deliberative Democracy* (Cambridge: Cambridge University Press, 1998); Amy Gutmann and Dennis Thompson, *Why Deliberative Democracy?* (Princeton: Princeton University Press, 2004).

47. See, e.g., Rawls, *Political Liberalism,* rev. ed. (New York: Columbia University Press, 1996), lectures VI, VIII.

48. See, e.g., Jürgen Habermas, *Between Facts and Norms* (Cambridge, MA: MIT Press, 1996).

49. See, e.g., Joshua Cohen, "Deliberation and Democratic Legitimacy," in Bohman and Rehg, eds., *Deliberative Democracy,* 67–92.

50. Though various results in social choice theory—most famously, Arrow's "impossibility theorem"—raise doubts about the capacity of democratic procedures to reliably reach the goal of collective utility maximization. Democracies, in this view, are those polities that grant universal franchise, count all votes equally, and decide according to majority rule.

51. See, e.g., Schumpeter, *Capitalism, Socialism, and Democracy,* 269.

52. Indeed, according to a familiar variety of "public choice theory," government should operate only to correct market imperfections, thus limiting democracy to dealing with (e.g.) externalities, certain public goods, etc.

53. In order to avoid these problems, polities must establish far more extensive rights than the franchise, speech, press, and assembly rights stressed in "market" theories. For instance, deliberative theorists argue, we may need rights to employment, education, welfare, health care (etc.), along with institutional guarantees of noncontrol by wealthy or special group interests (e.g., through public financing of political campaigns, formal arenas for public deliberation, etc.).

54. Which characterize what Ronald Dworkin calls the "partnership conception of democracy" (*Sovereign Virtue* [Cambridge, MA: Harvard University Press, 2000], 358–65).

Chapter 6

1. Locke certainly conceived of the state of nature in this *relational* fashion; Hobbes may have done so as well (or so Kavka claims). See my discussion of the relational character of the state of nature in *On the Edge of Anarchy,* 16–22 (see Ch. 2, n. 7).

2. See Richard Tuck, *The Rights of War and Peace* (Oxford: Oxford University Press, 1999), Ch. 3.

3. Hobbes, *Leviathan,* Ch. 13, para. 12.

4. See Charles Beitz, *Political Theory and International Relations* (Princeton: Princeton University Press, 1979), esp. Ch. 1, 2.

5. Locke, *Second Treatise,* sect. 14.

6. Hobbes, *Leviathan,* Ch. 14, para. 20.

7. Ibid., Ch. 15, para. 36–38.

8. Ibid., Ch. 13, para. 12.

9. Ibid., Ch. 13, para. 1.

10. Locke, famously, did not accept this view. A state of war exists, in his view, only where one person has declared "by word or action . . . a sedate settled design upon another man's life" (*Second Treatise,* sect. 16). This need not characterize either interpersonal or international relations in a state of nature. Mere aggressive posturing toward and a preparedness to fight (if attacked) against others are not sufficient to constitute a condition of war. See my *On the Edge of Anarchy,* Ch. 2.

11. I cannot here discuss just war theory at any length. Such theories typically offer distinct rules or criteria for the justice of going to war (e.g., to defend against attack) and for just conduct in the waging of war (e.g., refraining from deliberately harming noncombatants)—*jus ad bellum* and *jus in bello,* respectively. See, e.g., Michael Walzer, *Just and Unjust Wars* (New York: Basic Books, 1977), and J. B. Elshtain, ed., *Just War Theory* (New York: New York University Press, 1992).

12. Remember that we are speaking here of the *moral* rights of states. States' *legal* rights are a function of how international law identifies states and what legal rights statehood carries with it.

13. This, I think, is roughly the line of argument advanced by Beitz in *Political Theory and International Relations,* Part 2.

14. I assume here (with Locke) that, while persons are morally entitled to create no states at all or to create one legitimate world-state—which would be equally legitimate world conditions—the only legitimate international condition is the one just described.

15. See Copp, "The Idea of a Legitimate State," 18 (see Ch. 3, n. 6).

16. Here I draw on my paper "On the Territorial Rights of States," *Philosophical Issues* 11 (2001), 300–26.

17. Locke, *Second Treatise,* sect. 146.

18. But the differences in the concepts allow the possibilities of both legitimate but non-sovereign political institutions and sovereign but illegitimate ones.

19. As we might say in more familiar language, legitimate governments are those that represent or "speak for" the people as a whole (or, in the language of the Universal Declaration of Human Rights, "the will of the people shall be the basis of the authority of government"). Notice that legitimate states, in this model, are logically prior to and can exist without governments (or as "perfect democracies," to use Locke's term).

20. Since governments have both institutional and personal dimensions, we must ask both whether the institutions of government reflect the will of the people and whether the administration that is institutionally empowered to act on the people's behalf actually does speak for and represent the interests of the people as a body. Governments can clearly qualify as legitimate on either of these scores without qualifying on the other. Ideal institutions can be used in highly partisan ways, just as perfect trustees or representatives can be saddled with

illegitimate institutions. Traditional tests for governmental legitimacy in international legal thinking focus on whether or not a government exercises "effective control" over a population and territory or on whether a population "habitually obeys" a particular government (see, e.g., Brad R. Roth, *Governmental Illegitimacy in International Law* [Oxford: Oxford University Press, 1999], 136–42). Neither of these tests, however, reliably tracks *moral* legitimacy, for both control and obedience can be secured by governments in seriously immoral ways. There is also, of course, a purely domestic legal sense of "legitimacy" that governments achieve simply by coming to power in accordance with the relevant rules of domestic law.

21. For a more complete and more fully accurate account of Locke's views on territorial legitimacy, see my "On the Territorial Rights of States," 312–15.

22. See, e.g., Morris, *An Essay on the Modern State*, 262–63 (see Ch. 2, n. 5); David Miller, "Secession and the Principle of Nationality," in *National Self-Determination and Secession*, ed. M. Moore (Oxford: Oxford University Press, 1998), 68; and Allen Buchanan, "The Making and Unmaking of Boundaries: What Liberalism Has to Say," in *States, Nations, and Borders*, ed. A. Buchanan, M. Moore (Cambridge: Cambridge University Press, 2003), 232–34. Morris and Miller, perhaps correctly, actually ascribe this view to (respectively) Nozick and Hillel Steiner. But the view they reject is not Locke's view, and it is a far easier philosophical target than is the more plausible version I describe. Buchanan for some reason seems to think that the Lockean view *confuses* geographical territory with legal jurisdiction (232–33), when the view is in fact quite clearly intended instead to explain only how states can come to have morally defensible claims of jurisdiction over a territory. He also, even more oddly, suggests that because "jurisdictional authority includes the right to make legal rules that define property rights," one can hardly appeal to property rights (à la Locke) to explain jurisdictional authority over territory (233). But Locke's account is plainly an account of how *moral* rights to property in land can explain states' possession of legitimate jurisdictional authority (including the authority to institute a regime of *legal* rights to property).

23. For suggestions as to how to deal with these difficulties concerning historical rights, see my "Original-Acquisition Justifications of Private Property" and "Historical Rights and Fair Shares," both in *Justification and Legitimacy*, 197–248.

24. Legal doctrines of prescription establish gains (and losses) of rights from long use or enjoyment (or from nonprotest of others' use) of things—as when squatters and regular trespassers acquire certain rights (e.g., rights of way) against legal owners of property.

25. Margaret Moore, "The Territorial Dimension of Self-Determination," in *National Self-Determination and Secession*, 145. See also Brian Barry, "Statism and Nationalism: A Cosmopolitan Critique," in *Nomos XLI: Global Justice*, ed. I. Shapiro and L. Brilmayer (New York: New York University Press, 1999), 41.

26. Avishai Margalit and Joseph Raz, "National Self-Determination," *Journal of Philosophy* 87 (Sept. 1990), 459.

27. Rawls, *The Law of Peoples*, 38–39 (see Ch. 1, n. 17).

28. See my "On the Territorial Rights of States," 309.

29. These challenges are most difficult in cases of secession, as we will see in section 6.3. They are far less so in cases involving the reincorporation of a state, within previously recognized boundaries, that had dissolved into anarchy.

30. It is, of course, possible for groups to be in some reasonable measure politically self-determining without being (or becoming) autonomous, sovereign states. International law identifies various such standings for groups. And one clear theme in recent liberal political philosophy has been the argument(s) that liberal polities may in principled ways accommodate the needs of internal cultural or national groups for special protection or leeway. See, e.g., Will Kymlicka, *Liberalism, Community, and Culture* (Oxford: Oxford University Press, 1989) and Yael Tamir, *Liberal Nationalism* (Princeton: Princeton University Press, 1993).

31. In some recent political philosophy, *nation* is defined without reference to political or territorial aspects of nationality, the focus being entirely on the cultural or ethnic aspects. See, e.g., Hampton, *Political Philosophy*, (Boulder, CO: Westview, 1997), 222.

32. See, e.g., Margalit and Raz, "National Self-Determination," and David Miller, *On Nationality* (Oxford: Oxford University Press, 1995).

33. See Buchanan, *Secession* (Boulder, CO: Westview, 1991) and "Secession and Nationalism," in *A Companion to Contemporary Political Philosophy,* ed. R.E. Goodin, P. Pettit (Oxford: Blackwell, 1993), 586–96.

34. See, e.g., Daniel Philpott, "In Defense of Self-Determination," *Ethics* 105:2 (1995), 352–85; David Copp, "Democracy and Communal Self-Determination," in *The Morality of Nationalism,* ed. R. McKim, J. McMahan (New York: Oxford University Press, 1997), 277–300; and Christopher Wellman, *A Theory of Secession* (Cambridge: Cambridge University Press, 2005).

35. See Beitz, *Political Theory and International Relations,* esp. Part 2. Several of my criticisms do, however, share the spirit of Beitz's attack on the principle of state autonomy.

36. Buchanan, *Secession,* 68.

37. In the end, I think it is this simple problem that sinks the argument of Buchanan's *Justice, Legitimacy, and Self-Determination.* Buchanan there attempts to defend a theory of political legitimacy without solving the problem of political authority (and of subjects' correlative obligations of obedience) (pp. 234–35). But without a case for political authority in "legitimate" polities, Buchanan deprives his argument of the justification it needs for the legitimacy of democratic governance (by majority rule). And, as I suggest below, his theory also lacks, as a consequence, any acceptable account of the territorial rights of legitimate states.

38. According to Locke (as we saw in sections 5.3 and 6.2), mere consent to membership in a political society involves consenting to both majority rule and the joining of private (rightful) holdings in land to the society's territory (i.e., the placing of that land under the state's "jurisdiction").

39. Intervention by one state in a civil war or a secessionist movement in another state is particularly complicated in this regard since the intervention often enjoys the enthusiastic consent of one party to the dispute. It constitutes "intervention" precisely because it is not consented to by the other side.

40. See Buchanan, *Justice, Legitimacy, and Self-Determination,* 212–14; Thomas Pogge, *World Poverty and Human Rights* (Cambridge: Polity Press, 2002), Ch. 4.

41. Buchanan, *Justice, Legitimacy, and Self-Determination,* 216. This is, very roughly, the approach first defended by Beitz. Even if we think of domestic political societies as self-sufficient units, the moral arbitrariness of national boundaries (by itself) requires international redistribution to remedy inequalities in the resources available to persons within the established boundaries of different polities. But once we recognize that the self-sufficiency assumption is false (and that there are in fact international "cooperative schemes" in play), we can see that a stronger principle of international distributive justice is required: namely, a global version of the difference principle (Beitz, *Political Theory and International Relations,* Part 3). For a similarly egalitarian reading of the implications of Rawls' theory of justice for international duties, see Pogge, "An Egalitarian Law of Peoples," *Philosophy and Public Affairs* 23 (Summer 1994), 195–224.

42. Beitz refers to this position in political philosophy as "cosmopolitan liberalism" (*Political Theory and International Relations,* 199, 215).

43. Rawls' use of the term *peoples* rather than *states* seems to be mostly a function of his rejecting certain aspects of the traditionally recognized "sovereignty" of states (in particular, the right to make war for "reasons of state" and the right of domestic autonomy) (*The Law of Peoples,* 25–26). Given, however, that states need not be conceived of as possessing such rights and that Rawls regularly refers to peoples as being politically organized with territories and governments, not much seems to turn on the different terminology being employed.

44. Rawls, *The Law of Peoples,* 37.

45. Ibid., 111.

46. Beitz, *Political Theory and International Relations,* 215. For a related view, see Thomas Nagel, "The Problem of Global Justice," *Philosophy and Public Affairs* 33 (Spring 2005), 113–47.

47. Rawls, *The Law of Peoples,* 107.

48. Ibid., 117–18.

49. See, e.g., Robert Goodin's argument for closed borders to avoid the risk of "a particularly generous welfare state. . . . being swamped with immigrants" ("Free Movement: If People Were Money," in *Ethics in Practice,* ed. H. LaFollette [Cambridge, MA: Blackwell, 1997], 578).

Index